Woody Allen
and Philosophy

Popular Culture and Philosophy™

Series Editor: William Irwin

Woody Allen and Philosophy

*You Mean My Whole
Fallacy Is Wrong?*

Edited by

MARK T. CONARD

and

AEON J. SKOBLE

Foreword by Tom Morris

OPEN COURT
Chicago and La Salle, Illinois

Volume 8 in the series, Popular Culture and Philosophy™

To order books from Open Court, call toll free 1-800-815-2280, or visit our website at www.opencourtbooks.com.

Open Court Publishing Company is a division of Carus Publishing Company.

Copyright ©2004 by Carus Publishing Company

First printing 2004

Printed and bound in the United States of America

Library of Congress Cataloging-in-Publication Data

Woody Allen and philosophy : you mean my whole fallacy is wrong?
/ edited by Mark T. Conard and Aeon J. Skoble.
    p. cm. — (Popular culture and philosophy ; v. 8)
        Includes bibliographical references and index.
        ISBN 0-8126-9453-8 (pbk. : alk. paper)
        1. Allen, Woody—Criticism and interpretation.   I. Conard,
Mark T., 1965–   II. Skoble, Aeon J. III. Series.
PN1998.3.A45W67 2004
791.43'092—dc22
                                                            2004011805

Dedicated to the memory of John Atwell

Contents

Act III

Foreword:
Can We Not Talk about Sex
All the Time?

Philosophers love Woody Allen, in part, because he writes us into his movies. What other well-known filmmaker in our time has had philosophy professors as central characters in his films? For that fact alone, I believe the American Philosophical Association would give him a gold statue, if we could afford the gold. But even better, Woody Allen fills his films with the most important philosophical questions and ideas. Some are brilliantly expressed in dialogue. Others underlie the action. Since we have no award to present him for all this, we do the best we can. We show his movies in Philosophy 101. We crack his jokes in class. And we often see the surprised looks of students raised on Adam Sandler and Vin Diesel flicks when they first realize that you can actually grapple with important ideas on the big screen.

Of course, Woody Allen isn't the only creative thinker to deal with the deepest human questions in the context of drama. The ancient Greeks did a decent job of it long ago. And so did certain twentieth-century existentialists. But Woody is different. He's a bit like Sartre or Camus, only funnier. No one can lead us to the edge of the cosmic abyss like Woody, and then hit us with a joke that somehow makes it all easier, and even more memorable. "Not only is there no God," he quips, "but try getting a plumber on weekends." And this comedic genius isn't just a comic. He has made some thoroughly serious films as well, with no jokes whatsoever. These also tend to be the ones with no audiences whatsoever. But they are all very well done, and extremely powerful in their explorations of the human condition.

Despite all his great wit and personal charm, Woody Allen is an atheistic existentialist with, understandably, strongly pessimistic inclinations on even a good day, which in his own estimation means when it's raining hard. Every silver lining has a very dark cloud around it—and who needs silver when even gold can't buy off death? That's his perspective. But this cinematic genius is not just a messenger of gloom full of nihilistic neuroses, he's also a classic romantic as well. He's a master at depicting our hopes and dreams as well as our foibles and fears. Vivid scenes in his films help us to understand the practical psychological impact of the deepest questions about life and death, and how tenuous all our answers can appear, especially in the hour before an important exam.

Woody Allen is not at all a philosopher in any academic sense, and his short stories and essays often poke fun at the professorial approach to the perennial issues. But he calls us all back to those gripping questions that get people interested in philosophy in the first place. What is morality? Is there really an objective difference between right and wrong? What is the meaning of life? Can there be justice in the universe? Is there a God? How should we think of death? Is philosophy just the ultimate sublimation of sex on the part of very intellectual people who can't get a date?

In a scene worthy of one of his films, a Yale undergraduate once approached me at the end of a class, three weeks into the new semester, wanting to transfer into my section of philosophy. Her current instructor insisted on dragging her through Thomistic metaphysics and mind-numbingly complex arguments. She looked totally exasperated while explaining this to me and said, "He has no clue. I mean, the reason most of us take a philosophy class at all is so that, if we're at a cocktail party sometime in the future and somebody mentions Plato or Aristotle, we'll know what they're talking about." When you watch the films of Woody Allen, you may not come away with a lot about Plato or Aristotle, but you can end up quite well equipped to become a world-class cocktail party philosopher, with insights, anecdotes, and witticisms available for any theoretical occasion.

My own experience of the work of this great filmmaker and artist has been rich and varied. *Manhattan* is the only movie I have ever paid full ticket price to watch twice in the same week. I used clips from most of his movies in my most popular classes at Notre Dame, and found them endlessly stimulating for the students. I have written on his views concerning the meaning of life, and have as thoroughly enjoyed how he poses the problems as I have vigorously objected to how he gives his own answers. Woody will make you think. He may make you mad, or leave you depressed. But along the way he will make you laugh, and appreciate the ultimate questions in a deeper way than before.

I remember once sitting about twenty feet away from Woody as he played his clarinet with his incredibly good jazz band in a small club in New York. His concentration was astonishing. He seemed not to notice that there were other people in the room, in addition to the band. He was playing his music for the sake of the music itself, not to please the crowd. He didn't appear to be aware of the applause that ended each song, and the cheering that sometimes erupted after one of his solos. He was lost in the art itself, oblivious to all else.

That's the way he is as a filmmaker. He has total concentration and lives in the art. He doesn't seem to notice whether his movies are reviewed, or how much money they make. He didn't show up for his Academy Award. He was too busy working on the next project, as lost in his art as he thinks we all are in the universe. He probably won't even be aware that this book exists. But all his fans should know that, finally, a group of careful thinkers—real philosophers—has gotten together to explore and assess his work in a philosophical way. Some of these essays will make you laugh, and all of them will make you think. I believe that by the time you get to the end, you'll applaud Woody as an unusually insightful artist and thinker. Of course, he'll be too busy to notice your applause or mine, but he deserves it anyway.

TOM MORRIS

Acknowledgments

The editors wish to thank the contributors to this volume for all their hard work, insight, and patience. We would also especially like to thank Lisa Bahnemann, Andrew Clyde, William Irwin, David Ramsay Steele, and all the good folks at Open Court.

Introduction:
You Know Nothing of
My Work

This series in Popular Culture and Philosophy began with a book on *Seinfeld*, then came works on *The Simpsons*, *The Matrix*, *Buffy the Vampire Slayer*, and *The Lord of the Rings*. From the beginning, the idea (as well as the notion and concept) has been to introduce to philosophy people who might ordinarily have little or no experience of the discipline. Some people sign up for a philosophy class in college, find the professor annoying, and drop the class—but they nevertheless are intrigued by the ideas. College philosophy isn't for everyone: Woody Allen remarks that he got kicked out for cheating on his metaphysics exam—he "looked within the soul of the boy sitting next to him."[1] But philosophy itself *is* for everyone: questions about life, morality, and value are of universal appeal. So, this series uses popular culture to motivate philosophical thinking. Bill Irwin, the General Editor of the series, is fond of paraphrasing Mary Poppins: just as "a spoonful of sugar helps the medicine go down," a bit of *The Simpsons* helps the Descartes or Aristotle go down. The present work, *Woody Allen and Philosophy*, begins essentially with the same goal in mind, but with a twist: in this case, the subject matter is often more deliberately philosophical. Even in his "earlier, funnier" period, Woody Allen's films were designed to have highbrow appeal, combining slapstick and farce with satire and jokes derived from literature, psychology, or philosophy. (On psychoanalysis: "I haven't seen my analyst in 200 years. He was a strict Freudian. If I'd been going all this time, I'd probably almost be cured by now."[2]) Later films, some not even comedic at all, seem to specifically raise and explore a variety of philosophical issues, often using humor to do so. (On the problem of evil: "If there

---

[1] *Annie Hall* (1977).
[2] *Sleeper* (1973).

1

is a god, why were there Nazis?" "How the hell should I know why there were Nazis, I don't even know how the can opener works!"[3]) Woody says that art is just "entertainment for intellectuals"[4], so it shouldn't come as a surprise that his movies should be literate and philosophically interesting as well as funny. Intellectuals need fun too—it's not as if we just sit around mispronouncing words like "allegorical" and "didacticism."

Unlike the initial volume on *Seinfeld*, this book has been preceded by a good deal of academic work on Woody Allen, including, of course, books by two contributors to this anthology, Sander Lee and Mary P. Nichols. This one, though, is *not* primarily directed at academics (although they'll enjoy it if they're Woody Allen fans), but to the typical Woody Allen fan, the sort of person who takes the *New York Review of Books* or *The New Republic*, who likes to think about philosophy, and uses "take" to describe subscriptions. The sort of person who can have a sense of humor about being an intellectual, and thus laugh at Woody's frequent skewering of intellectuals. The sort of person who knows how to pronounce "Van Gogh" properly. (The sort of person who will notice the sentence fragments in this paragraph, but realize they're deliberate, an affectation.)

Like all the other volumes in the series, the book's genesis is its editors', and later its contributors', appreciation of the subject matter. With all this in mind, we have collected fifteen essays about Woody Allen's work, both his films and his writing, which we hope and believe will appeal to regular people who are philosophical as well as to professional philosophers: our aim is merely (!) to facilitate some philosophical thinking by using explorations into Woody Allen's work. Familiarity with lots of academic theories and jargon is *not* a prerequisite for this course.

The first part of the book explores some recurring themes concerning morality and the meaning of life. Just to make you do some of the work yourself, two of the essays in this section offer different interpretations of these themes—Mark Conard interpreting a more or less consistent pessimism in Woody's work, Ian Jarvie seeing a kind of pragmatic optimism. Wow, two philosophers disagreeing about interpretation of art—go figure.

---

[3] *Hannah and Her Sisters*, 1986.
[4] Stig Björkman, *Woody Allen on Woody Allen* (New York: Grove Press, 1993), p. 103.

Also, Aeon J. Skoble examines the virtue of integrity as it appears in *Manhattan*, and James Lawler uses a Kantian interpretation of *Crimes and Misdemeanors* to examine the idea of morality and its intersection with religion.

The second section of the book is chiefly a look at philosophically significant aspects of Woody's techniques as a filmmaker, or, in the case of James Wallace's essay, a writer. Jason Holt details a theory of aesthetic appreciation as a balance between intellectual and emotional responses, which he claims is present in Woody's films. As one of Woody's alter egos puts it, "It's very hard to get your heart and head together in life. In my case they're not even friendly,"[5] so the balance is certainly worth considering. Jerold Abrams discusses the picture of American culture in Woody's films as voyeuristic, or as a "surveillance society." James South talks about the very important relation between music and emotion in Woody's films. Lou Ascione argues that Woody ingeniously uses humor in a very special way for social and cultural analysis and critique. Per Broman discusses the influence of Ingmar Bergman, one of Woody's cinematic heroes ("If she had said one more word about Bergman, I'd have knocked her other contact lens out"[6]).

The third section contains five essays, each of which focuses on a particular Woody Allen film. Sander Lee argues that *A Midsummer Night's Sex Comedy* provides us with a moral lesson on the dangers of hedonism, and the nihilism and lack of personal integrity which often accompany it. David Detmer looks at Woody's treatment of personal identity and the way inauthenticity—fitting in and going along with the crowd—can lead to fascism in *Zelig*. John Pappas uses Plato's "ring of Gyges" myth to explore issues of vice, virtue, good and evil in *Crimes and Misdemeanors*. In her essay, Jill Gordon discusses the way the central character, Marion Post, gains crucial, life-transforming self-knowledge by seeing herself reflected in "another woman." Last, Mary P. Nichols discusses the relation between *The Curse of the Jade Scorpion* and *The Maltese Falcon*, and argues that Woody presents a much more positive image of moral character than that found in the bleak and noirish world

---

[5] *Crimes and Misdemeanors* (1989).
[6] *Manhattan* (1979).

of the earlier film. Yes, even comedy can be edifying—good, and good for you, as Aristotle is alleged to have said. Woody's character Mickey Sachs discovered the meaning of life at a Marx Brothers movie.

"Millions of books written on every conceivable subject by all these great minds, and, in the end, none of 'em knows anything more about the big questions of life than I do."[7] Well, maybe that's an exaggeration, but it's true that one must think about philosophical issues for oneself. Woody Allen's films prompt us to consider some of them. Consider this a guide to doing so. Or at least, as proof that some of us philosophers have a sense of humor.

_____

[7] *Hannah and Her Sisters* (1986).

Act I

Morality, Interpretation, and the Meaning of Life

1
God, Suicide, and the Meaning of Life in the Films of Woody Allen

MARK T. CONARD

I think what it boils down to, really, is that I hate reality. And, you know, unfortunately, it's the only place where we can get a good steak dinner.

—WOODY ALLEN[1]

Other than sex and art, the one thing that the characters in Woody Allen's movies talk about most is the meaning of life, in one form or another. So, throughout Allen's body of films and writing, is there a consistent position on the meaning and value of life that's expressed by his characters?[2] Despite all the jokes and gags in his work, the focus on romantic love, and the desire and struggle of his characters for self-expression through art, I think the answer is yes, there is a position on the issue, and it's that life is inherently and utterly meaningless. What's more, in

---

[1] From Stig Björkman, *Woody Allen on Woody Allen* (New York: Grove Press, 1993), p. 50.

[2] I'm not claiming that this is necessarily Woody Allen's own position. It's a rather thorny issue whether an idea or set of ideas expressed in the thoughts and speech of various fictional characters scattered throughout various works of art can be attributed to the artist. However, it's probably not a bad inference to claim that if there is a consistent position, it's one that the artist holds, especially—in this case—since in interviews Allen at times confirms that he does in fact accept at least some of the views which I'll be discussing here.

the end Allen seems to tell us that, instead of discovering or creating real meaning and value (through relationships and artistic creativity, for example), all we can ever really hope to do is distract ourselves from, or deceive ourselves about, the meaninglessness of our lives, the terrifying nature of the universe, and the horrible anticipation of our own personal annihilation in death.

Meaning and Permanence

One usual path of reasoning is to claim that, because I am mortal, because I will die, my own personal destruction renders all that I do, my whole life, meaningless. This view is expressed by various characters in Woody Allen's films, perhaps most notably by Mickey Sachs (Woody Allen) in *Hannah and Her Sisters*. When Mickey receives the news that his tests for cancer are negative, he initially celebrates, but then begins to reflect on his own mortality. Back at the office, he tells Gail (Julie Kavner) about his results, and then asks her:

> MICKEY: Do you realize what a thread we're hanging by?
> GAIL: Mickey, you're off the hook. You should be celebrating.
> MICKEY: Can you understand how meaningless everything is? Everything, I'm talking about—our lives, the show, the whole world—meaningless.[3]

Mickey concludes that because he's going to die, because he's only hanging onto life by a "thread," everything, his life, the universe, is without meaning.[4] This recognition of his own mortality then leads him to questions about God's existence, and he soon begins to equate the issue of meaning in life with the existence or nonexistence of God, more than with his own mortality. I'll discuss this in a moment.

Mickey's reasoning about human mortality and the meaning of life is one approach to the problem. However, the more common, and perhaps more sophisticated, approach to the issue in Allen's films is to say that our lives are inherently meaningless

---

[3] *Hannah and Her Sisters* (1986).
[4] Likewise, in *Interiors* (1978), for example, Renata (Diane Keaton) claims, "it's hard to argue that in the face of death life loses real meaning."

because there is no absolute or objective value or meaning built into the universe as a whole. Further, the latter is due to the nature of the universe; it is because everything is impermanent and fleeting that there is no ultimate value or meaning.

In an early (and hilarious) scene in *Annie Hall*, a young Alvy Singer's mother (Joan Neuman) brings him to a doctor (Chris Gampel). She tells the doctor that the boy has stopped doing his homework because of something he has read. When asked to explain what it is that has made him depressed, Alvy (Jonathan Munk), in monotone voice, tells us: "Well, the universe is expanding, and if it's expanding, then someday it will break apart and that will be the end of everything."[5] Consequently, he concludes, it's futile to do anything, including his homework. The point here is clear: since the universe is impermanent, since everything will someday be destroyed, and nothing will eternally endure, life is pointless.

This view, that the universe is fleeting, and that life is thus meaningless, appears in a number of Allen films. In *September*, for example, Lloyd (Jack Warden), a physicist, explains to Peter (Sam Waterston) what he does for a living. He didn't work on the atomic bomb, he tells Peter, but rather on "Something much more terrifying than blowing up the planet." Peter asks, "Is there anything more terrifying than the destruction of the world?" Lloyd replies:

> Yeah—the knowledge that it doesn't matter one way or the other, that it's all random, radiating aimlessly out of nothing, and eventually vanishing forever. I'm not talking about the world. I'm talking about the *universe*. All space, all time, just a temporary convulsion. And I get paid to prove it.[6]

Likewise, in *Stardust Memories*, Sandy Bates (Woody Allen), a filmmaker, is struggling with the meaning of his life and his work. In a telling scene, he asks the people around him, his 'handlers':

> Hey, did . . . did anybody read on the front page of the *Times* that matter is decaying? Am I the only one that saw that? The universe

---

[5] *Annie Hall* (1977).
[6] *September* (1987).

is gradually breaking down. There's not going to be anything left. I'm not talking about my stupid little films here—eventually, there's not going to be any . . . any Beethoven or Shakespeare . . .[7]

Sandy Bates is frightened by the impermanence of his life and the universe at large. The fact that "matter is decaying," that nothing lasts, as we'll see, threatens to render his life meaningless.

Towards the end of the film, Sandy imagines being shot and killed by a deranged fan. During this sequence, his analyst (Leonardo Cimino) claims:

> I treated him. He was a complicated patient. He saw reality too clearly—faulty denial mechanism, failed to block out the terrible truths of existence. In the end, his inability to push away the awful facts of "being-in-the-world" rendered his life meaningless, or as one great Hollywood producer said: "Too much reality is not what the people want."
>
> Sandy Bates suffered a depression common to many artists in middle age. In my latest paper for the *Psychoanalytic Journal*, I have named it, "Ozymandias Melancholia."[8]

"Melancholia" may refer to Freud's use of the term; he employed it to designate many (of what we now describe as) states of depression.[9] "Ozymandias" refers to the Shelley poem of that name, in which a "traveler from an antique land" reports having seen a crumbling statue in the middle of the desert, on which is inscribed: "My name is Ozymandias, King of Kings / Look on my Works, ye Mighty, and despair!" The traveler then says: "Nothing beside remains. Round the decay / Of that colossal Wreck, boundless and bare / The lone and level sands stretch

---

[7] *Stardust Memories* (1980).

[8] *Ibid.*

[9] In "Mourning and Melancholia," Freud compares the healthy process of mourning, the "reaction to the loss of a loved person," to the neurotic/depressive condition, melancholia. The latter is characterized by "a profoundly painful dejection, cessation of interest in the outside world, loss of the capacity to love, inhibition of all activity, and a lowering of the self-regarding feelings to a degree that finds utterance in self-reproaches and self-revilings, and culminates in a delusional expectation of punishment." Sigmund Freud, "Mourning and Melancholia," *The Complete Psychological Words of Sigmund Freud*, trans. and ed. James Strachey (London: Hogarth Press, 1957), p. 246.

far away."[10] Besides being perhaps a clue into Sandy's self-importance, the point of this is clear: Sandy's despair (his "melancholia") is derived from the knowledge that nothing lasts, not even great works and kingdoms. This "terrible truth of existence," this awful fact of "being-in-the-world," "rendered his life meaningless."

Last, in *Deconstructing Harry*, Cookie (Hazelle Goodman), a black prostitute, asks Harry Block (Woody Allen), whom she has just finished servicing, why he is so sad and why he takes so many pills. Harry replies that he is "spiritually bankrupt," and "empty." He then clarifies:

> HARRY: You know that . . . that the universe is coming apart? Do you know about that? Do you know what a black hole is?
> COOKIE: Yeah, that's how I make my living.
> HARRY: You know, I gotta tell you, Cookie, a great writer named Sophocles said that it was probably best not to be born at all.[11]

Like Sandy Bates and his concern that matter is decaying, like young Alvy Singer and his dread of the universe breaking apart, and like Lloyd's terror that the universe is just a "temporary convulsion," Harry likewise is worried about the universe "coming apart," and seems to conclude with Sophocles that, because of that fact, it's "probably best not to be born at all," meaning that because of the lack of anything enduring, permanent, or eternal, life is meaningless, pointless, and therefore not worth suffering through.

This argument is a broader and more sophisticated approach to the question of meaning than the one concerning mortality voiced by Mickey Sachs. It says: because the universe at large is impermanent, it is without meaning and value, since (and here's the unstated premise) real value would have to be permanent, enduring, eternal; consequently, since I'm a part of that universe, my own life is likewise impermanent and therefore without meaning and value. This may be an example of what logicians call the fallacy of division, when one unjustifiably attributes the

---

[10] "Ozymandias," Percy B. Shelley. *The Norton Anthology of English Literature*, fifth edition (New York: Norton, 1986) p. 691.

[11] *Deconstructing Harry* (1997).

qualities of the whole of something to the parts of that thing, but it is a more subtle and interesting claim than to say merely that I'm going to die, ergo my life is without meaning.

Further, Allen tells us, we are at times able to grasp the larger point about the universe, and it may in fact be the limit of human understanding. *Hannah and Her Sisters* includes "sections titles," phrases in white lettering on a black screen that divide up the film. One of these titles is a quote by Tolstoy: "The only absolute knowledge attainable by man is that life is meaningless."[12]

Depression and Suicide

When we do have this insight and attain the understanding that life is meaningless, the knowledge of it is often crushing and debilitating. When asked why he won't do his homework any longer, young Alvy responds simply: "What's the point?" As an adult, Alvy (Woody Allen) tells Annie (Diane Keaton) that he has a "very pessimistic view of life," and that he believes that "The world is divided into the horrible and the miserable." The horrible are terminal cases and crippled and blind people, Alvy says. The miserable are the rest of us, struggling through our awful, meaningless lives. "So when you go through life," he tells her, "be thankful that you're miserable."[13]

Perhaps naturally, some are driven by this knowledge and understanding to suicide. For example, in *Crimes and Misdemeanors*, the philosophy professor Louis Levy (Martin Bergmann) admits that "The universe is a pretty cold place," that it is inherently valueless and meaningless. It is because of this, then, that we sometimes come to realize or believe that "the thing isn't worth it,"[14] that life isn't worth living. Levy, coming to this realization himself, subsequently commits suicide.

---

[12] In Björkman (p.156), Allen claims that this is the real message of the film, despite its happy ending, which he sees as a cop out: "It [the Tolstoy quote] was not a point of departure for *Hannah*, but it's certainly what my story was about, what my thread was about. I think, if I'd had a little more nerve on that film, it would have been confirmed it somewhat more. But I copped out a little on the film, I backed out a little at the end."
[13] *Annie Hall*. About Alvy's view, Allen says: "That's a reflection on my own feelings. Be happy that you're just miserable" (Björkman, p. 85).
[14] *Crimes and Misdemeanors* (1989).

In *Play it Again, Sam*, Allan Felix (Woody Allen) attempts to pick up a woman (Diana Davila) at an art museum. She's examining a painting, and he approaches her:

ALLAN: It's quite a lovely Jackson Pollock, isn't it?
WOMAN: Yes, it is.
ALLAN: What does it say to you?
WOMAN: It restates the negativeness of the universe, the hideous lonely emptiness of existence, nothingness, the predicament of man forced to live in a barren, godless eternity like a tiny flame flickering in an immense void with nothing but waste, horror, and degradation, forming a useless, bleak straightjacket in a black, absurd cosmos.
ALLAN: What are you doing Saturday night?
WOMAN: Committing suicide.

In *Another Woman*, Marion (Gena Rowlands) recalls an argument she had with her first husband, Sam (Philip Bosco), about having children. She asks him: "Oh, do you want to bring a child into this world really? You're the one who hates it so much. You're forever lecturing me on the pointlessness of existence."[15] Her husband later kills himself.

In the same film, Marion overhears the therapy session of a woman named Hope (Mia Farrow). During the session, Hope tells her doctor (Michael Kirby):

I began having troubling thoughts about my life, like there was something about it not real, full of deceptions, that these . . . these deceptions had become so many and so much a part of me now, that I . . . I couldn't even tell who I really was.

And suddenly I began to perspire. I sat up in bed with my . . . my heart just pounding, and I looked at my husband next to me, and it was as if he was a stranger. And I turned on the light and woke him up, and I asked him to hold me. And only after a long time did I finally get my bearings.

But for one moment earlier it was as if a curtain had parted and I could see myself clearly. And I was afraid of what I saw and what I had to look forward to, and I wondered . . . I wondered about ending everything.[16]

---

[15] *Another Woman* (1988).
[16] *Ibid.*

Once Hope looked through the deceptions and saw herself clearly, she was afraid of what she saw and what her future held, and so she contemplated suicide. She doesn't make explicit what it was exactly that she saw or what was in her future that terrified her so, but it's quite conceivable that it's the perceived meaninglessness of her existence, which her self-deceptions had previously hidden, and which drove her to contemplate suicide.[17] I'll talk more about these self-deceptions in a moment.

God and Meaning

At times, Allen makes the (perhaps natural) connection between the existence of God and the meaning of life. This connection is quite ingeniously expressed in *The Purple Rose of Cairo*. In this film the fictional movie character Tom Baxter (Jeff Daniels) has stepped off the screen and entered the real life of Cecilia (Mia Farrow). She is showing him around town, when they stop for a moment inside a church. The setting naturally leads to a discussion about God:

> TOM: It's beautiful. I'm not sure exactly what it is.
> CECILIA: This is a church. You do believe in God, don't you?
> TOM: Meaning?
> CECILIA: That there's a reason for everything, for our world, for the universe.
> TOM: Oh, I think I know what you mean: the two men who wrote *The Purple Rose of Cairo*, Irving Sachs and R.H. Levine. They're writers who collaborate on films.
> CECILIA: No, no, I'm talking about something much bigger than that. No, think for a minute. A reason for everything. Otherwise, it would be like a movie with no point, and no happy ending.[18]

In this brilliant exchange, Cecilia expresses the position well: God is the "reason for everything," and if there were no God, then life would have no point at all and no happy ending, sim-

---

[17] Eve in *Interiors* also commits suicide, and Lane in *September* once attempted suicide and contemplates it again.
[18] *The Purple Rose of Cairo* (1985).

ilar, I suppose, to a film that was accidentally made, with no intention or purpose behind it, just a random and chaotic sequence of scenes that don't mean anything and don't go anywhere. We should note, of course, that (while not being chaotic or purposeless) Allen's *Purple Rose* is without a happy ending. Allen himself refers to it as "tragic."[19]

God and the meaning of life, then, are at times quite naturally linked to the question of whether or not life is worth living. In *Love and Death*, for example, Boris (Woody Allen) expresses to Sonja (Diane Keaton) his skepticism about God:

> BORIS: Sonja, what if there is no God?
> SONJA: Boris Dimitrovich! Are you joking?
> BORIS: What if we're just a bunch of absurd people, who are running around with no rhyme or reason?
> SONJA: But if there is no God, then life has no meaning. Why go on living, why not just kill yourself?
> BORIS: Well, let's not get hysterical; I could be wrong. I'd hate to blow my brains out and then read in the papers they found something [pointing upwards].[20]

Sonja unflinchingly makes the inference that if God doesn't exist, then life has no meaning and one might as well commit suicide. Boris claims that if God doesn't exist, then humans are "absurd," (without meaning), and he seems to accept Sonja's inference, insofar as he implies that if God does exist, then one shouldn't commit suicide[21]—he'd hate to pull the trigger and then learn that God really does exist.

Similarly, in *Hannah and Her Sisters*, subsequent to his search for answers about the meaning of his life, Mickey contemplates suicide when he can't seem to find any definitive proof of the existence of God. He clearly believes that life is only worth living if God does in fact exist. In attempting to find some reason to believe in God, he considers becoming Catholic:

---

[19] *Woody Allen: A Life in Film* (Turner Classic Movies, 2002. Directed by Richard Schickel).

[20] *Love and Death* (1975).

[21] Strictly speaking, this is invalid. That is, from the claim that if God doesn't exist, one ought to commit suicide it doesn't (logically) follow that if God does exist, one ought not to commit suicide.

PRIEST: Now, why do you think that you would like to convert to Catholicism?
MICKEY: Well, because, you know, I've got to have something
to believe in. Otherwise, life is just meaningless.[22]

Mickey goes on to tell the priest: "I need to have some evidence. I've got to have some proof. You know, if . . . if I can't believe in God, then I don't think life is worth living." Ultimately, he doesn't find the answers he is looking for, and because of this comes close to attempting suicide. Subsequently, as he relates the story to Holly (Dianne Wiest), we see that Mickey's attitude about the issue is the same as that of Boris, at least initially:

And I remember thinking at the time, I'm going to kill myself. Then I thought, What if I'm wrong? What if there *is* a God? I mean, after all, nobody knows that.[23]

Like Boris, Mickey wouldn't want to live if there is no God, but, at the same time, he doesn't want to kill himself, for fear that God might in fact exist. However, in the end, he interestingly divorces the two issues, and decides that, since life isn't "all a drag," it may be worth living on its own terms, even without God, because of the zaniness of it all (as manifested, for example, in Marx Brothers films). Thus, the suggestion in *Hannah*, at least from the point of view of Mickey, seems to be that the question of God is simply an unanswerable one, out of the reach of human understanding, and thus that we ought not waste our time worrying about it.

I believe that Mickey's response is not only incorrect, but that it is at odds with the overall view presented in Allen's films. (This may well be part of the "cop out" of the film, one of the reasons Allen is disappointed in it.) The absence or nonexistence of God is the precondition of the meaninglessness of life and the universe. Again, the reason that everything is meaningless and valueless is that nothing is permanent. But that certainly wouldn't be the case if God really existed. In that case, and probably *only* in that case, would there be anything absolute and eternal in the universe which could provide absolute and

---

[22] *Hannah*.
[23] *Ibid*.

objective meaning to the world and our lives. Since the view in the films is that nothing is permanent and, because of that fact, life is inherently meaningless, that must mean that the question of God's existence has already been answered negatively.[24]

In some films, Allen also expresses this view when he hints that belief in God is a naïveté or a self-deception. For example, in *Manhattan*, Mary (Diane Keaton) off-handedly remarks, "Hey listen, hey listen, I don't even wanna have this conversation. I mean, really, I mean, I'm just from Philadelphia, you know, I mean, we believe in God. So, okay?"[25] This seems at first like a non sequitur, and Isaac (Woody Allen) certainly takes it to be so. However, the remark is actually quite revealing. It means that the belief in God is a mark of naiveté and innocence, Philadelphia being the more provincial, backward place, as opposed to the sophisticated New York. In New York, in other words, people have sophisticated conversations about orgasms and similar matters, but in Philadelphia, people are still naive and backward enough not to do so. Belief in God, therefore, is likewise an indication of the backwardness of Philadelphians.[26]

Further, in *Crimes and Misdemeanors*, Judah's father, Sol (David S. Howard), a very religious man, claims that if forced to choose between God and the truth, he will always choose God. That juxtaposition is quite telling: God is opposed to truth; and thus God is tantamount to falsity. Consequently, belief in God is a self-deception. Referring to the literal and figurative blindness of Rabbi Ben (Sam Waterston) in *Crimes*, Allen says:

---

[24] This is also what makes the question of individual mortality less important than the question of permanence. That is to say, if God really exists, and Mickey, for example, leaves open that possibility, then my death doesn't render my life meaningless, because, in effect, I never *really* die—my soul will live on after me.

[25] *Manhattan* (1979).

[26] Let me also note that Mary tends to get things completely backwards. She is, for example, wrongheaded in her appreciation of art—everything that Isaac and Tracy like in the museum, she hates; everything they hate, she loves. Further, and interestingly, she claims that we glorify our neuroses by attaching them to grandiose philosophical problems; but the truth, as Isaac reveals it in the end, is quite the other way around: we invent our neuroses in order to avoid the grander philosophical problems. This might suggest that Mary is wrong or has got it backwards on the God issue, as well.

Ben is the only one that gets through it, even if he doesn't really understand the reality of life. One can argue that he understands it more deeply than the others. I don't think he does myself. I think he understands it less, and that's why I wanted to make him blind. I feel that his faith is blind. It will work, but it requires closing your eyes to reality.[27]

Ben's faith in God enables him to get through the hardships of life, including his progressive literal blindness. However, according to Allen, blind faith is truly blind: it's a matter of not understanding reality, of closing one's eyes to reality, of self-deception. It's important to note too that in the documentary, *Woody Allen: A Life in Film*, Allen reports that one of the central messages of *Crimes* is that: "there's no God, and that we're alone in the universe, and that there is nobody out there to punish you"[28]

Last, in *Deconstructing Harry*, Harry argues with his sister, Doris (Caroline Aaron), about the orthodox views she has adopted from her husband:

Harry: . . . and then you go away to Fort Lauderdale and you meet this fanatic, this zealot, and you . . . you . . . he fills your head full of superstition.
Doris: It's tradition.
Harry: Tradition is the illusion of permanence.[29]

Harry here affirms, or reaffirms, the lack of permanence in the universe. Religion and belief in God are superstitions which give us the illusion of something permanent, and therefore of meaning and value, in the world and our lives.[30]

Distractions

As I mentioned above, Sandy Bates's psychiatrist claims that the root of Bates's great melancholy was his inability to distract him-

---

[27] Björkman, pp. 224–25.
[28] *Woody Allen: A Life in Film*.
[29] *Deconstructing Harry*.
[30] Further, a number of the Woody Allen characters are explicitly identified as atheists: Miles Monroe (*Sleeper*) identifies himself as an atheist; Sandy Bates (*Stardust Memories*) is identified as an atheist; the eponymous Danny Rose claims not to believe in God; Harry Block (*Deconstructing Harry*) is identified as an atheist.

self from the "terrible truths of existence" and the "awful facts of 'being-in-the-world'" which "rendered his life meaningless."[31] That one needs to distract oneself, or that one is in fact continually distracting oneself, likewise becomes apparent to Mickey Sachs after his brush with death. In his discussion with Gail about the meaninglessness of life in the face of his own mortality, he tells her that this awful truth is something that he usually manages not to think about. She reminds him that he's not dying, and he says:

> MICKEY: No, I'm not dying now, but, you know, when I ran out of the hospital I was thrilled because they told me I'm going to be all right. I'm running down the street and it hit me: All right, so I'm not going to go today, but eventually I'm going to be in that position.
>
> GAIL: You're just realizing this now?
>
> MICKEY: No, I don't realize it now. I know it all the time, but I manage to stick it in the back of my mind because it's a very horrible thing to think about.[32]

Again, we find ways to push this horrible truth to the backs of our minds, we find ways to deceive and distract ourselves, for if we don't, we—like Sandy Bates and others—will be crushed by the weight of the knowledge, driven to despair and perhaps suicide.[33]

In *September*, prior to the opening of the story, Lane (Mia Farrow) once attempted suicide because of a deep depression. In the course of the film, we see her again depressed and again contemplating suicide. Her friend, Stephanie (Dianne Wiest), tries to help her:

> STEPHANIE: Now give me those pills. Tomorrow will come and you'll find some distractions. You'll get rid of this place, you'll move back to the city, you'll work, you'll fall in

---

[31] *Stardust.*

[32] *Hannah.*

[33] Allen says: "That's really what we're all talking about is the tragedy of perishing. Ageing and perishing. It's such a horrible, horrible thing for humans to contemplate, that they don't contemplate it. They start religions, they do all kinds of things not to contemplate it. They try to block it out in every way. But sometimes you can't block it out" (Björkman, p. 105).

love, and maybe it'll work out, and maybe it won't, but
you'll find a million petty things to keep you going, and
distractions to keep you from focusing on—

LANE: On the truth.[34]

Again, the point is clear: we need distractions, we need illusions
and self-deception, in order to help us avoid the terrible truths
of our lives. In *Shadows and Fog*, Kleinman (Woody Allen) is
caught up in a Kafkaesque plan to catch a brutal murderer who
strikes randomly and without mercy. This can be read as an alle-
gory for our lives: that they're random, impenetrable to understanding, with evil and death awaiting us at every turn. At the
end of the film, Kleinman has decided to accompany a traveling
magician-illusionist on the road, to be his assistant. He imagines
it a wonderful job. Someone says, "It's true—everybody loves
his illusions." And Omstead the magician (Kenneth Mars)
exclaims, "Loves them? They need them, like they need the
air!"[35] We need our illusions, our self-deceptions, in order to
survive. Without them, the crushing weight of the truth would
perhaps be fatal.[36]

Okay, so we need to distract ourselves from thinking about
awful things. However, most of us still live our lives—and most
of Allen's characters live their fictional lives—as if, despite the
chaos, emptiness, and coldness of the universe at large, we
could invest those individual lives with meaning and value
through our various pursuits and relationships. So the message
in Allen's films is not only that we need to distract ourselves
from the awfulness of the truth, but, further (and pessimistically)
that these individual projects, activities, relationships, and other
concerns, which we pursue in order to give ourselves meaning
and value (in the microcosms of our lives), are ultimately

---

[34] *September*.

[35] *Shadows and Fog* (1992).

[36] In *Manhattan*, while making some notes for a writing project, Isaac (Woody
Allen) reports that this is the source of many of the neurotic personalities he
encounters: "An idea for a short story about people in Manhattan who are constantly creating these real unnecessary neurotic problems for themselves 'cause
it keeps them from dealing with more unsolvable, terrifying problems about
the universe." One way in which we distract ourselves from the "terrifying
problems" of life and the universe is by creating "unnecessary" and mundane
problems.

doomed to failure. This is, again, precisely because of the lack of permanence and value and meaning in the universe as a whole (and, therefore, also in our individual lives). Because of that impermanence, these projects and relationships are ultimately no more than the mere distractions and self-deceptions which help us to avoid facing the terrible truths of existence.

The Failure of Our Attempts at Meaning

One of the ways in which we attempt to provide meaning for our lives is through our relationships to other people, and particularly (at least in Allen's films) through our romantic relationships. The claim that these relationships, like everything else, turn out to be mere distractions is rather dramatically made in *September*, in the exchange between Peter and Lloyd, part of which I cited above. After Lloyd explains that he is paid to prove that the universe is meaningless, that it doesn't matter one way or the other whether or not we destroy the world in an atomic holocaust, the scene (remarkably) concludes thus:

> PETER: You feel so sure of that when you look out on a clear night like tonight and see all those millions of stars? That none of it matters?
> LLOYD: I think it's just as beautiful as you do, and vaguely evocative of some deep truth that always just keeps slipping away, but then my professional perspective overcomes me, a less wishful, more penetrating view of it, and I understand it for what it truly is: haphazard, morally neutral, and unimaginably violent.
> PETER: Look, we shouldn't have this conversation. I have to sleep alone tonight.[37]

The exchange is remarkable not only because of Lloyd's description of the universe as "haphazard, morally neutral, and unimaginably violent," which is quite striking on its own; it's utterly remarkable because of Peter's seemingly incongruous response to that claim, that they shouldn't be having the conversation because he has to sleep alone. This is a wonderfully

---

[37] *September.*

interesting and telling statement. It means, really quite cynically (or realistically, as the case may be), that relationships are important distractions, or buffers against the harsh nature of reality. In the film, Peter's romantic advances have been rejected by Stephanie, and thus that night he has nothing to distract him from the ugly truths about the universe which Lloyd is laying before him. The scene thus not only presents us with the view of the universe that I discussed above, that it's devoid of meaning and value, but it also exposes the truth about our individual pursuits, in this case our romantic relationships: that they're ultimately mere distractions, ways of deceiving ourselves about the awful truths of the universe and our lives. This view is also expressed quite nicely in Allen's "God, (A Play)," from *Without Feathers*:

> DORIS: But without God, the universe is meaningless. Life is meaningless. We're meaningless. (*Deadly pause*) I have a sudden and overpowering urge to get laid.[38]

Like Peter, Doris needs sex, needs a romantic relationship, to distract her from the knowledge that the universe and life are meaningless. Granted, these passages don't indicate that this is the *only* possible function of a relationship, that a relationship *couldn't possibly* provide meaning and value in one's life. However, again, this is necessarily the case, given the nature of meaning and value according to Allen: Since value and meaning could only be provided by, or exist as, some eternal and permanent feature of the universe, and since our individual projects and lives can by no means produce something eternal and permanent, these projects can never produce meaning and value. Consequently, as I've said, these pursuits are—at best—mere distractions.

Besides relationships, one other very common means of pursuing meaning for Allen's characters is through art and creativity.[39] In *Interiors*, for example, the three sisters are artists of one variety or another. One central part of the story, then, is Renata's

---

[38] "God, (A Play)," *Without Feathers* (Ballantine, 1975, p. 150).
[39] In *Annie Hall*, Alvy uses art in the form of a play to try and correct what he doesn't like about reality. In *Interiors*, most of the characters are artists or writers. In *Manhattan*, Mary and Isaac are both writers. In *Stardust*, Sandy Bates is a filmmaker. In *September*, Lane is a photographer, and Peter is a writer. In

(Diane Keaton) realization that her art won't ultimately provide meaning to her life. She tells her therapist:

> Increasing thoughts about death just seemed to come over me . . . a preoccupation with my own mortality, these feelings of futility in relation to my work. I mean, just what am I striving to create anyway? I mean, to what end? For what purpose? What goal? I mean, do I really care if a handful of my poems are read after I'm gone forever? Is that supposed to be some sort of compensation? I used to think it was, but now, for some reason, I . . . I can't . . . I can't seem to . . . I can't seem to shake this . . . the real implication of dying—it's terrifying. The intimacy of it embarrasses me.[40]

Renata realizes that the idea that she will achieve immortality— the elusive permanence, which might give our lives true meaning and value—through her art is a self-deception. In an interview, Allen tells us that this is one of the messages in the film:

> I wanted to show three sisters, first off, one who was genuinely gifted, that is, Diane Keaton, who is a writer, and who based everything in her life on art, who put all her faith in art, and had come to the realization that art was not going to save her. And the notion of posterity, of achieving immortality through posterity is the artist's Catholicism; it's the artist's sense of an afterlife, which I don't believe in at all, and I . . . Catholics do believe in an afterlife. I don't. And artists do believe in an afterlife, which I believe is equally as fallacious.[41]

Again, any hope that, through art, one might achieve the permanence, the immortality required to create real meaning and value is "fallacious," it's a self deception on the part of the artist, comparable to the theist's belief in the survival after death of the soul: Both are ways of deceiving and thus comforting ourselves about the harshness of reality, the ultimate meaninglessness of our lives, and our own personal destruction in death.

Hannah, Frederick is a painter, Mickey is a writer for TV, and Holly becomes a playwright. In *Crimes*, Cliff is a filmmaker. *Bullets Over Broadway* is essentially about artists and morality.

[40] *Interiors.*

[41] *Woody Allen: A Life in Film.* Allen gives a very similar account in Björkman's book, p. 103.

2
Integrity in Woody Allen's *Manhattan*

AEON J. SKOBLE

Towards the end of Woody Allen's 1979 film *Manhattan*, Allen's character Isaac chastises his friend Yale (Michael Murphy): "you're too easy on yourself, don't you see that? You know, that's your problem, that's your whole problem. You rationalize everything. You're not honest with yourself."[1]

Isaac is referring here not only to the justifications Yale offers Isaac for his otherwise unjustifiable actions, but also to the sorts of self-deceptions he engages in which allow the actions to proceed. Isaac can be taken as making a more general claim, of course, about people's self-deceptions and rationalizations. Having integrity, or fidelity to one's own principles, seems to require both that we act in certain ways and that we think in certain ways, for if we allow ourselves too much latitude in "rationalization," we will have no reliable guide to action. Since integrity is major theme of *Manhattan*, this chapter will examine the ways in which that film treats it, as a vehicle for some philosophical reflection on the nature and value of integrity.

The Hobgoblin

We would be well advised to distinguish integrity from mere *consistency*, as well as from *stubbornness*, although both of those seem to reside in the same general vicinity as integrity.[2]

---

[1] *Manhattan* (1979).
[2] For a related discussion, see Robert A. Epperson's *"Seinfeld* and the Moral

"Having integrity" is always intended as moral praise. Although being consistent may be part of integrity, mere consistency doesn't capture the moral praiseworthiness intended by "integrity." One can be consistent in a variety of morally neutral ways, for example, consistently following a certain aesthetic in home decorating, and one can be consistent about actual moral wrongs, for example a consistent Nazi who doesn't fail to kill any of the Jews he encounters. A character flaw can appear as a consistency also; for example the Alvy character (Allen) in *Annie Hall* consistently sabotages his relationships. The common phrasing "being true to yourself" might be part of integrity, but by itself it is too subjective to be useful. A vain narcissist (such as the Lester character (Alan Alda) in *Crimes and Misdemeanors*) is typically committed to being "true to himself," but this isn't seen as a moral good.

A more sophisticated contrast is with stubbornness. "Being stubborn" is generally something discouraged, perhaps because it implies an unwillingness even to consider contrary views. A person of integrity might show unwavering fidelity to a principle, but we would assume that such a person would, in theory, be open to discussing the grounding of those principles, whereas the stubborn person is one who "won't listen to reason." Both integrity and stubbornness seem to imply "being uncompromising," but in the latter case this is thought to be unfortunate, the product perhaps of stupidity, while in the former case it is thought to be a good thing. The difference, it seems, is that while it may be good to be uncompromising about principles one ought to have, it is bad to be uncompromising about principles one ought not to have. Does this mean that we should only value integrity after we are sure we are right? That would make integrity a bit more inaccessible than we normally conceive of virtues as being. Let me sketch an account of integrity which accounts for these distinctions without falling into that trap.

Parts and Wholes

We might begin by noticing the etymological similarity between "integrity" and "integrated"—in this context, it is one's charac-

---

Life," in William Irwin ed., *Seinfeld and Philosophy* (Chicago: Open Court, 2000).

ter which might be said to be "fully integrated." Plato, for example, describes the just person as having attained a state of inner harmony, harmony with respect to himself. The just person "rules himself. He puts himself in order, is his own friend, and harmonizes the three parts of himself. . . ., and from having been many things he becomes entirely one, moderate and harmonious."[3] On this view, the three "parts" (namely, reason, emotions, and appetites), are made to work together for the sake of one's overall psychological well-being. (As the Clifford character [Allen] in *Crimes and Misdemeanors* laments, "it's very hard to get your heart and head together in life. In my case they're not even friendly."[4] But they should be, on Plato's view—his point is that one would be happier if they were.) One way to understand integrity, then, is to see it as involving the pursuit of a kind of psychological wholeness, wherein internal conflicts are minimized. That would eliminate, for example, the temptation to violate one's own principles for the sake of expediency, since one's desires and one's sense of principles would have been brought more in line with each other.

The question would still remain, though, of whether having integrity presupposes a correct underlying morality. Is integrity a secondary virtue, like loyalty? Some philosophers have argued that loyalty is not a virtue in and of itself, but a trait the goodness of which is contingent on the moral value of its object. (On that view, we wouldn't lavish moral praise on a loyal Nazi, since Nazism is something to which morality requires disloyalty.) Should we understand integrity like that, so that we do not praise a Nazi with integrity? Actually, I think that is not right. It seems more accurate to say instead that a person of integrity could not remain a Nazi after careful consideration, that integrity requires abandoning obviously false moral principles. The person of integrity might, through ignorance or error, embrace Nazism initially, but upon reflection would have to reject it. Integrity seems to imply, if not the holding of, at least the openness to, some correct underlying morality. Its connotations of "the whole" and "integration" must imply some connection to reality, in the sense that being

---

[3] Plato, *Republic* (Indianapolis: Hackett, 1992), 443d.
[4] *Crimes and Misdemeanors* (1989).

whole is an objective matter. So integrity seems to be a matter of fidelity to correct moral principles, as a product of an integrated psychological makeup in which desires and reason are largely in agreement, not in perpetual conflict, and where reason plays a role in discovery and examination of the principles one holds. Using this as a working definition, at least, let us turn to the treatment of integrity as a theme in *Manhattan*, and see whether the film helps illuminate our understanding of the virtue, or vice versa.

One of the Beautiful People

First, here is a more complete account of the scene where Isaac confronts Yale. To set the stage for this scene, we need to know a little background. Yale had been having an affair with Mary (Diane Keaton), and Isaac, who had become interested in her, did not start seeing her until the affair had ended. But then Isaac discovers that Yale (still married) has taken up with Mary again, in effect cheating on his wife and (in a way) on Isaac.[5] Here is the dialogue for the confrontation scene. They are in a science classroom at the school where Yale teaches, and there is a skeleton of some early hominid hanging next to where Isaac is standing.

> YALE: Well, I'm not a saint, okay.
> ISAAC: But you're too easy on yourself, don't you see that? You know, that's your problem, that's your whole problem. You rationalize everything. You're not honest with yourself. You talk about, you want to write a book, but in the end you'd rather buy the Porsche, you know. Or you cheat a little bit on Emily and you play around the truth a little with me, and the next thing you know, you're in front of a Senate committee and you're naming names, you're informing on your friends!
> YALE: You are so self-righteous, you know. We're just people, we're just human beings, you know. You think you're God!
> ISAAC: I gotta model myself after someone!

---

[5] I don't mean to imply that Yale and Isaac were lovers, but Yale has betrayed Isaac by sneaking around with Mary, who at this juncture is seeing Isaac.

YALE: Well, you just can't live the way you do, you know. It's all so perfect.

ISAAC: What are future generations going to say about us? My God, you know, someday we're gonna, we're gonna be like him [pointing to the skeleton]. I mean, you know, he was probably one of the beautiful people. He was probably dancing and playing tennis, and everything. Now look, this is what happens to us. It's very important to have some kind of personal integrity. I'll be hanging in a classroom someday, and I want to make sure that when I "thin out" that I'm well thought of.[6]

The significance of this scene, for present purposes, is the questions it raises about integrity, which Isaac specifically mentions here. Three in particular seem worth special attention: Why is "you'd rather buy the Porsche" a failure of integrity? Is the slippery-slope argument (next thing you know, you're informing on your friends) in that passage justified? What is the relevance of how one is "thought of" after "thinning out" to integrity?

Buying the Porsche is, of course, a *symbol* for Isaac of Yale's lack of integrity, not literally *evidence* of it. Let us examine how this is so. Earlier in the film, we see that Yale wants to write a book, but never quite gets around to it. When he should be devoting energy to his work, he is agonizing about unnecessary extravagances and extramarital affairs. This is indicative of a poor sense of priorities. On a Platonic model, we might describe Yale's desires as being not integrated with his reason. This is why he is internally conflicted, and vacillates on whether he wants, or should want, to leave his wife and take up with Mary. His vacillation about the Porsche is similar in nature, and reveals the same character flaw. He gives in to his desires without subjecting them to rational scrutiny—for example, a person living in Manhattan will not typically be in a position to benefit from owning a Porsche, and, more substantially, Yale leaving his wife for the emotionally unstable Mary ("the winner of the Zelda Fitzgerald emotional maturity award"[7]) doesn't seem like a bright idea. Yale keeps talking about how he should write his

---

[6] *Manhattan.*
[7] *Manhattan.*

book, but lacks the emotional commitment to do so, but ultimately decides in favor of acting on his desires for the Porsche and for Mary. He deceives himself, as Isaac notes, into thinking that he is fulfilling his life plan by doing these things, yet he never does what would genuinely do so.

Turning next to the slippery-slope argument,[8] is it true that by deceiving Isaac about Mary, Yale is becoming the sort of person who would inform on his friends? Without invoking it specifically, Isaac here appeals to the Aristotelian notion that our character traits are formed over time by the actions we perform and the decisions we make. Just as a talented athlete makes certain physical tasks "second nature" by practicing, a person develops virtues (or vices) by habituating himself to such actions. In other words, by continually choosing and doing right acts, one becomes virtuous, and by continually choosing and doing wrong acts, one becomes vicious.[9] Isaac is noticing a pattern of habituation in Yale's actions: he lies to his wife, he lies to Isaac, he lies to himself. His deceptions and self-deceptions are the product of mere expediency ("you're too easy on yourself")—he doesn't even attempt to justify them in terms of some greater good. He is forming his character based on habituation, and the more often he lies for the sake of expediency, the easier it becomes to do so, the more natural it seems. Hence, it is not hyperbole for Isaac to claim that Yale is becoming the sort of person who would inform on his friends. This is in fact an accurate diagnosis of Yale's character flaw.

Why Not to Buy the Porsche

Why is it, as Isaac claims here, important to have integrity? He claims here that he wants to be sure that he is "well-thought-of"

---

[8] In logic, a "slippery-slope" argument is one in which either (a) a series of small differences are taken to not add up to a large difference, or (b) a small step is taken to unavoidably entail much greater ones. Isaac's concern here is of the latter variety, that if you allow yourself to do X, you will end up doing Y, and since Y is obviously bad, you have good reason not to do X. For two different perspectives on slippery-slopes, see Greg Bassham *et al.*, *Critical Thinking* (Boston: McGraw-Hill, 2002), p. 173, and Eugene Volokh, "The Mechanisms of the Slippery Slope," *Harvard Law Review* 116 (2003), p. 1026.
[9] See Aristotle, *Nicomachean Ethics* (Indianapolis: Hackett, 1999), especially Book II, Chapters 1–2.

by future generations. That could be taken to imply that the sole value of integrity, or of virtue generally, is that future generations remember one well. But that probably isn't what Isaac has in mind: after all, he has no way of knowing whether the skeleton was a person of integrity or not. When he becomes "just like" the skeleton, it won't matter to him what anyone thinks anyway.

Indeed, we know that Isaac thinks that moral merit can't be ascertained by majority opinion in the first place. Earlier in the film, he questions the claim that a comedy sketch is funny because people laugh: "Why do you think this is funny? You're going by audience reaction? This is an audience that's raised on television, their standards have been systematically lowered over the years."[10] This is odd in a way, since the fact that people laughed might be taken as tautologically implying that the sketch is in fact funny, but his larger point is that people's judgments can be called into question if they don't have appropriate standards to begin with. If a roomful of Yales were making retrospective judgements about people's characters, they might very well praise compromisers and self-indulgent types (like themselves). So when Isaac refers to retrospective judgments of character by posterity, he can only mean the judgments of people with the right standards. In other words, what he really wants is to be well thought of by morally good people. By asking how (idealized) future generations will remember him, he is asking whether he will have actually *been* good, by an objective measure.

Another point Isaac is making in this speech is that we *do* become skeletons: we die. So we ought to be concerned with what it is that makes life good "while we're here." Is it "dancing and playing tennis" (or buying Porsches and having affairs) that constitutes a good life? As Yale's increasingly corrupted character indicates, perhaps we should take a broader view of what constitutes happiness.

Later in the film, Isaac notes certain specific things that make life worth living,[11] but the scene in the lab seems to point to the

------

[10] *Manhattan.*
[11] "Well, There are certain things I guess that make it worthwhile. uh . . . Like what . . . okay . . . um . . . For me, uh . . . ooh . . . I would say . . . what, Groucho Marx, to name one thing . . . uh . . . um . . . and Willie Mays . . . and

importance of integrity, or virtue generally, to a well-lived life. Without integrity, one can't bring reason and emotion together, and this disharmony results in internal conflicts, endless unsatisfied longings, and an inability to follow through on valuable commitments. Without virtue, only superficial or ephemeral pleasures are available.

A broader conception of the happy life would include the necessity of psychological harmony and well-being over time. Isaac himself is not flawless in this regard: he is conflicted about his relationship with Tracy (Mariel Hemingway), but he does at least attempt to be honest about it. Is his breaking up with Tracy an example of integrity, or an example of a lack of integrity? He will not date both women simultaneously—his sense of integrity dictates that his wish to see Mary entails his breaking up with Tracy. On the other hand, one might argue that if Isaac had more integrity, he would not have let himself get involved with Mary in the first place, that *that* was self-deception on his part.[12] But as the story unfolds, we see that his involvement with Mary was unplanned, she initially seemed a better match than Tracy (if only because of being older), and when it did begin, he refused to deceive Tracy. At any rate, when he realizes he has treated her poorly, he rushes to make amends, for the sake of his own psychological well-being. He had not lied to her as Yale had to his wife, but Isaac's inability to commit to Tracy is similarly the result of internal conflicts (though not of self-deception). He realizes later that he needs his commitment to Tracy to be whole.

---

um . . . the second movement of the Jupiter Symphony . . . and um . . . Louis Armstrong's recording of "Potato Head Blues" . . . um . . . Swedish movies, naturally . . . *Sentimental Education* by Flaubert . . . uh . . . Marlon Brando, Frank Sinatra . . . um . . . those incredible Apples and Pears by Cézanne . . . uh . . . the crabs at Sam Wo's . . . uh . . . Tracy's face . . ." On Aristotle's view, there's a variety of "external goods" which *contribute to* the happy life, but virtue is *a necessary condition* of the happy life. See *Nicomachean Ethics*, Books VII–X. See also Douglas Rasmussen, "Human Flourishing and the Appeal to Human Nature," in Paul, Miller, and Paul, eds., *Human Flourishing* (Cambridge: Cambridge University Press, 1999).

[12] I leave aside the argument as to whether integrity allows or forbids a man of Isaac's age from dating a high-school girl. The viewer will note that Isaac is at least aware of the potential problem the age difference presents, but at the same time, it is Tracy who is dismissive of it.

Integrity, then, isn't merely of instrumental value in terms of one's reputation, but is one of the yardsticks by which a person's moral status can be objectively appraised. If we understand integrity not as mere stubbornness, but as consistency with respect to correct moral principles, involving integration of reason and emotion, and hence the willingness to examine oneself and be honest with oneself, then it really would be as important as Isaac claims it is. We *should* want to be well-thought-of in that sense, after we "thin out."[13]

---

[13] Thanks to Mark Conard for his helpful comments on this chapter.

3

Does Morality Have to Be Blind? A Kantian Analysis of *Crimes and Misdemeanors*

JAMES LAWLER

Woody Allen's *Crimes and Misdemeanors* directly confronts the problem of meaning in a world in which the eyes of justice have apparently been blinded. According to Immanuel Kant, the highest goal of morality consists in creating a just world, or what Kant called "the Highest Good." This is a world in which happiness is "in exact proportion to morality,"[1] or, in other words, a world in which those who are morally upright are happy, while those who violate moral duty in one way or another suffer as a result.

Consequently, the greatest scandal for morality is that the world as we see it seems to operate on completely different, non-moral principles. This is stated clearly in the Bible's classic *Book of Job*, where the innocent, suffering Job complains against God: "Why does he look on and laugh, when the unoffending, too, must suffer? So the whole world is given up into the power of wrong-doers; he blinds the eyes of justice. He is answerable for it; who else?"[2]

---

[1] Immanuel Kant, *The Critique of Practical Reason* (New York: Library of Liberal Arts, 1993), p. 117.
[2] "Book of Job," in *The Holy Bible*, Knox translation, (New York: Sheed and Ward, 1956), p. 458; 9:23–24.

Two Visions of Life

In *Crimes and Misdemeanors* four central stories deftly inter-
twine. One is that of a high and terrible crime. Judah Rosenthal,
a successful eye-doctor, family man, and pillar of the community, commits murder under the all-seeing eyes of God. At least
that is what his father had always affirmed:

> I'll say it once again. The eyes of God see all. . . . There is
> absolutely nothing that escapes his sight. He sees the righteous and
> he sees the wicked. And the righteous will be rewarded. And the
> wicked will be punished, for eternity.[3]

Applauded by an admiring wife and daughter, Judah is seen
at the beginning of the film attending a banquet in honor of his
philanthropic work. In the eyes of society he is a happy family
man, a successful doctor, and a benefactor of humanity. In reality, underneath this glowing image, he is an adulterer, a liar, and
an embezzler of his charities' funds. At least that is what his mistress, Dolores, tells him as she threatens to expose both his adultery to his wife, and his fraudulent use of the charity monies
entrusted to him.

Judah turns for help to his brother Jack, who has shady connections with the underworld. At first he balks at the final solution Jack proposes. "I can't believe I'm talking about a human
being. She's not an insect. You don't just step on her." "I know,"
Jack replies. "Playing hard ball was never your game. You never
like to get your hands dirty. But apparently this woman is for
real, and this thing isn't just going to go away." Judah finally
agrees to have Jack arrange the murder.

The second is a tale of petty misdemeanors, jealousy and
amorous rivalry, together with the frustration of lofty moral
intentions. The good guy, as he sees himself, is Cliff, who makes
documentaries on some of the major issues of our time regarding homelessness, disease, injustice. His current effort is a high-
minded documentary on the life and ideas of an elderly
German-Jewish philosopher, Louis Levy. Cliff is trying to create
a better world, a world of fundamental justice. The trouble is,

---

[3] Where not otherwise indicated, the citations are from Woody Allen's film,
Crimes and Misdemeanors (1989).

few see his films and no one is interested enough to pay him any serious money for them. His marriage is all but dead, and he is looking for someone to love.

The bad guy, as Cliff never tires of telling his would-be girlfriend Halley, is his brother-in-law Lester, a producer of commercially successful TV comedies. Cliff is supposed to make a favorable documentary about Lester for a TV series on "Great Minds." He owes this financially interesting opportunity, resentfully, to Lester's condescending generosity in offering his sister's husband the opportunity to make some real money.

The third and fourth tales provide commentary on the first two from the higher plane of philosophical reflection.

The third story is that of the existentialist philosopher and university professor Louis Levy, whose life and ideas are being recorded by Cliff in one of his idealistic documentaries. Levy, we learn, is a survivor from the Nazi anti-Semitic persecutions which destroyed his entire family. According to Levy's existentialist philosophy, we live in a blind, uncaring universe that is completely indifferent to issues of justice and human happiness. The challenge for those who recognize the heartlessness of nature is to affirm life themselves by creating loving relationships. Levy describes the God of the Jewish culture as a projection of a society only partly able to envision the possibility of such a loving world:

> The unique thing that happened to the early Israelites was that they conceived a God that cares. He cares but he also demands at the same time that you behave morally. But here comes the paradox. What's one of the first things that that God asks? That God asks Abraham to sacrifice his only son, his beloved son to Him. In other words, in spite of millennia of efforts we have not succeeded to create a really and entirely loving image of a God. This was beyond our capacity to imagine.

The fourth tale is about one of Judah's patients, Cliff's other brother-in-law, the good Rabbi Ben. At first glance, the tale of Rabbi Ben seems to reinforce the pessimistic existentialism of Levy. Ben learns from Judah that his sight is fatally compromised. This, together with the outcome of the first two stories, suggests that the universe must be indifferent to any sense of justice, since it permits the morally suspect (Lester) and outright criminal (Judah) to rise in fame and fortune and punishes the good (Cliff and Ben himself). But while Cliff endlessly laments his fate, Rabbi Ben does not seem to notice this contradiction between the axioms of his faith and clear-sighted empirical appraisal of reality. Ben therefore seems blind even before he goes blind.

Ben recommends that Judah confess his betrayal to his wife, Miriam, and hope for forgiveness. But Judah sees no chance that Miriam will ever forgive him for his lies and her humiliation. Ben believes there is a basic difference in their respective philosophical visions, in the way they see the world:

> It's a fundamental difference in the way we see the world. You see it as harsh and empty of values and pitiless. And I couldn't go on living if I didn't feel with all my heart a moral structure, with real meaning, and . . . forgiveness. And some kind of higher power. Otherwise there's no basis to know how to live. And I know you well enough to know there's a spark of that notion somewhere inside you too.

This basic conflict between two radically opposed visions of life is the central theme of Judah's recollection of a family dinner as he revisits the home of his youth. Vividly conjuring a scene from his past, he watches from the side as his youthful self and family members are celebrating the Jewish festival of Passover.

> *At the head of the table, his father Sol conducts prayers before eating.*

> Aunt May (*impatiently*): Come on Sol. Get on with it. I'm hungry. . . . It's nonsense anyway. What are you putting everyone through this mumbo jumbo? Bring on the main course.
>
> SOL: Spare us your Leninist philosophy just this once.

An argument breaks out over the fundamental nature of reality. Is there a moral structure to the universe? Is there justice—punishment for the wicked and reward for the good? If God punishes the wicked, says Aunt May, what about Hitler?

> AUNT MAY: Six million Jews, and millions of others. And they got off with nothing. . . . Because might makes right. Until the Americans marched in. . . .

SOMEONE: What are you saying, May? There's no morality any-where in the whole world?

MAY: For those who want morality there's morality. Nothing's handed down in stone.

WOMAN: Sol's kind of faith is a gift. It's like an ear for music, or the talent to draw. He believes and you can use logic on him all day long and he still believes.

SOL: Must everything be logical?

JUDAH (*intervening from the side into this vision from his past*): And if a man commits a crime, if he kills?

SOL: Then one way or another he will be punished.

AN UNCLE: If he's caught, Sol.

SOL: If he's not, that which originates in a black deed will blossom in a foul manner. . . . Whether it's the Old Testament or Shakespeare, murder will out.

AUNT MAY: And I say if he can do it, and get away with it and he chooses not to be bothered by the ethics, then he's home free. Remember. History's written by the winners. And if the Nazis had won, future generations would understand the story of the World War Two quite differ-ently.

SOL: Your aunt is a brilliant woman, Judah, but she's had a very unhappy life.

AN UNCLE: And if all your faith is wrong, Sol? I mean, just what if? If?

SOL: Then I'll still have a better life than all of those that doubt.

AUNT MAY: Wait a minute. Are you telling me you prefer God over the truth?

SOL: If necessary, I'll always choose God over the truth.

A WOMAN: I agree.

As the scene fades, another woman chimes in: I say, what goes around, comes around.

Conflicting Conclusions

The threads of the four stories come together during the final scene, which takes place at the wedding of Ben's daughter.

Cliff and his wife are finally splitting up. Lester and Halley are engaged and Cliff is completely crushed. Judah finds Cliff brooding alone over a drink, and says, "You look very deep in thought." Cliff replies, with unconscious irony, "I was plotting the perfect murder." Knowing that Cliff is a film maker, Judah tells him that he has an interesting story—his own story in fact—for a movie. He concludes:

> And after the awful deed is done, he finds that he is plagued by deep-rooted guilt, little sparks of his religious background which he'd rejected are suddenly stirred up. He hears his father's voice. He imagines that God observes his every move. Suddenly it's not an empty universe at all, but a just and moral one. And he's violated it. Now he's panic-stricken. He's on the verge of a mental collapse, an inch away from confessing the whole thing to the police. Then one morning he awakens. The sun is shining, and his family is around him. Mysteriously the crisis is lifted. . . . As the months pass he finds he's not punished. In fact he prospers. The killing gets attributed to another person, a drifter who has a number of other murders to his credit. So, what the hell, one more doesn't even matter. He's scot-free. His life is completely back to normal, back to his protected world of wealth and privilege.

> CLIFF: I think it would be tough to live with that. Very few guys could actually live with something like that on their conscience.
> JUDAH (*suddenly angry and self-defensive*): People carry awful deeds around with them. What do you expect them to do, turn themselves in? This is reality. In reality we rationalize, we deny, or we couldn't go on living.
> CLIFF: Here's what I would do. I would have him turn himself in. Because then, you see, your story assumes tragic proportions, because in the absence of God or something he is forced to assume that responsibility himself. Then you have tragedy.
> JUDAH: But that's fiction. That's movies. You've seen too many movies. I'm talking about reality. If you want a happy ending you should see a Hollywood movie.

Cliff is in fact borrowing his ending from Dostoevsky's tragic novel, *Crime and Punishment*. There, the student Raskolnikov confesses to the police that he has committed a murder, although he could have escaped punishment. And Cliff does luxuriate in the harmony of morality and happiness that permeates his favorite Hollywood movies.

Judah admits that occasionally the murderer may have twinges of guilt, "But it passes. In time it all fades." He then leaves Cliff, embraces his wife, and, in the glow of apparent happiness, walks off into his protected world of wealth and privilege.

The first two stories therefore end with a lesson that contradicts what Kant calls the moral vision of the Highest Good. In what Judah calls "reality," it seems, the wicked person prospers, while the good person, who tries to contribute to creating a just society, is left with his life in tatters.

But on the second, philosophical level, something different is suggested. Levy has committed suicide, thereby ruining Cliff's opportunity to make a successful film. How could Levy do this, after being so affirmative, after saying "yes" to life? The answer is suggested in Cliff's documentary, where Levy explains:

> But we must always remember that when we are born we need a great deal of love in order to persuade us to stay in life. Once we get that love it usually lasts us. But the universe is a pretty cold place. It's we who invest it with our feelings. And under certain conditions, we feel that the thing isn't worth it any more.

This statement provides an important perspective on the idea that in the absence of a just and loving God, the individual should take responsibility for life. If there is no intrinsic moral structure to existence, why should the choice of a "yes" to life be worth any more than the choice of a "no"? If there were no "moral structure with real meaning and forgiveness and some kind of higher power," as Rabbi Ben puts it, why should one not simply see, behind our arbitrary projections onto the universe— our brave "yeses" to life—the cold face of indifference that we suppose is really there? Levy here answers. It is not enough merely to affirm life. Life is worth living only if love sustains us. But it seems that Levy's efforts to find and to project love in what he believes is an essentially loveless universe had finally proved to be futile.

This message regarding the importance of love is amplified in Levy's voice-over that provides philosophical comment to the concluding sequence of the film. This sequence begins with Ben alone on the dance floor, the loving father dancing with the beautiful bride, his daughter. There follows a montage of major events in the film, and finally concludes, at the final sentence, with Ben embracing his daughter.

Levy's words are the following:

We are all faced throughout our lives with agonizing decisions, moral choices. Some are on a grand scale. Most of these choices are on a lesser scale. But we define ourselves by the choices we have made. We are in fact the sum total of our choices. Events unfold so unpredictably, so unfairly. Human happiness does not seem to have been included in the design of creation. It is only we with our capacity to love that give meaning to the indifferent universe. And yet most human beings seem to have the ability to keep trying, and even to find joy from simple things, like their family, their work, and from the hope that future generations might understand more.

The film ends with a double message. On the one hand, we hear the voice of the atheist philosopher, who lucidly underscores the meaninglessness of existence, where all too often the good suffer while the evil prosper. In the moral vacuum of a cold, indifferent, essentially loveless universe, we must somehow have the strength to love and the luck to be loved. On the other hand, what we see before us is the blind man of faith actually enfolded in such love. Perhaps then in order to find real love and happiness it is necessary to have Ben's seemingly blind faith that the universe is itself an inherently loving place. Aunt May, for all her clear-sightedness regarding the injustices of life, had an unhappy life—if we can believe Sol, who seems to have had a happy one. Can we trust the final picture we see of Judah embracing his wife? Does Judah find love and happiness, as Ben surely does with his daughter? We are more likely to trust Dolores' perception of the hollowness of Judah's alleged happiness. She once said to Judah, "You're always so much more relaxed away from home. You come to life. Your whole face changes."

And when does Cliff find meaning and happiness? When, in the company of someone he loves, like his niece, Jenny, or Halley, he is elevated into the ideal world of Hollywood endings where the good are rewarded with the one they love, while the wicked are exposed and deservedly punished. It is this willing suspension of disbelief in the apparent injustices of life, in those moments of faith that the universe ultimately does have a moral structure, that provides Cliff with his periodic moments of happiness. No doubt he is also happy in making his morally conscious documentaries, when he allows himself the belief, constantly renewed but never materializing in concrete evidence, that he is contributing to advancing human welfare, to creating the Highest Good.

From Knowledge to Faith

The philosophical conflict between the apparent clear-sightedness of Professor Levy and the blind faith of Rabbi Ben is addressed by Kant, who writes that "It is necessary to deny knowledge, in order to make room for faith."[4] This is not however a blind faith, but a rationally defensible faith based on a critique of mechanistic science. This critique makes room for the faith that is implied in the moral vision of the world.

On the one hand, natural science shows us a physical world governed by mechanical cause and effect, with no intrinsic moral structure. In social science this deterministic framework is transposed to the plane of practical life. Social science portrays individuals as motivated primarily by self-centered desires or passions, which in turn are caused by their biology, education, and circumstances.

Morality, on the other hand, involves a completely different vision—that of the "Highest Good." This is a vision of a world in which people who freely choose what is right, and who fulfill their responsibilities despite the costs, ultimately find happiness. This is the vision of the Bible—Job is ultimately rewarded for his goodness—of Shakespeare, and of classic Hollywood movies. But if the so-called "realistic," scientific view of the world is the correct one, Kant says, the moral vision "must be fantastic, directed to empty ends, and consequently inherently false."[5]

Kant's *Critique of Pure Reason* argues that the so-called real world, the universe as portrayed by science as a morally indifferent place, is not so real after all. It is only an "appearance," built up in part out of the underlying structures of the mind that we employ when we seek to organize knowledge. When we pursue scientific knowledge, we inevitably employ categories of strict causality. But these categories reflect the structure of the human understanding and its "transcendental logic," not the

---

[4] Immanuel Kant, *Critique of Pure Reason* (New York: Macmillan, 1961), p. 29; B xxx.

[5] Kant, *Critique of Practical Reason* (New York: Macmillan, 1993), p. 120.

nature of reality as it is in itself. "Does everything have to be logical?" Sol asks rhetorically. Kant replies that the "logical" categories of a deterministic science are in fact subjective, not
objective. They express the way in which human beings, in their
scientific enterprise, subjectively organize experience, not the
nature of reality itself. Beyond the "logic" of a mechanistic science is a more fundamental truth, expressed in religious traditions, in the aspirations of the human heart, and in the implicit
assumptions of moral consciousness. This is the truth that the
universe in fact has meaning and purpose—that of fostering the
Highest Good.

The natural and social sciences therefore are inherently
biased in the sense that the scientific approach *presupposes*
determinism; it doesn't prove that the universe itself is deterministic. In the most advanced social science of Kant's day,
Adam Smith's classic work of economic theory, *The Wealth of
Nations*, modern socio-economic life is portrayed as the outcome of the self-interested actions of individuals. "It is not from
the benevolence of the butcher, the brewer, or the baker, that
we expect our dinner," Smith says matter-of-factly, "but from
their regard to their own interest."[6] But what happens to people
who can't pay for their dinner? Cliff warns his niece Jenny about
the purely self-interested character of life in Hollywood: "It's
worse than dog-eat-dog. It's dog doesn't answer other dog's
phone calls." Before Smith, Hobbes had described the world of
self-interested individuals as a war of all against all, a dog-eat-
dog world. But in the economic version of egoism advocated by
Adam Smith, the situation gets even worse. Better to be eaten,
Cliff says, than to be ignored completely.

The indifferent universe presented to us by a mechanistic science, which Professor Levy believes to be real, is essentially a
projection onto nature of our indifference to one another. In his
third formulation of the Categorical Imperative, Kant argues
against the relativism of economic value, and for the subordina-
tion of economic life to the intrinsic dignity of each human individual:

> What is relative to universal human inclinations and needs has a
> *market price*. . . . but that which constitutes the sole condition

---

[6] Adam Smith, *Wealth of Nations* (New York: Modern Library, 1965), p. 14.

under which anything can be an end in itself has not merely a relative value—that is, a price—but has an intrinsic value—that is, *dignity.*[7]

A way of looking at life that is not "logical" in the strictly economic sense is nevertheless morally required of us. The purely economic approach is in fact a subjective one, the result of a human decision to behave in a certain way, not a necessary requirement imposed by human nature or the causal structure of the universe. An alternative way is therefore equally valid. This is the way of morality, with its exalted vision of a just world. To show the legitimacy of an alternative way of viewing life, Kant proposes his own story of crime and misdemeanor. The story has two parts. The first has to do with misdemeanors. Kant writes:[8]

> Suppose that someone says his lust is irresistible when the desired object and opportunity are present. Ask him whether he would not control his passion if, in front of the house where he has this opportunity, a gallows were erected on which he would be hanged immediately after gratifying his lust. We do not have to guess very long what his answer would be.

Judah seemingly can't resist his sexual desire for Dolores, until Dolores threatens to destroy his life. He then finds it very easy to resist his passion for her. Does this mean that Judah is free from causal determinism? No. It means that there is an even greater force than sexual desire determining our actions: love of life in the face of the threat of death.

To find real freedom, Kant thinks, it is necessary to move to a higher level. We must go from the level of the misdemeanor to that of the serious crime. Kant continues:

> But ask him whether he thinks it would be possible for him to overcome his love of life, however great it may be, if his sovereign threatened him with the same sudden death unless he made a false deposition against an honorable man whom the ruler wished to destroy under a plausible pretext. Whether he would or

---

[7] Immanuel Kant, *Groundwork of the Metaphysics of Morals* (New York: Harper Torchbooks, 1964).

[8] *Op. cit.*, p. 30.

not he perhaps will not venture to say; but that it would be possible for him he would certainly admit without hesitation. He judges, therefore, that he can do something because he knows that he ought, and he recognizes that he is free—a fact which, without the moral law, would have remained unknown to him.

Faced with the choice between saving his own life and being responsible for the death of an innocent person, the individual transcends the level of ordinary passion or desire and enters the realm of morality. Here, Kant says, he discovers the true possibility of freedom. He finds that he is able to decide to die rather than to commit a crime against an innocent person. Whether or not he will actually make this decision, Kant says, is not the point. What is important is that he feels he *could* make that decision. This feeling of possibility in the face of death is the experience of authentic freedom. Through moral experience of this kind, we discover our capacity to go beyond all the deterministic laws of physics and biology, psychology and social science, and live or die according to our own capacity for self-determination.

Judah has to choose between his own life and killing an innocent person. According to Kant, this is where he should have the experience of authentic freedom. And yet Judah is intent on denying just such a possibility. He rationalizes and denies. In a dream-like sequence Judah argues with Rabbi Ben:

JUDAH: What choice do I have Ben? Tell me. . . . I will not be destroyed by this neurotic woman.
BEN: It's a human life. You don't think God sees?
JUDAH: God is a luxury I can't afford.
BEN: Now you're talking like your brother Jack.
JUDAH: Jack lives in the real world. You live in the kingdom of heaven. I managed to keep free of that real world but suddenly it's found me.

As in Kant's moral imperative, God sees the intrinsic dignity of Dolores. Judah should see that too—see with God's eyes of love. Judah locks himself into one view of the world, that of "reality," the worse than dog-eat-dog, indifferent, loveless world of egoism and survival. But this "real world" that Judah chooses is in fact an appearance, as Kant says, and as the characters of the film themselves acknowledge. Judah's "real world" is a carefully crafted construct made of denial and rationalization, of lies and crime. The "real world" is Judah's artificially protected world of wealth and privilege. His actual deeds are hidden in a darkness where, eventually, even he can no longer see them. In this sense, it is Judah, not Ben, who has become blind.

But there is another world—that of the kingdom of heaven in which Ben lives. It is founded on two pillars. One is faith, and the other is love. The alternative that Ben holds out to Judah is the possibility of forgiveness and mature love. But for this possibility of love, a certain kind of faith is needed. Faith in what?

The moral vision of the Highest Good, Kant writes, requires that we make three assumptions or "postulates."[9] One is that, contrary to the deterministic assumptions of science, human beings are fundamentally free. We must believe in our ability to rise above the level of survival, of dog-eating-dog, and, far worse, of dog-indifferent-to-dog, and live from out of an inner power to create our own reality, and to attract the love we need. Ultimately, Levy says, we create our own reality. Each of us is the sum of our choices. But this affirmation of freedom contradicts all that science tells us about a mechanistic, indifferent universe. It is an expression of moral faith. If Levy believes with Kant in freedom, why then does he not take a further step? Why, after implicitly rejecting the power of the supposedly indifferent world of mechanistic science, in order to affirm his freedom, does he insist on the truth of that deterministic conception in other respects?

The second postulate is the postulate of God. "By moral faith," Kant writes, "I mean the unconditioned trust in divine aid, in achieving all the good that, even with our most sincere efforts, lies beyond our power."[10] Belief in God means the belief that where we appear to be powerless to achieve the Highest Good, there is in fact power working through our moral actions

---

[9] For a parallel treatment of the postulates in the film, *The Matrix*, see my article, "We Are (the) One! Kant Explains How to Manipulate the Matrix," in William Irwin, ed., *The Matrix and Philosophy* (Chicago: Open Court, 2002), pp. 144–151.

[10] Letter to J.C. Lavater, April 28th, 1775, in *Philosophical Correspondence, 1759–99* (Chicago: University of Chicago Press, 1967), p. 81.

that will ultimately prevail. The God of morality does not demand the sacrifice of innocent human beings, but their triumph. To persist in moral endeavor supposes faith in a God of love who can accomplish miracles through us. She sees what is in our hearts and will somehow, we trust, work out results that correspond to what She finds there. For the moral vision to survive, it is necessary to trust that out of our efforts to do what is right, good will be accomplished. If he doesn't trust in the power of such a loving God, if he doesn't have confidence that the Universe is somehow in sync with his highest intentions and efforts, if he believes that his efforts for the good disappear into an empty void, then the good person, like Professor Levy, will finally despair.

The third postulate of morality is the postulate of immortality. Dolores asks Judah: "Do you agree the eyes are the windows of the soul? . . . My mother taught me that I have a soul and it will live on after me when I am gone. And if you look deeply into my eyes, you can see it." But Judah sees only her body. In Dolores he might have finally seen the soulful eyes of a deathless love looking out at him, calling him to leave his artificial, essentially unreal world of denial and rationalization, but he didn't notice. With her eyes of love, she sees a transformed, truly happy Judah: "You come to life. Your whole face changes."

In Kant's fable, freedom means to be able to choose between the apparent necessities of survival and respect for the infinite dignity of the human person. This means that the human person is more than just her body, more than a mere thing. Judah once said to Jack, "She's not an insect. You don't just step on her." In the end that is in fact what he sees in her, the black eyes of an insect. After his trip to the dead woman's apartment, he recounts to Jack: "I saw there, just staring up, an inert object. . . . Behind her eyes when you looked into them, all you saw was a black void."

When Judah imagines the eyes of God, he sees the destruction of his own vision of himself. Caught up in his worse than dog-eat-dog world of survival, he can only imagine a God who punishes, a God who destroys. For such destruction is the negative side of morality. The moral vision of the world is incompatible with the worldview of egoism, and is its destruction. The alternative that Judah refuses to imagine is to die to this "real world."

When Judah momentarily leaves that world behind, and lives in the eyes of Dolores's love, he finds true happiness. Then he too lives in the kingdom of heaven. Cliff finds such moments in the movie theater with a loving companion. There he transports himself into a world of justice—of love and happiness for those who struggle for the good. The hero is ready to sacrifice his life, and in the end he finds love. Murder on the other hand only brings murder in return—the murder of a higher life, of the possibility of true happiness.

When Judah kisses his wife and walks off into his carefully gilded version of happiness, we are looking at an "appearance," a staged performance, not at Judah's reality. With the aid of Kant's critique of the idea of a morally indifferent universe, an intelligent, rationally grounded faith becomes possible. Such faith enables us to see the final performance of Judah with the eyes of the Bible, of Shakespeare, and of the classic Hollywood films, and so to agree with old Sol that "that which originates in a black deed will blossom in a foul manner."

4

Arguing Interpretation: The Pragmatic Optimism of Woody Allen

IAN JARVIE

Woody Allen is a pragmatic optimist. "Pragmatic" because to go on making thoughtful films is to affirm optimism by action. Allen's optimism is not to be identified with that expressed by some of his characters.

The standard rubrics of optimism and pessimism yield fruitful interpretations of several of Allen's later films. How best to argue for such interpretations? The arguments to be preferred are those that appeal neither to some pronouncement of, or biographical fact about, the author; nor to the predilections of the interpreter. Allen's work helps us avoid both of these moves: the biographical fallacy and the reading in or "eisegetic" fallacy (reading a meaning into the text, rather than interpreting what the text might have to say),[1] because he presents the alternatives of optimism and pessimism in dramatic rather than discursive form. This enables Allen the author to stand at one remove from positions defended in the works, clearly apparent in his deployment in the drama of what I shall call secret knowledge—knowledge shared by the audience but not by all of the characters. The dramatic use of secret knowledge should alert the audience to the pitfalls of naively identifying author and work, author and character. This does not mean that Allen's views are hidden. There is

---

[1] For my discussion, I draw on some of the criteria of interpretation proposed in my *Philosophy of the Film* (London: Routledge, 1987), where earlier Woody Allen films are discussed.

a straightforward optimism displayed in the films, in Allen's making them, and in his expressed intentions. It amounts to the claim that getting on with one's creative work is an antidote to pessimism. Thus pragmatic optimism: it is worthwhile to continue.

Dramatizing versus Arguing

The philosophy dramatized in Allen's films is mostly existentialist, centering around topics such as the meaning of death, existence, responsibility, and personal integrity in one's relations with others.[2] Life is short. Love, despite its pains, disappointments, and transience is the main, indeed the essential, counterbalance. Love is one of only two ways to deny death; the other is through creative work. Creative work outlasts us and can become a source of enduring value.

My particular focus will be *Hannah and Her Sisters* (1986), *Crimes and Misdemeanors* (1989), *Husbands and Wives* (1992), and *Deconstructing Harry* (1997).[3] In these movies there is much raking over of the philosophical ground mentioned in the previous paragraph. I confine myself to their treatment of the two polarized attitudes to life: optimism and pessimism. Optimism is the view that life is good, things will work out for the best. Its strongest form is the view that this is the best of all possible worlds. Pessimism is the view that life is a torment, that things will only get worse. Its strongest form is the view that it would be better to escape it or that it had never existed.[4] As philoso-

---

[2] See Sander Lee, *Woody Allen's Angst* (Jefferson: McFarland, 1997), p. 1.

[3] Given that Allen is now in his sixties, it may be helpful to periodize his work, albeit arbitrarily, as follows: the three films, *Annie Hall* (1977), *Interiors* (1978), and *Manhattan* (1979) can be seen as inaugurating his early mature period. The immediately subsequent films now look like a middle period. These differ in a number of ways from the early mature ones. The protagonists are usually in long-standing relationships, some of which are satisfactory. Hence issues of managing to stay together, of having and raising children, and of career trajectory are more prominent. Now perhaps in his final mature period, we might see that as inaugurated by the confidence and gravitas of *Crimes and Misdemeanors* (1989).

[4] Optimism is described by one source as "general hopefulness regarding the balance of pleasure and pain" in the world. Pessimism is "the view that hope is unreasonable and that happiness, if attainable, lies beyond the sphere of ordinary experience. The prevailing tone of a particular philosophical system

phies, both extremes are difficult to defend; as dramatic devices
they are powerful. Optimism tends to go with hope; pessimism
with despair. An extreme expression of despair is suicide.

Suicide figures in several Allen films, including *Interiors*
(1978), and *September* (1987). To bring out the difference
between dramatizing and discussing, consider the treatment of
suicide in *Hannah and Her Sisters*. Allen himself plays Hannah's
ex-husband Mickey, a self-described loser and hypochondriac.
Mickey goes through agony waiting to find out if he has a brain
tumor, even buying a gun—in case. When he is told he is fine,
he dances in the street. This is an extraordinary moment in
which we share Mickey's extroverted joy. Almost immediately,
however, we find out that matters were not so simply settled.
Despair set in after the cancer scare had been dispelled: the
brush with death left Mickey with the insistent thought that the
reprieve was temporary. Having previously ignored or denied
death, he could no longer do so.

Although Mickey's panic is satirized, his subsequent despair
is not. After quitting his job, and having comic encounters with

---

depends mainly upon that system's cosmology and its account of man's role in
the universe" (Antony Flew, *A Dictionary of Philosophy* [London: Pan, 1984], p.
257). An older view with more religious overtones describes pessimism and
optimism as follows: "These rival interpretations of existence have one circum-
stance in common: both are designated by superlatives; and the loose employ-
ment of the terms in ordinary phraseology renders it needful to point this out.
To justify their use in a philosophical sense it is not enough that a given view
of things should dwell by preference on their more forbidding or more engaging aspect respectively. The terms are more strictly opposed than this, and each
is to be understood in its literal sense. For pessimistic theory this is the worst
of worlds; if it were to be a world, it could not have borne to be worse than it
is. Some rudiments of order and well-being Schopenhauer himself will allow to
it, since otherwise it could not cohere or continue in existence at all. But, so
much being granted, the contention is that its irrationality, misery, and worth-
lessness could not be more than they are. And optimism also expresses itself
in the same unqualified way, maintaining that all is for the best in this best of
all possible worlds" (Alexander Martin, "Pessisism and Optimism," in James
Hastings, ed., *Encyclopedia of Religion and Ethics* [Edinburgh: Clark, 1917], p.
803). Runes's *Dictionary of Philosophy* (Patterson: Littlefield, Adams, 1942) adds
that optimism holds that "the world as it exists is not so bad, or even the best
possible, life is good, and man's destiny bright"; while pessimism considers
"this world the worst possible, holds man to be born in sorrow, and thinks it
best if neither existed." There is a pretty discussion of some of the historical

different religions, it is revealed in flashback that at one point he sank low enough to hold a gun to his head. Reprieved by accident (the gun slipped off his forehead), alone, tired, he regained his sense of proportion from an encounter with the Marx Brothers in *Duck Soup*.[5] In voice-over Mickey describes wandering the streets alone afterwards, going to a movie, and "trying to put the world back into a rational perspective." Then comes epiphany, not argument:

> I started to *feel* how can you even think of killing yourself? I mean, *isn't it so stupid?* . . . what if the worst is true? What if there is no God, and you only go around once and that's it? Well, you know, don't you want to be part of the experience? And *I'm thinking to myself*, geez, I should stop ruining my life . . . searching for answers I'm never gonna get, and just enjoy it while it lasts. . . . And . . . then, *I started to sit back*, and I actually began to enjoy myself. (Italics mine.)[6]

I felt, isn't suicide stupid?, I'm thinking, I sit back—these are conclusions, not reasons. As philosophy, they are trite. This description of the film's philosophy is not meant as criticism; commonplaces are worth re-telling. Indeed, in popular philosophy it may be the case that familiar truths reiterated, modernized, and dramatized are entirely sufficient for the purposes at hand. Characters and situations that absorb the audience, matters presented with drama and humor, are more than sufficient. If the resolution is not going to be argued—and while Mickey may mull things over, it hardly reaches the level of argument—but dramatized and embodied, the philosophical problems and the offered solutions need to be accessible to audience common sense. It is particularly noteworthy that the four films on which I am concentrating are, dramatically speaking, ensemble pieces. Their author thus gives himself wide latitude to express different versions of ideas and to keep his overall dramatic point of view detached.

---

background in Joseph Agassi, "The Philosophy of Optimism and Pessimism," in C. Gould and R. Cohen, eds., *Artifacts, Representations, and Social Practice* (Dordrecht: Kluwer, 1994), which treats both poles as myths.

[5] Groucho Marx tops Isaac's list in *Manhattan* of things that make life worth living. However, Ike in that movie never comes near to the degree of despair that is portrayed through Mickey. Cliff, in *Crimes and Misdemeanors*, regularly views *Singin' in the Rain* to keep his spirits up.

[6] *Hannah and Her Sisters* (1986).

Depicting Pessimism

In *Hannah and Her Sisters*, Allen has built some of the philosophizing into the staging, composition, and camerawork of each
shot (the *mise-en-scène*) as well as the editing together of suc-
cessive shots. This allows the filmmaker to present Mickey and
his suffering in different ways, now comic, now empathetic,
now slightly detached. Almost all Mickey's expressions of
despair are done in medium long shot. One obvious reading of
the use of this shot, and the eschewal of close-ups, is as a way
of standing back from both the characters and the action. The
closest the film comes to Mickey's face is when he has the gun
at his head, a medium close-up in profile from behind.

Mickey is only one of four variations on pessimism verging
on despair that appear in *Hannah and Her Sisters*. Lee (Barbara
Hershey), Holly (Diane Wiest), and Lee's partner, Frederick
(Max von Sydow) all evidence pessimism. Lee confirms that five
years before the action she was a serious alcoholic who began
drinking at 10:00 A.M. When Holly asks for a loan from Hannah,
Hannah asks directly if she still uses cocaine. On the date
between Mickey and Holly, arranged by Hannah, Holly is quar-
relsome and takes cocaine several times. It is tempting to see
their substance abuse and distancing behavior as indications of
despair—an extreme form of pessimism.

Lee's artist partner and mentor, Frederick, is a permanently
gloomy soul who tells Lee "you are my only connection to the
world." He acts like a sourpuss with a client and then announces
that it is humiliating that the client wants to consult a decorator
before he decides what to buy. While artistic work is a form of
satisfaction in these films, something is amiss when Frederick uses
it to withdraw from contact with the world. Why, though, are we
invited to laugh at Mickey; indeed, why the element of comedy
in all four of the films? One obvious answer is that comedy itself
creates distance, distance permits a sense of proportion. The comedy in Allen's films embodies, perhaps, his sense of proportion.
Detachment is also maintained in *Hannah and Her Sisters* by
means of the character of Hannah (Mia Farrow), the link between
all the others. She is the least explored. We get to know very little about her. Her optimism is partly sustained by her obliviousness: the adultery of her husband Elliot with her sister goes

unnoticed by her. Her marriage might survive such disclosure but it is hard to imagine sororal harmony at the Thanksgiving dinner would.

Pessimism figures differently in *Deconstructing Harry*. The eponymous author is accused of humiliating the people he knows by putting them into his work. His pessimism expresses itself through jaundiced comments, heavy drinking, and loveless sex with prostitutes. Perhaps his pessimism is most clearly manifest in his failure to work; Harry suffers from writer's block. By the end of the story he has regained his zest for life and is back at work. He achieves this partly via self-knowledge: he tells the greeters at his *alma mater* that he is working on a story about a man whose true love is kidnapped by the devil and who follows them to hell to retrieve her. Ignoring the Orpheus myth overtones, Harry admits the questionable claim that the main character is himself thinly disguised; in fact, he muses on whether there is any point in disguising it any more. Perhaps that is a Woody Allen joke at the expense of his commentators.

Secret Knowledge

What are we to make of the importance of secret knowledge in Allen's films? I am thinking of the importance of overheard confessions in *Another Woman*, and *Everyone Says I Love You*; the snooping in *Manhattan Murder Mystery* (1993) and *Mighty Aphrodite* (1995); the successful concealment of adultery and the unsuccessful concealment of prostitution in the latter; and the adultery also concealed in *Hannah and Her Sisters* and *Crimes and Misdemeanors*.

Consider secret knowledge in *Hannah and Her Sisters*: it opens with the audience being privy to Elliot's (Michael Caine) ruminations on his secret desire for Lee, his sister-in-law. They have an affair, he betraying his wife, Hannah; Lee betraying both her sister and her partner, Frederick. Such rationalized treachery may be treated as another variant of pessimism, as both so despair about the state of their "official" relationships that they are willing to risk them on a secret fling. As the plot works out, neither confesses the truth; Elliot re-affirms his love for Hannah, Lee leaves Frederick and finds a husband. Hannah recognizes that a script of Holly's displays knowledge of her conversations with Elliot that he must have leaked. But her suspicion is not followed up, and in the final scenes all is love and devotion. Elliot and Lee are portrayed as untroubled by their secret knowledge, happy despite their deception of a loved one. Hannah is portrayed as untroubled by the suspicious clue. In not choosing to contradict them the filmmaker seems to allow that happiness can supervene in the absence of openness and candor. Allen presents a stronger version of this pessimistic view of life in *Crimes and Misdemeanors*.

Secret knowledge can be seen as a version of the view that truth is hidden, that appearances deceive. If only one could access people's real thoughts and feelings, one's actions in relation to them could be better calculated. The eponymous *Alice* (1990), for example, once made invisible, discovers she has been naively trusting of people. But some secret knowledge is treated as better kept that way if we are to go on enjoying life. At the end of *Hannah and Her Sisters* Elliot is depicted as close to his wife again, and Lee radiates happiness as she talks to her new husband. Even Mickey, the near-suicide, has ended up happily with a pregnant Holly. The theme of wanting children and enjoying children, which is scarcely present in the films of the 1970s, is strong in these later films. A jarring episode in *Hannah and Her Sisters* shows Hannah to be capable of lack of understanding. When Mickey and Hannah were married he was found to be infertile. The usually so supportive Hannah is shown in that crisis as accusing and blaming Mickey, rather than comforting him. The audience is shown a side of Hannah she keeps from the world.

Optimism in *Hannah and Her Sisters* is found mainly in reaching out to other people with the hope of finding the right one. Elliot and Lee reach out to one another but battle guilt all the way. Hannah's parents are shown in a roller-coaster relationship—at times all bitter recriminations, other times a couple of nostalgic seniors. Mickey's second attempt to get together with Holly succeeds. Lee breaks away from the depressed Frederick and his excessive demands, enters Columbia and marries a professor.

The film takes place over two years, beginning on a Thanksgiving dinner and ending on a Thanksgiving dinner two years later. These feasts are occasions for stocktaking. The first

Thanksgiving dinner sees the beginning of Elliot's resolve to commit adultery. The second sees Lee breaking off with Elliot. Frederick and Mickey are absent from both dinners. In the final Thanksgiving, all the main characters are coupled with someone they love. Pessimism in its various forms has been overcome by love, love that works partly with the help of lies and concealment. There is evidence that Allen originally intended a darker film. Maurice Yacowar quotes Allen expressing disappointment that the film turned out to be too upbeat.[7] I venture that Allen tried not to make that mistake with *Crimes and Misdemeanors*.

Husbands, Wives, and Harry

Pessimism is taken furthest in *Crimes and Misdemeanors*, so I shall treat it after the next two films, although it was made before them.[8] First, *Husbands and Wives* and *Deconstructing Harry*. *Husbands and Wives* dramatizes several versions of optimism and pessimism through the intricacy of romantic relationships, degrees of self-deception, compromises, and the attempt to learn from experience. Jack (Sidney Pollack) runs off with a younger woman with whom he soon becomes bored. His wife Sally (Judy Davis) takes up with the charming Michael (Liam Neeson), but does not return his passion. By the end Jack and Sally are back with one another, none of their original problems solved, but ever ready with self-deceiving rationalizations to persuade themselves that this is the best they can get. Thus do they mask their underlying pessimism. Their friend, Gabe Roth (Woody Allen), a professor, is sorely tempted by one of his students, Rain (Juliet Lewis), who seems quite casually promiscuous and unconcerned about the broken hearts she has left behind.

---

[7] Maurice Yacowar, *Loser Takes All: The Comic Art of Woody Allen* (New York: Ungar, 1991), p. 252. Ralph Rosenblum, the film editor, describes the evolution of the shooting script "Anhedonia," a pessimistic title if ever there was one, into the romantic comedy *Annie Hall* as having taken place mainly in the editing room (*When the Shooting Stops* [New York: Viking, 1979]). Of course, where the filmmaker happened to change his intentions is irrelevant, merely that he did so, sometimes to his satisfaction, other times not.

[8] "Allen's pessimism is portrayed most powerfully in *Crimes and Misdemeanors* (1989)" (Lee, p. 4).

These revelations, and perhaps the example of Jack's experience, result in Gabe rejecting an affair with her both in self-protection (his previous proclivity for "kamikaze women") and out of loyalty to his wife Judy (Mia Farrow). However, his faith in his marriage is misplaced. At the end of the film Judy and Michael are a couple, equally ready to offer rationalizing rewrites of the origin of their relationship to the unseen Interviewer-Narrator who questions them. Gabe faces the camera alone at the end, affirms that he is not despairing, indeed that he is working on a new novel, but then abruptly asks: "Is it over? Can I go now?"

Perhaps the most intriguing character in the film is Judy, played by Mia Farrow. Her first husband describes her as a classic passive-aggressive personality who affects helplessness yet gets just what she wants. In brief scenes we see her ensnare Gabe this way, and then, later, Michael. She does not suffer doubts or despair, partly at the expense of displacing all of her misery onto others. The student, Rain, is a younger variant of the same personality type. Aware that Gabe has a soft spot for her, she pleads to read his work in progress. After offering a few anodyne words of praise she proceeds systematically to trash it. This, of course, only makes Gabe the more interested. However, in the end he does not succumb, either to Rain or to pessimism. Like the deceived couples at the end of *Hannah and Her Sisters*, the reconstituted couples at the end of *Husbands and Wives* are mired in self-deception, and Gabe, who may have gained some self-understanding, at least of a self-protective kind, is alone. Self-deception is another form of secret knowledge possessed by the audience but not by the characters. The drama asks the audience to allow that self-deception may be essential for some people and some relationships to function. By using the dramatic distancing device of his characters talking to an unseen interviewer the filmmaker brackets his characters' affirmation of contentment. The ending is enigmatically bleak.

Deconstructing Harry parallels *Husbands and Wives* in several ways. Woody Allen plays Harry. Harry's self-deceptions are deeply buried under a readiness to catalogue his own faults. To a degree he knows what he is: a chronic womanizer, a man who prefers paid-for sex, a writer who exploits the lives and problems of those he knows, a heavy drinker and pill popper, possessed of a really foul mouth. His self-absorption is complete.

Encountering a friend with heart problems he tries to change the subject of conversation to his own writer's block. When accused by his ex-mistress, and by his sister, of betraying and humiliating them in his fiction, he protests feebly. When his psychiatrist wife is apoplectic over his seduction of one of her patients, he blames her because they don't have sex, don't go out, hence, her patients are the only people he meets.

At the center of the story is a journey Harry makes upstate with his son, his friend Richard (Bob Balaban), and a hooker, Cookie (Hazelle Goodman). Along the way there are interludes and flashbacks in which the way Harry uses his nearest and dearest in his writing is sometimes illustrated and sometimes discussed. Literally en route to a rendezvous with his wife's sister, he takes up with a young blonde fan, Fay (Elizabeth Shue). Harry tries to argue this young mistress out of falling in love with him and then, when she tries to move on, makes a frantic last-minute attempt to stop her, claiming to have fallen in love himself.[9] In his foul language, his drinking, his resort to prostitutes, as in all other things, Harry acts ruthlessly for his own pleasure and desire, and expresses very little in the way of self-doubt. He tries to demonize his friend and rival Larry (Billy Crystal), but the effort fails. His trail of destructive behavior is not redeemed by the time he turns back to his work at the close.

Heavy drinking, nasty talk, callous behavior are, of course, symptoms of some sort of despair, some sense that hope is naive and indulgence is the way to go. Harry is an unpleasant character, one of the most unpleasant Allen has created, and certainly the most unpleasant he has ever decided to play himself. He is pictured as a writer good enough to be taught in his alma mater, and also successful enough to be able to afford two-hundred-dollar hookers at will. He is the center of the film in a way in which there is no clear center to the ensemble pieces, *Hannah and Her Sisters* or *Husbands and Wives*. The *mise-en-scène* mostly keeps its distance through medium shots, the screenplay by humor.

Some of the humor is made possible by the dramatization of fragments of Harry's fiction, especially scenes which correspond closely to real-life events. Other humor is derived from

---

[9] This parallels Issac's behavior at the end of *Manhattan*.

incongruity.[10] Harry is deconstructed in various ways. In a scene where he meets all his fictional characters a college student tells him that although his work seems sad on the surface, she likes deconstructing it because underneath it is happy. Harry himself has just said that his story is that of a person who can't function in life, only in art; and such a story is sad but also funny. Other people's pessimism can be funny; perhaps other people's optimism (*Hannah and Her Sisters, Husbands and Wives*) can be sad. This neat thought addresses no popular or professional philosophical issue, but it is fruitful for filmmaking.

Interpretation and Its Problems

In each of the films discussed, characters express some degree of pessimism and others find some kind of hope, some way to get on with and enjoy life. Remarkably, *Crimes and Misdemeanors*, while it explores pessimism in various manifestations, offers an ending without optimism or comfort. It also exploits the idea of coping with secret knowledge to the maximum. Just how it should be interpreted, and just what Woody Allen is saying, has been controversial since its release. One main character, Cliff (Woody Allen), has failed in everything: he has seen his hero commit suicide, making it impossible to complete the documentary film he wanted to make; he has been dumped by his wife; he has failed to get the girl, indeed seen her happily married to a despised rival. In a controversial closing scene, he is sharing a drink and a moment with Judah (Martin Landau), who has successfully concealed corruption, adultery, and murder, is portrayed as immensely successful and respected in his community, and who obliquely confesses that he is happy and guilt-free. Judah's friend the Rabbi, Ben (Sam Waterston), who insists there is, indeed must be, a moral structure in the universe, has gradually gone blind; that is, can't see the world at all, still less see what Cliff and Judah see.

---

[10] Who can forget the hysterically funny scene in which Joan, his psychiatrist wife, having discovered his affair with a patient, berates him ever-more ferociously, pausing momentarily to admit a patient, twice excusing herself to scream at Harry some more, and finally yelling her last sally from her analyst's chair, whereupon her patient dissolves into tears?

The attitude which the *mise-en-scène* strikes towards all this is unmediated, neither detached, nor preachy. Although many remember the film as dark in mood, there is nonetheless a good deal of humor, especially involving Cliff and Lester. The gloomy developments are shown to us in a manner that asks us to take them quite seriously. Not only are the good not always rewarded, they may be humiliated and left frustrated. The bad are not only not punished, they may get away with murder—literally, psychologically, and spiritually. Halley (Mia Farrow), on whom Cliff has a crush, simply insists that his former brother-in-law Lester (Alan Alda), is, in fact, a very nice guy. Judah looks set to go on enjoying his domestic and public life untroubled any longer by severe pangs of conscience.

Nothing in the text of the film suggests that these wrongs are to be righted. It is tempting to say that the attitude of the film is itself without hope. It dramatizes a world without justice. Professor Levy, the expert on the Holocaust, whom Cliff has interviewed and filmed, and who seems to have confronted the abyss and come back able to make sense of it without abandoning optimism, has thrown himself out of a window. His voice affirming that qualified optimism is the last we hear in the film. Allen dramatizes all these points of view, but need not share any of them to do so. The pragmatic argument I make is that since he goes on making films rather than going out the window, he does not share the despair.

Judah, who fears losing all that he has worked for if his mistress Dolores (Angelica Huston) informs his wife (Claire Bloom) about their affair, and the community about his corruption, approaches his underworld brother Jack (Jerry Orbach) for help. Jack sees at once that murder is the only way to ensure Dolores's silence, and offers to arrange it. When it is done he telephones his brother to tell him to forget about it and go on with his life. Judah is at first sick to his stomach, but not too sick to go to Dolores's apartment to retrieve evidence that would implicate him, and to confront the staring eyes of Dolores's corpse. But her eyes are dead and do not see; much as Ben is depicted as blind to Judah's amorality before he literally goes blind. A man of science, not faith, Judah is able to overcome his father Sol's admonition that "the eyes of God are always upon you." Those of the dead Dolores and the live Ben are equally unseeing. What happens to Judah—he gets over it and goes on

with an enjoyable life—and what happens to Cliff offer no comfort at all to those who want a just world. Jack arranges for a
stranger and a professional to murder Dolores, so there is no
clue pointing to Judah. Judah manages to remain calm when the
police ask him about his knowledge of Dolores. Desperate
though these moments are, they pass. The wicked are not necessarily unhappy; the good may be left miserable.

In scenes that recall those in *Annie Hall*, childhood is revis-
ited in *Crimes and Misdemeanors*, but the discussion of religious doubts is tortured rather than funny; there are
celebrations and a wedding, but only as backgrounds to grim
revelations. Cliff suggests that Judah's idea for a film (which
happens to be his actual story) needs a different ending, where
the protagonist accepts responsibility and turns himself in.
Judah responds, knowing that Cliff is an aspirant filmmaker,
that that may be so in Hollywood, but life does not resemble
Hollywood movies. It would not be lost on the audience that
Woody Allen's movies, like Cliff's, are made in New York, not
in Hollywood.

Justice, Crime, and Pessimism

In *Crimes and Misdemeanors* Allen pushed his dramatic exploration of pessimism very hard, perhaps to the limit of what
would engage an audience. He deploys many familiar themes,
and variations on previous characters. Yet he says farewell to his
characters without giving any of the plotlines an upbeat twist.
Halley may be correct that Lester is a nice guy and they are
going to be happy, though the audience, like Cliff, may be
incredulous. No magic bullet is about to arrive and make Cliff a
success, whether with women or in his work. His not very nice
wife has met someone new, his nice sister has not. Judah, mean-
while, acts quite relaxed and untroubled. His means have suited
his ends, and he is able to enjoy the ends he strove for and put
the evil of his means behind him. Thus does Allen test his audience to the limit, refusing to offer any straw of comfort either
through the screenplay or the *mise-en-scène*. The naiveté of
Ben's moralistic optimism is strongly suggested. His physical
blindness parallels his blindness to the way things are. He himself has said that the lack of a moral structure in the world
would mean that there is no hope.

Does the film argue, as it were, for philosophic or philo-sophically motivated pessimism, for this being a world where the guilty go free and the innocent suffer? Dramatization is not argument. Clearly, the film is not optimistic. This may be the rea-son why it is possibly the least philosophically trite of Allen's films, especially as it seems to allow that optimism and despair are not mutually exclusive options, we can vacillate between them or even experience them together.

Sander Lee, in what is by far the most philosophically inter-esting of the many books on Woody Allen, argues differently.[11] He stresses that the final shots of the blind Ben dancing with his daughter, and the voice-over of the late Louis Levy, are not with-out hope. Cliff *might yet* utilize Judah's story to make a success-ful movie, Lee continues. Judah *might* drink too much another day and let slip the truth. His marriage *can't* be happy because he finds his wife boring and because he hides a terrible secret. Lee candidly admits that when he put this interpretation to Woody Allen the latter flatly denied it, insisting that Judah feels no guilt, and that his occasional pang of uneasiness is negligible.

Lee counters with two arguments: the film text permits his reading; and authors do not have the last word on interpretation. These are fair points. They do not, however, amount to reasons for rejecting Allen's interpretation. Authors are not privileged, it is true; but they should not be disregarded without good reasons. Lee gives a reason: philosophical disagreement. He affirms Sol's affirmation earlier in the film that, "If necessary, I will always choose God over truth."[12] Is philosophical disagreement a good reason for rejecting the author's interpretation?

Lee's interpretative probing helps to reveal Allen's brilliance. Judah's father Sol is a character in an Allen screenplay. Lee finds his philosophy congenial and wishes it to control his interpreta-tion. He thus sides with one character. Allen, however, in his writing and direction does not. He devised all the characters and worked out the *mise-en-scène*. The father Sol's point of view, his defiant optimism in the face of his sister's skeptical questioning, is powerfully dramatized, as Lee admits.[13] However, if we take

[11] Lee, *Woody Allen's Angst*, pp. 286–89.
[12] Lee, *Woody Allen's Angst*, pp. 267, 289.
[13] Lee, *Woody Allen's Angst*, p. 264.

Allen's powerful presentations of a philosophy as proof that the latter is the philosophical point of view of the film, we end up with contradictions produced by the incompatible views that are dramatized. Allen's intentions do not control the interpretation of the film, but neither does the point of view of one character.

The work asks to be taken as a whole, as a drama. Judah's reminiscences of his father, the latter's optimism and conviction that the eyes of God are always upon us, occur when Judah is trying to come to terms with the evil that he has done. I take it that this is explored precisely in order to set up the impact of the revelation of the final scene that all that has passed and some kind of ataraxia has been achieved. Lee seems to me to try to find optimism in the outlook of this film to the point of eisegesis. The *mise-en-scène* shows us Judah calm and relaxed, full of his secret knowledge. Cliff is unhappy and rueful, and finds Judah's story too pessimistic for a movie. Ben, the believer in moral structure, dances happily with his daughter, blissfully ignorant of Judah's secret knowledge of the way the world is.

Criteria for Interpretation

Now to draw together the various points made about interpretation, as well as to apply them to the interpretation presented here of Allen as a pragmatic optimist.

Attributing views to the author of dramatic works is notoriously difficult and, in a sense, self-defeating. An author who wants simply to expound a line on something can choose a literary form that lends itself to assertion; the essay for example. When an author chooses drama or dialogue the motive could be exploratory, and/or it could be a form of disguise. Allen in his movies mulls over different kinds of reactions to a small set of problems. The different characters being fictional, I can discern no simple one-to-one correspondence between the philosophy articulated and the author. In particular, there are plenty of philosophical and artistic reasons for not treating the speeches and fates of the characters acted by Allen himself as expressions of "his" philosophy.[14]

---

[14] The familiar problems of trying to find Plato in Plato's dialogues come to mind.

Lee writes: "we have absolutely no reason for choosing a truth that destroys life's joy over the fulfilling subjective values we can create for ourselves."[15] But is this endorsed in *Crimes and Misdemeanors*? The author flatly denies it.[16] Yet clearly one *can* read the film as Lee does. How best to handle such disputes? One way is to articulate our principles of interpretation so that they can be subjected to scrutiny. Lee writes little on this topic. It seems that he is caught in a difficulty. He admires the film (and its author). He finds it difficult to admire the cold view of the world as one in which some of the deserving suffer and some of the guilty prosper. Hence he does not want to read the film as saying that. He wants it to say something he can agree with. The interpretative principle involved might be formulated: "Interpret works of art so that they articulate a philosophical thesis with which you can agree." Let me call this "The Agreement Principle."

Put baldly, this does not sound promising. Yet in Lee's favor is the fact that this principle is widely utilized in philosophy. Philosophers often study a figure because they find his views sympathetic; or they study only those aspects with which they are sympathetic. Where an author says things they find unpleasant, beautification is attempted.[17] All of this is entirely understandable. One may also criticize it rationally. As philosophers and teachers of philosophy we have a duty to expound and defend views with which we may not agree. We must be able to do this if we are to present the range of philosophical options to our students, and in order make use of the dialectic, the clash of views as an engine of the search for truth. As a principle of interpretation in the arts, The Agreement Principle would permit interpretative proliferation. Yet just because the text permits my reading it does not therefore support my reading. Rather, the text supports readings that present its ideas for what they are, no matter how difficult, off-putting, or wrong-headed they may seem. This kind of interpretative work entails trying hard to set the text in its time and context, including that of other works of

---

[15] Lee, *Woody Allen's Angst*, p. 289.
[16] Lee, *Woody Allen's Angst*, p. 374.
[17] See Karl Popper, *The Open Society and Its Enemies* (London: Routledge, 1945), Volume I, on the beautification of Plato.

the same author. It means trying to read it sympathetically. It means avoiding eisegesis.

While the principle that authors do not have the last word is sound, most of what that principle tries to capture can be achieved by a principle of interpretation that does not over-throw authorial interpretation without overwhelming argu-ment.[18] That an interpretation fits a text is a weak principle, since all too many do so. Texts underdetermine their correct interpretations. To claim that a film affirms a philosophy when most viewers and the author think it does not, strikes me as needing far stronger argument than Lee offers. Were Lee to say only that the philosophy of Judah's father Sol, choose God over truth, is articulated in the film as an affirmation of hope in the face of despair, then he would not need to meet any special interpretative criterion. He could also tell us that he agrees with that point of view. Where he goes too far, in my view, is in try-ing to impute this thesis to the film. It is a bit like arguing that Thrasymachus's claim that justice is the interest of the stronger is the thesis of *The Republic*.[19]

Lee does not, however, foist his interpretation onto Allen, only on the film as he reads it. Mary Nichols is less cautious. "Is Lester Allen's spokesman?" she asks.[20] Since Allen chose to make a dramatic film it would seem an obvious criterion that the film, not merely a part of it, is his spokesman. Yet this can lead to inconsistency. A happy ending, or a downer ending, if attributed to Allen, would make his philosophy shift from film to film as moods do. He has created bad central characters who are happy and fulfilled—Judah (*Crimes and Misdemeanors*) and Harry (*Deconstructing Harry*) come to mind—and he has unhappy and unfulfilled good ones—Frederick (*Hannah and Her Sisters*),

---

[18] Ian Jarvie, *Philosophy of the Film* (London: Routledge, 1987), pp. 289–294.

[19] This gets more intricate if one looks at authorial strategy. If Plato caricatures Thrasymachus, that very choice is telling. If, in *Crimes and Misdemeanors*, Allen caricatures the religious attitudes of Judah's father, or of Ben, that is equally telling. To my reading, the argument at the dinner table between Judah's father and his atheistic aunt caricatures them both—perhaps merely for comedy, perhaps because Allen does not think much of the level such debates usually reach.

[20] Mary Nichols, *Reconstructing Woody: Art, Love, and Life in the Films of Woody Allen* (Lanham: Rowman and Littlefield 1998), p. 154.

Cliff (*Crimes and Misdemeanors*), and Gabe (*Husbands and Wives*) for example.

Sometimes Allen puts the words of a character into his own mouth—by playing the character himself—but that is as likely to be a dramatic device as it is to be a tacit endorsement of the doctrine or arguments the character advances. It was partly to stave off such threatened inconsistency that I have tried to shift discussion to the organizing notion of pragmatic optimism as embodied in the output and its continuation. This gives an over-all philosophical point of view to the work without getting mired in the possibly contradictory evidence or claims found in any particular film.

To sum up, while lots of interpretations are permitted, per-haps we should impose on ourselves such restraints as respect for (not deference to) authorial intentions where known; respect for context, including that of the author's other work; and respect for form, since the choice of literary form has philo-sophical aspects.

Hope and Despair

I offer one final argument for my own interpretation. I do not know what weight to give it. Pragmatic optimism not only does not contradict the films, it is articulated in some of them, at least since *Annie Hall*. Like his characters Holly, Gabe, and Harry, and just possibly Cliff, Allen goes on working: writing and directing movies. Creative work is presented in these films as an affirmation in the face of the terrors of existence, the disap-pointments of human relations, even the lack of just desserts.

Even if Allen experiences despair, he yet affirms optimism in the very continuation of his output. Perhaps, as in the quotation from Mickey earlier in this chapter, he does not know the answers to the questions his characters return to again and again; perhaps he thinks it naive to expect answers. Creative work, however, represents hope. Creative work is forward-look-ing in and of itself—regardless of what problems and doctrines its characters and situations embody.

Act II

Woody's Craft

5

The Mousetrap:
Reading Woody Allen

JAMES M. WALLACE

The play's the thing
Wherein I'll catch the conscience of the king.

—Shakespeare, *Hamlet*, II.2., 609–610

Woody's Mousetraps

My first taste of Woody Allen's work came in 1972 at Radio City
Music Hall, where as a timid child I watched *Play It Again, Sam*
during my Catholic school's eighth grade trip to New York City.
I remember little about the experience except watching Sister
Anne twitch at every mention of orgasms, homosexuality, and
nymphomania.

While I've relished Allen's movies since then and perhaps
understand them better these days, I must confess that his allusions and especially his philosophical references are often suited
for a palate more refined than mine. In his films, references to
Nietzsche or Kierkegaard have often left me less amused by his
humor and more awestruck by his knowledge. In his writings,
even the historical and cultural references can be awfully
impressive and elusive:

> Not since the evanescence of Hubert, whose Flea Museum
> enchanted the naïfs on Forty-second Street, has the Broadway area
> seen a shyster to rival that peerless purveyor of schlock, Fabian
> Wunch. Balding, cheroot-sucking, and as phlegmatic as the Wall of

China, Wunch is a producer of the old school, resembling physically not so much David Belasco as Kid Twist Reles. Given the consistency and dimensions of his exaltation of flops, it has remained a puzzle on a par with string theory how he manages to raise money for each fresh theatrical holocaust.

Hence, when a beefy arm in a Sy Syms suit curled itself around my shoulder blades the other day as I perused some Rusty Warren at the Colony Record Shop, and the heady conflation of lilac Pinaud and White Owls subverted my hypothalamus, I could feel the wallet in my pocket instinctively clenching like an endangered abalone.[1]

Maybe Kid Twist Reles rings a bell, but Hubert? Rusty Warren? Without footnotes, these opening paragraphs of "Sing, You Sacher Tortes," would be unintelligible to a reader unfamiliar with the geography, history, and culture of New York City, and with sideshows, gangster lore, Jewish history, Yiddish, Las Vegas lounge acts, the theater, modern physics, the fashion industry, French grooming products, Viennese pastries, cigars—and probably much more; we can never be certain that we've registered every reference in the literary soup. Of course, it's possible, this being fiction, that he means someone other than, for example, *the* Rusty Warren, the "Knockers Up Gal," "the mother of the sexual revolution" (she has a website); it's possible that the story's ostensibly real-life references were created entirely in Allen's imagination. I've fallen for this before: I spent a little time one embarrassing day trying to find more information on the great jazz guitarist Emmett Ray, the subject of Allen's parodic biopic *Sweet and Lowdown*. But let's make the very safe assumption that in "Sing" the references are grounded in the world outside the text, as they are in most of Allen's short stories. When in "The Kugelmass Episode" Professor Kugelmass, a humanities professor at City College, turns up in *Madame Bovary*, it's *the Madame Bovary*.

For a reader without a brain like Allen's, even a complete liberal arts education and a good search engine are only partially helpful in disentangling his work. He demands much more than simply recognizing allusions and references; there's difficult mental work to be done—the work of interpreting beyond the

---

[1] Woody Allen, "Sing, You Sacher Tortes," *The New Yorker* (4th March, 2002), p. 34.

literal level—and the possibilities appear endless. A reader of "Sing, You Sacher Tortes," should know not only that David Belasco wrote and produced Broadway plays and that Abraham Reles was a member of Murder Incorporated, but also what each looked like, since Wunch apparently has Reles's heavy, thick, dim-witted, hirsute appearance rather than Belasco's softer, more ethereal, intelligent face.

Someone steeped in New York City history might recall that "Kid Twist" Reles ratted out his crony Louis Buchalter, who made his fortune, like Sy Syms, in the garment industry, or that Belasco's original theater was on 42nd Street, not far from Hubert's Museum and Flea Circus, a similarity that helps cement Allen's suggestion that the legitimate theater and the world of con artists were not all that different.

Fabian Wunch's first name, while recalling the 1950s teen idol, echoes more significantly and quite ironically the progressive think tank founded by socialist Sidney Webb and boasting such members as the playwright George Bernard Shaw. In fact, it becomes quite clear that Allen has created in Wunch a prototype of the overly perfumed, cigar-chomping producer-capitalist, a shyster who, with his "beefy arm . . . curled around my shoulder blades" (strong arming him, as it were, or riding the backs of the workers and playwrights), intends to squeeze money from the truly aesthetic (shopping for records), feministic, environmentally aware ("engendered abalone") narrator with a few bucks in his pocket. Allen's short story is a jigsaw puzzle that can be assembled in infinite ways, and he demands of the reader the perspicuity, acumen, and background to make the connections, especially if one is to understand the Marxist implications of his work.

This is the point in my essay, of course, where Woody Allen himself might pop out between the lines to ask incredulously, "Do you believe this guy?" Maybe he'd declare my Reles-Buchalter-Syms connection ludicrous, my Fabian observation pretentious, and the rest of my reading way off the mark. Like Marshal McLuhan in *Annie Hall*, maybe he'd say, "You know nothing of my work . . . How you ever got to teach a course in anything is totally amazing."[2] Writing an interpretation or analy-

---

[2] The omitted sentence, "You mean my whole fallacy is wrong," will be addressed later in the essay.

sis of Woody Allen, while difficult and painstaking, is perilous since Allen attacks in a number of his writings scholars, intellectuals, and literary critics—those of us trained not so much to create, but to learn, and, in the process of learning, to dissect, interpret, explain, and sometimes evaluate in political, social, and theoretical terms.

Allen, because of his extraordinary intellect, presents an unusual problem: like most serious writers, he invites us to recognize and connect allusions, to forage deeply in his works for intellectual nourishment, but he has laid a trap that is hard to resist for modern readers accustomed to considering literature something to interrogate and expose rather than a place to turn to for guidance and insight. Taken as a whole, his writings are a literary mousetrap, inviting educated readers to nibble at an appetizing and complex work of literature and ensnaring pretentious academics like the one in *Annie Hall*. The problem, of course, is in knowing exactly what springs the trap.

The Bait

Allen's best work is written for the same intelligent audience he enjoys poking fun at—intellectuals. Because of his colossal, boundless imagination and expansive knowledge of politics, philosophy, literature, theory, sociology, economics, popular culture, science, and just about every other category of learning, reading Allen is a task more easily accomplished by readers with as vast a store of knowledge and as fluid a mind as his, or at least something close. Surely his biggest fans (and even his more perceptive critics) are exceptionally well educated and well read. A large part of the enjoyment of reading Allen comes from the self-congratulations we most likely feel upon recognizing a more obscure reference or connecting a more complicated set of allusions.

Two of his funniest and best known short stories, "The Whore of Mensa" and "The Kugelmass Episode," would require courses in literature and contemporary theory to explicate. In "The Whore of Mensa," Word Babcock, an intellectual married to a woman who won't discuss Pound or Eliot, has been satisfying his craving for "quick intellectual stimulation" with a Vassar student AND prostitute provided by Flossie, "a madam with a master's degree in comparative lit.," who's now blackmailing Babcock for ten grand. Narrated by a private detective, Kaiser Lupowitz, in the pared-down, hard-boiled, simile-drenched style of Mike Hammer, the story centers on Lupowitz's entrapment of one of Flossie's mental hookers:

> "Shall we begin?" I said, motioning her to the couch.
>
> She lit a cigarette and got right to it. "I think we could start by approaching *Billy Budd* as Melville's justification of the ways of God to man, *n'est-ce pas?*"
>
> "Interestingly, though, not in a Miltonian sense." I was bluffing. I wanted to see if she'd go for it.
>
> "No. *Paradise Lost* lacked the substructure of pessimism." She did.
>
> "Right, right. God, you're right," I murmured.
>
> "I think Melville reaffirmed the virtues of innocence in a naïve yet sophisticated sense—don't you agree?"
>
> I let her go on. She was barely nineteen years old, but already she had developed the hardened facility of the pseudo-intellectual. She rattled off her ideas glibly, but it was all mechanical. Whenever I offered an insight, she faked a response: "Oh, yes, Kaiser. Yes, baby, that's deep. A platonic comprehension of Christianity—why didn't I see it before?"
>
> We talked for about an hour and then she said she had to go. She stood up and I laid a C-note on her.
>
> "Thanks, honey."
>
> "There's plenty more where that came from."
>
> "What are you trying to say?"
>
> I had piqued her curiosity. She sat down again.
>
> "Suppose I want to—have a party?" I said.
>
> "Like, what kind of party?"
>
> "Suppose I wanted Noam Chomsky explained to me by two girls"?[3]

The blending of sex and intellectualism reaches a climax when detective Lupowiz investigates at Flossie's, where he finds out that

> For a hundred a girl would lend you her Bartók records, have dinner, and then let you watch while she had an anxiety attack. For

---

[3] "The Whore of Mensa," *Without Feathers*, p. 35. From this point forward, abbreviations will be used in reference to Allen's three books: *Without Feathers* (*WF*), *Side Effects* (*SE*), and *Getting Even* (*GE*).

one-fifty, you could listen to FM radio with twins. For three bills,
you got the works: A thin Jewish brunette would pretend to pick
you up at the Museum of Modern Art, let you read her master's, get
you involved in a screaming quarrel at Elaine's over Freud's conception of women, and then fake a suicide of your choosing—the
perfect evening, for some guys. Nice racket. Great town, New
York.[4]

In a story about the need for intellectual stimulation, that paragraph is especially gratifying to a modern reader.

"The Kugelmass Episode" turns the tables: in this case an
intellectual seeks better sex—"romance . . . music . . . love and
beauty," as he calls it—which he doesn't get from his shrewish
wife, and finds help in The Great Persky, a magician who has
invented a machine for transporting lonely men into any novel
they choose. Kugelmass selects *Madame Bovary*. After his first
dalliance with Emma, Kugelmass returns to New York:

> Kugelmass hailed a cab and sped off to the city. His heart danced
> on point. I am in love, he thought, I am the possessor of a won-
> derful secret. What he didn't realize was that at this very moment
> students in various classrooms across the country were saying to
> their teachers, "Who is this character on page 100? A bald Jew is
> kissing Madame Bovary?" A teacher in Sioux Falls, South Dakota,
> sighed and thought, Jesus, these kids, with their pot and acid. What
> goes through their minds![5]

Eventually Emma Bovary joins Kugelmass in New York City,
where she gets temporarily stranded because of a malfunction
in Persky's machine. Kugelmass panics: Emma turns out to be
as demanding and unforgiving as the professor's wife; his wife
is growing suspicious, and his colleague, "Professor Fivish
Kopkind, who teaches Comp Lit and who has always been jealous of me, has identified me as the sporadically appearing character in the Flaubert book."[6] Finally, Emma is returned to the
novel and Kugelmass asks to be transported to the Monkey
scene in *Portnoy's Complaint*. An irreversible malfunction in the

---

[4] *Ibid.*, p. 37.
[5] "The Kugelmass Episode," *SE*, p. 47.
[6] *Ibid.*, p. 53.

machine sends him instead to *Remedial Spanish*, where he is last seen "running for his life over a barren, rocky terrain as the word *tener* ('to have')—a large and hairy irregular verb—raced after him on its spindly legs."[7]

What is a literary critic to do faced with stories so entertaining, comical, and appetizing to intelligent readers? Point out the misogyny that runs through both stories? Expose the social and cultural stereotyping? Analyze the ways in which humor masks the undercurrent of despair and loneliness in the two men whose marriages are unsatisfying? Trace the existential themes of helplessness and loss of power? Uncover the ideological content of the narratives? Deconstruct the machine-human binary, or the choice each protagonist is given between living in words or living in the world? Subject the stories to a psychoanalytic interpretation that includes a discussion of the author's own relationships with women? Allen's literature, like any other, is fair game for critical analysis, right?

The Trap

But it seems that any approach might only reveal the shortcomings of the critic and end up sounding exactly like Allen's brilliant "Fabrizio's: Criticism and Response," an essay in which "Fabian Plotnick, our most high-minded restaurant critic, reviews Fabrizio's Villa Nova Restaurant, on Second Avenue," demonstrating the excesses of modern criticism. Here are the first paragraph and part of the second:

> Pasta as an expression of Italian Neo Realistic starch is well understood by Mario Spinelli, the chef at Fabrizio's. Spinelli kneads his pasta slowly. He allows a buildup of tension by the customers as they sit salivating. His fettuccine, though wry and puckish in an almost mischievous way, owes a lot to Barzino, whose use of fettuccine as an instrument of social change is known to us all. The difference is that at Barzino's the patron is led to expect white fettuccine and gets it. Here at Fabrizio's he gets green fettuccine. Why? It all seems so gratuitous. As customers, we are not prepared for the change. Hence, the green noodle does not amuse us. It's

---

[7] *Ibid.*, p. 55.

disconcerting in a way unintended by the chef. The linguine, on the other hand, is quite delicious and not at all didactic. True, there is a pervasive Marxist quality to it, but this is hidden by the sauce. Spinelli has been a devoted Italian Communist for years, and has had great success in espousing his Marxism by subtly including it in the tortellini.

I began my meal with an antipasto, which at first appeared aimless, but as I focused more on the anchovies the point of it became clearer. Was Spinelli trying to say that all life was represented here in this antipasto, with the black olives an unbearable reminder of mortality? If so, where was the celery? Was the omission deliberate? . . .[8]

The review is a hilarious send-up of the modern critic's wish to consider every sneeze and hiccup a text to be interpreted and to see connections where none exist ("Who can forget his scampi: four garlic-drenched shrimp arranged in a way that says more about our involvement in Vietnam than countless books on the subject?"[9]). The *responses* to Fabian Plotnick's review, written as letters to the editor, are even better at capturing perfectly the tone and habits of uppity, well-educated, parochial intelligentsia—especially, sorry to say, literary critics—determined to show off their erudition, accustomed to speak and write in an elegant, allusive manner, and insistent on viewing everything through their ideological lenses:

---

[8] "Fabrizio's: Criticism and Response," *SE*, pp. 123–24. This is only one of Allen's many essays dealing with scholars. Another of his best pieces is "The Metterling Lists," (*GE*, pp. 3–11), a satirical review of *The Collected Laundry Lists of Hans Metterling*, Vol. 1, recently published by "Venal and Sons" "with an erudite commentary by the noted Metterling scholar Gunther Eisenbud," who cites such scholarly works as Anna Freud's "'Metterling's Socks as an Expression of the Phallic Mother', *Journal of Psychoanalysis*, Nov., 1935." Other essays aimed at scholarly pretensions or parodying academic dissertations include "Hassidic Tales, with a Guide to Their Interpretation by the Noted Scholar" (*GE*, pp. 63–69); "Lovborg's Women Reconsidered" (*WF*, pp. 26–31), an academic essay on "the great Scandinavian playwright Jorgen Lovborg," whose early works included "the series of plays dealing with anguish, despair, dread, fear and loneliness (the comedies)"; and "But Soft . . . Real Soft" (*WF*, pp. 185–87), which looks at the debate over who wrote Shakespeare's plays.
[9] "Fabrizio's: Criticism and Response," *SE*, p. 126.

To the Editor:

In his review of Fabrizio's Villa Nova, Fabian Plotnick called the prices "reasonable." But would he call Eliot's Four Quartets "reasonable?" Eliot's return to a more primitive stage of the Logos doctrine reflects immanent reason in the world, but $8.50 for chicken tetrazzini! It doesn't make sense even in a Catholic context. I refer Mr. Plotnick to the article in *Encounter* (2/58) entitled "Eliot, Reincarnation, and Zuppa di Clams."

Eino Shmeederer[10]

Other readers aggressively challenge Plotnick's interpretation, arguing that Fabrizio's Villa Nova Restaurant, rather than conforming "to the classic Italian nuclear-family structure," is "modeled on the homes of pre-Industrial Revolution middle-class Welsh miners"; that Plotnick's "logic breaks down linguistically" since he has failed to consider the paradox that the odd-numbered noodles equal the combined total of the odd- and even-numbered noodles; and that the review is "yet another shocking contemporary example of revisionist history." Plotnick's reply to the letter-writers is a dead-on parody of an author's defense:

I'm grateful to Dove Rapkin for his comments on the nuclear family, and also to Professor Babcocke for his penetrating linguistic analysis, although I question his equation and suggest, rather, the following model:

(a) some pasta is linguine
(b) all linguine is not spaghetti
(c) no spaghetti is pasta, hence all spaghetti is linguine.

Wittgenstein used the above model to prove the existence of God, and later Bertrand Russell used it to prove that not only does God exist but He found Wittgenstein too short.[11]

In this short passage, Allen captures the patronizing, but professional tone of authors' responses to critics, spoofs ridiculous syllogisms of the kind that drive students of logic mad, and

---

[10] *Ibid.*, p. 126.
[11] *Ibid.*, p. 128.

alludes ironically to Wittgenstein's opposition to arguments intended to prove God's existence. That's what I see, anyway. There may be many more philosophical insights and connections incomprehensible to me, but whatever quotations, echoes, allusions or references lie within the text, they depend for their existence on a reader: "a text's unity lies not in its origin but in its destination."[12] A reading gives life to a text. Why then the satire against intellectuals and scholars? Why target the same audience you depend on?

The Mechanism

In one sense, Allen's works could be seen as a bulwark against the onslaught of structuralist and reader-response critics writing at the same time his three books, *Getting Even* (1971), *Without Feathers* (1975), and *Side Effects* (1980) appeared. Perhaps these essays and short stories, the work of so fertile and expansive a mind, restore the concept of the Romantic genius, the creative, independent consciousness purposely selecting and manipulating raw material from the experiential and literary worlds to create something new, unique, complex, and profound (and very funny). His work, in such a reading, would stand as evidence that the talented author is the first and best determiner of what a literary work means, that creative works are not simply the expression of unconscious structures whose meanings are left to individual readers.

But such a position would make reading Allen's works a battle of egos, his against the reader's, as we try desperately to guess what he may have intended and step lightly so as not to exceed our boundaries lest we incur his wrath. It seems more likely that Allen, rather than beating us with allusions in a show of intellectual superiority, invites our participation in creating meaning. In fact, his works could serve not as challenges to, but as exemplars of, several of the ideas scripted in Barthes's famous "The Death of the Author."

Allen demonstrates an extraordinary negative capability by refusing to write in a voice identifiable as his own and writing

---

[12] Roland Barthes, "The Death of the Author," trans. Stephen Heath, In William Irwin, ed., *The Death and Resurrection of the Author?* (Westport: Greenwood, 2002), p. 7.

instead in the personas of, for example, lunatics, burglars, detectives, and, of course, scholars. Even the apparent first-person essays ("My Apology," "My Speech to the Graduates," "My Philosophy," and the like) reveal nothing reliable about the "real" author as they are filled with outlandish comments and biographical fabrication, showing perhaps that Allen has no illusions about the biographical or historical connection between a man and his work. In Allen's works, it is the "language which speaks, not the author"[13] in, for instance, the many shocking, jolting non sequiturs that characterize his work. Reading Allen means immersing ourselves in the slippery, shifting qualities of language, not in the stable, knowable biography of a writer. Moreover, his many allusions and references make him a sort of cultural amanuensis, scribing "the tissue of quotations drawn from the innumerable centres of culture"[14] that form the text.

Allen might even agree with Barthes that the critic died with the author in the 1970s since traditional criticism had been devoted to "deciphering" a text, to "discovering the Author" and, hence, the intended, ultimate, "secret" meaning of the author's work. Indeed, Allen mocks such criticism in works like "The Irish Genius" (*Without Feathers*), in which a poem by Sean O'Shawn, a poet "considered by many to be the most incomprehensible and hence the finest poet of his time,"[15] is annotated by a literary scholar. The poem begins, "Let us sail. Sail with / Fogarty's chin to Alexandria."[16] The gloss explains that "Fogarty's chin," is "undoubtedly a reference to George Fogarty, who convinced O'Shawn to become a poet and assured him he would be invited to parties."[17] The humor here may be a bit broader and sillier than Allen's other, more precise and subtle zingers, but the point is clear (I think): he certainly (maybe) intends to skewer the practice of literary interpretation that pretends to reveal the absolute and authoritative meaning in a text.

It's this pretension toward certain knowledge that seems most troubling to Allen. His writings suggest that he disdains not readers who make connections and interpret texts, but crit-

---

[13] *Ibid.*, p. 4
[14] *Ibid.*, p. 6.
[15] "The Irish Genius," *WF*, p. 117.
[16] *Ibid.*, p. 117.
[17] *Ibid.*, p. 119.

ics who have co-opted the text, who argue for the certainty of particular interpretations (his silly scholars use words and phrases like "clearly," "undoubtedly," "certainly," and "the truth is") and who pontificate loudly and aggressively, turning an author's work into an occasion for grandstanding and self-aggrandizement and a forum for browbeating opponents or discounting alternative viewpoints in the battle for critical supremacy. His works suggest to me that while we might have welcomed the birth of the reader in the 1970s and rejected once and for all the idea that a text can be interpreted "correctly," the baby should not be allowed to grow up without rules that prevent indulgent readings.

All interpretations are subject to revision. Taken as a whole, Allen's gentle satires caution readers against believing that they can ever claim with absolute certainty what a word, sentence or work means. His brilliantly intelligent works accomplish this, ironically, by demonstrating the limits of individual intelligence. What Allen does in his writing is not only to warn against egotistical readings, but also to write in such a way as to preclude them by inviting intelligent readers to make sense of complicated, intellectual works that often reveal the inadequacy of intellect.

Avoiding the Trap: Reader Response Criticism

The reader-response approaches to critical analysis that emerged during the 1970s may seem to justify subjective, run-away interpretations of the sort that appears to trouble Woody Allen. In sum, reader-response methods are based on the notion that the meaning of a literary work is produced not by an autonomous, objective text, but by the individual reader engaged in the act of reading. While a few reader-oriented theorists have promoted completely subjective responses to the text (it means what I want it to mean), reader-response theory does not necessarily include the idea that a reader is completely free to impose upon a text whatever interpretation he desires.

Wolfgang Iser, a student of Hans-Georg Gadamer, laid out a comprehensive statement of a phenomenological approach to reading in his seminal work, *The Implied Reader: Patterns of Communication in Prose Fiction from Bunyan to Beckett* (1974). The "implied reader" is not, for Iser, one who has complete freedom to interpret a text in whatever way he or she pleases, but one who, while guided by the text, "takes[s] an active part in the composition" of the text's meaning. A foundation for interpretation is provided by the text, but the text also implies—that is, involves as a *necessary* condition—the actions of a reader who is not a passive receptor, but an active participant, discovering, questioning, amending his expectations, as he proceeds through a text. The resulting interpretation of a work of literature, then, is not an objective and static fact, nor is it purely subjective, since the text controls much of the reader's reactions. The reader's role in the production of meaning was, for Iser, as one who filled in the "gaps" or "indeterminacies" in the text in an ever-moving process of creating what he called "the virtual text," the result of a reader's engagement with the work of art.[18]

It seems to me that Iser's theories—also contemporary with Allen's writings—are perfectly applicable to his humor. Allen is clearly aware in many of this works of the presence of a reader or, in the case of his plays and movies, an audience who he occasionally addresses directly. In several of his written works, especially those written as personal narratives, the daffy, neurotic persona pleads for the reader's sympathy or understanding ("Pity my dilemma, good reader! This maddening predicament that afflicts perhaps a good many of my contemporaries."[19]). In other cases, he makes the reader or audience part of the action, as he does in "God (A Play)," where a Greek playwright named Hepatitis, unable to think of an ending, asks the audience, "Do you folks have any suggestions?" Moments later, when the question "Is freedom chaos?" comes up, Hepatitis turns to the audience and asks, "Did anybody out there major in philosophy?" The best he can find is Doris, who "majored in gym, with a philosophy minor."[20] Allen, employing here one of his favorite strategies, blurring the distinction between reality and fiction, keeps readers alert to their involvement in the process of reading.

---

[18] Wolfgang Iser, "The Reading Process: A Phenomenological Approach," *The Implied Reader: Patterns of Communication in Prose Fiction from Bunyan to Beckett* (Baltimore: Johns Hopkins University Press, 1974), pp. 274–294).
[19] "The Lunatic's Tale," *SE*, pp. 76–77. The story is a satire on the apparent inability among men to be content with whatever woman they are currently with.
[20] "God (A Play)," *WF*, pp. 130–31.

The Gap Is the Meaning

Perhaps the most obvious way in which Allen engages the reader, and, in this case, challenges the reader's desire to know the text fully, is in his infinite jests, his constant use of non sequiturs, reversals, puns, illogic, and incoherent statements. Examples abound, but a few will suffice:

> I am plagued by doubts. What if everything is an illusion and nothing exists? In that case I definitely overpaid for my carpet.[21]

> Now he emerged from the hotel and walked up Eighth Avenue. Two men were mugging an elderly lady. My God, thought Weinstein, time was when one person could handle that job. Some city. Chaos everywhere. Kant was right. The mind imposes order. It also tells you how much to tip. What a wonderful thing to be conscious! I wonder what the people in New Jersey do.[22]

> As philosophers they relied heavily on logic and felt that if life existed, somebody must have caused it, and they went looking for a dark-haired man with a tattoo who was wearing a Navy pea jacket.
> When nothing materialized, they abandoned philosophy and went into the mail-order business, but postal rates went up and they perished.[23]

> DORIS: But without God, the universe is meaningless. Life is meaningless. We're meaningless. (*Deadly pause*) I have a sudden and overpowering urge to get laid.[24]

In "My Philosophy," from *Getting Even*, the incongruities pile up:

> These "particles" [atoms or monads] were set in motion by some cause or underlying principle, or perhaps something fell someplace. The point is that it's too late to do anything about it now, expect possibly to eat plenty of raw fish. This, of course, does not explain why the soul is immortal. Nor does it say anything about

---

[21] *Ibid.*, p. 6
[22] "No Kaddish for Weinstein," *WF*, p. 197.
[23] "Fabulous Tales and Mythical Beasts," *WF*, p. 184.
[24] "God (A Play)," *WF*, p. 143.

an afterlife, or about the feeling my Uncle Sender has that he is being followed by Albanians.[25]

What's especially notable about these examples, and many other occurrences of non-sequiturs in Allen's writing, is that he begins with abstract, metaphysical, or psychoanalytical statements and questions—suggesting an educated, knowledgeable, contemplative reader who has perhaps struggled with questions of immortality, the beginning of time, the meaning of existence—and undercuts the abstractions with outlandish but concrete images or reminders of the realities and necessities of life—often the need and desire for more sex, food, and money.

Much humor is built on incongruity, but many of Allen's non sequiturs follow a specific pattern: the humor depends on readers' recognizing the usual seriousness of the straight-line and on their surprise at seeing so serious a topic brought down brusquely, bathetically to a mundane, more comprehensible level.[26] Rather than the line carrying an objective statement about the often esoteric and impractical nature of philosophical inquiry, the meaning of the line is *in* the reader's experience of it: the universe is not a coherent, easily understood, well-organized, or ultimately understandable place, and attempts to comprehend the universe philosophically or intellectually are futile and, in fact, secondary to the need merely to survive. In Iser's terms, Allen's constant—some might say maddening—use of non-sequiturs creates gaps in the text that the reader is required to fill, but in Allen's case, the *gaps* themselves are the meaning. There are no answers, just voids, and the reader must admit that the text—like the phenomenal world—is really beyond his ability to control or to know completely even though he is immersed in it.

Allen explicitly addresses the limits of knowledge in a number of his works. After attempting to understand the writings of several philosophers ("True, the passage was totally incomprehensible to me, but what of it as long as Kierkegaard was having fun?"[27]), he decides to spell out his philosophy:

---

[25] "My Philosophy, II: Eschatological Dialects as a Means of Coping with Shingles," *GE*, p. 30.

[26] For more on the idea of humor as incongruity, see Chapter 9 in this volume.

[27] "My Philosophy," *GE*, p. 28.

> In formulating any philosophy, the first consideration must always be: What can we know? That is, what can we be sure we know, or sure that we know we knew it, if indeed it is at all knowable. Or have we simply forgotten it and are embarrassed to say anything?[28]

In several works, Allen's protagonist awakens to a confusing or absurd situation that is beyond his comprehension, such as the arrival of Death in "Death (A Play)" (*Without Feathers*). Allen in other works examines the effort to understand or make sense of something beyond understanding. In "A Little Louder Please" (*Getting Even*), an art-loving, phony intellectual discovers "a chink in my cultural armor": he doesn't understand the meaning of pantomime.[29] In "The Query," a one-act play (*Side Effects*) Abe Lincoln attempts to discover the reason someone asked him how long a man's legs should be. He discovers that there is no reason; Abe "was right. It was a non sequitur."[30]

But Allen is at his best when he lets the reader's confusion prove the point, when he pulls the reader into a kind of epistemological trap, as he does when he structures his argument using common syntactical and rhetorical devices such as the quotation marks and transitional tags (so, then, thus) in the following passage:

> So, then, to know a substance or an idea we must doubt it, and thus, doubting it, come to perceive the qualities it possesses in its finite state, which are truly "in the thing itself," or "of the thing itself," or of something or nothing. If this is clear, we can leave epistemology for the moment.[31]

Anyone who has struggled through a work of philosophy will recognize in the last two sentences the precision of Allen's parody, but the individual reader's experience of the passage, it seems to me, begins with confusion and then moves to recognition that the sentences lampoon obscure philosophizing. I can't imagine I'm the only reader who several times read the sentence beginning, "So, then, to know a substance . . .," trying

---

[28] *Ibid.*, pp. 28–29.
[29] "A Little Louder Please," *GE*, p. 105.
[30] "The Query," *SE*, p. 120.
[31] "My Philosophy, I: Critique of Pure Dread," *GE*, p. 29.

to make sense of it. In other words, the sentence does not make a *statement* that compels our attention; the meaning is what the statement *does* to us as we read it even before we recognize it as parody. When McLuhan says in *Annie Hall*, "You know nothing of my work. You mean my whole fallacy is wrong. How you ever got to teach . . .," one can almost anticipate the pompous academic's efforts to make sense of the gibberish in McLuhan's second sentence, when, in fact, the *confusion* created in the mind of someone trained to make meaning of words is, in this case, the message. Such a complicated blending of form and content strikes me as a deliberate, conscious effort of the writer to demonstrate that the reader or critic is not in complete control of the text and that discovering, let alone imposing, a stable meaning is futile. Getting caught in one of Woody Allen's stories is, or at least should be, a very humbling experience.

Interpretive Communities

Sometimes, for Allen, entire stories serve as traps. Almost every work in his three books is a parody of conventional literary and popular genres—newspaper articles, sociological reports, manifestoes, memoirs, notebook entries, plays, college catalogs, religious exegesis, letters, personal essays, book excerpts, diary entries, detective fiction, reviews, guidebooks, Theater of the Absurd, Old Testament stories, Father Brown mysteries, scholarly articles, graduation speeches, Socratic dialogues, and others I'm not aware of. Our experience of reading Allen is dependent on our familiarity with the genres he is working within or parodying since getting at least part of the joke requires recognizing the accuracy or cleverness of his imitation: "More than any other time in history," begins "My Speech to the Graduates," "mankind faces a crossroads. One path leads to despair and utter hopelessness. The other, to total extinction. Let us pray we have the wisdom to choose correctly."[32] Only if we're familiar with the genre being parodied can we get the joke. Similarly, familiarity with literature allows us to snag at least some of the references in the parodies. Allusions in "God (A Play)" include Greek tragedies and comedies, Shakespeare, *Uncle Tom's*

---

[32] "My Speech to the Graduates," *SE*, p. 57.

Cabin, Nietzsche, Marx Brothers comedies, *A Streetcar Named Desire*, and others (I'm sure). His writing recalls either by name or imitation Kafka, Bellow, Malamud, Beckett, Sartre, Camus, and Dostoevsky. My own membership in what Stanley Fish calls "interpretive communities" allows me to hear those echoes, connect intertextually some allusions and references, determine what broader theme might be suggested by Allen's imitation of, for example, Sartre, and "write" the stories and essays I'm reading.[33]

But my lack of membership in others surely limits me. To be specific about it, I get the feeling throughout Allen's works that I am missing a large part of the Jewish humor. Perhaps my sense of exclusion as I read is part of the experience, the *meaning* of Woody Allen; perhaps the uncomfortable, contradictory sensation of being aware that I am not getting some jokes helps remind me of the futility of desiring knowledge I can never possess, or lets me experience, in a very comparatively minor way to be sure, the feeling of being marginalized and excluded. Ironically, it is the wealth of allusion and the appeal to our intelligence that gets Allen's point: if I read according to the conventions of genre to understand the parody, if I recognize allusions and references because of experience, I must admit that I can't know everything there is to know in a text. All readings or interpretations or analysis would have to begin and end with admitting the possibility of a very narrow, incomplete reading.

Of course, I could ask a Jewish friend or read analysis from Jewish commentators or surf the Internet to have the Jewish references, allusions, jokes and genres explained to me. After all, interpretive communities grow and decline; they overlap, we can pass between them. But perhaps of all human expressions, humor, notoriously difficult to translate, depends most of all on context, on the community whose strategies or protocols we have absorbed over time. Someone could carefully explain to me the humor in a joke based on Jewish history, philosophy, culture, and experience, but still I most likely will not laugh. If I learned the structure and even the content of Jewish humor, an unfamiliar joke would probably still not

---

[33] See "Interpreting the Variorum," *Critical Inquiry* 2:2 (1976), p. 182.

strike me as funny.[34] I might understand better, but cognition can't necessarily produce the spontaneous laughter, the moment of recognition, of "getting" it that someone of the original community experiences. Can I ever fully "get" "No Kaddish for Weinstein"(*Without Feathers*)?[35] In *Annie Hall*, if a viewer's very first thought is that pastrami on white with mayonnaise is ridiculous, he gets the joke and laughs immediately—but it has to be the first thought, and such a thought comes more from experience and practice than from the learning and applying of theory and criticism.

Allen's limitless variety demonstrates the limits of learning; moreover, work as rich as Allen's is a humbling reminder not so much that we are limited by the communities of which we are part but that we are surrounded by other communities with abilities, strategies, and knowledge that may be denied us. Allen reminds readers that our readings of a work of literature may be enhanced, but also may be disproved or contradicted, by textual clues that are inaccessible to us because of our limitations. Getting Woody Allen's humor is part of the enjoyment of reading him, but not getting it—and the humbling sensation that comes with recognizing that we don't know it all—is an important part of the meaning of Woody Allen.

With his extraordinary talent, Allen creates inexhaustible literary gems that can be enjoyed by a number of interlocking interpretive communities, no community having the luxury of fully recognizing every and all of the potential meanings in a single piece. And no single reader can ever feel that he has mastered Allen. Perhaps it is not surprising that Woody Allen, in part, lures the unsuspecting intellectual into a potentially humiliating trap: the self-satisfaction of "getting it" when we are the

---

[34] See Ted Cohen, *Jokes: Philosophical Thoughts on Joking Matters* (Chicago: University of Chicago Press, 2001).

[35] Besides containing many references a non-Jewish reader might miss, the story explicitly deals with confusion, the limits of knowledge, and the indeterminacy of meaning: "Weinstein rang the bell to Harriet's apartment, and suddenly she was standing before him. Swelling to maculate giraffe, as usual, thought Weinstein. It was a private joke that neither of them understood" (p. 198). ("Swelling to maculate giraffe" is the fourth line of Eliot's poem, "Sweeney Among the Nightingales," one of the most celebrated of twentieth-century modernist works.)

ones gotten by our pretensions and our pride, our faith in the power of the intellect and in the educations that we feel put us in league with Allen. His gentle satire targets the intellectual, the philosophical, the academic—the very audience he most attracts. Allen shows us all the limitations of "knowing" in a world of confusion and the absurdity of absolutism in a relativistic, subjective, or simply unknowable world. Intelligence, of course, has its place, and if we exercise it with humility—admitting with Iser that we are never entirely free to impose our individual will—we will more fully appreciate Allen's works. While Allen's writings are never overtly political, the rhetorical impact of his texts speaks clearly for a social theory of reading. Words and works of art are complicated things that don't contain only the meaning I pour into them. Perhaps what the genius of Allen engenders is a hermeneutics of modesty, an interpretive practice that admits that there are more things in a work of literature than can ever be accounted for in our philosophy.[36]

---

[36] I am grateful to Louis Rader for his many suggestions on the drafts of this chapter.

6
Woody on Aesthetic Appreciation

JASON HOLT

Woody Allen is not a philosopher. He'd be the first to admit it. Much of his work does, however, have philosophical significance. This is hardly surprising if one observes that while good philosophy tends to be aesthetically piquant, good art likewise tends to be philosophically insightful. Now Woody might reject the label *artist*. There are certainly clues to this effect, possibly ironic, possibly sincere. The label might, at the very least, cause him some discomfort. But as we already know, the label is appropriate, and not just by common standards. Woody is, if nothing else, an entertainer, and he entertains, as a matter of fact, "on a very high level," bringing "a great sense of excitement, stimulation, and fulfillment to people who are sensitive and cultivated."[1] This, by his own standards, makes him not only an artist, but a very good one.

The philosophical relevance of many Woody Allen films is most evident in the exploration of such topics as the meaning of life, existential angst, and moral crisis. Other matters of concern are addressed more subtly, often humorously. The effect is twofold. While the humor distracts us from the matter at hand, obscuring its own foundations, its own implicit assumptions, it also lends credence to those assumptions. It's not that what's funny is true. There are different ways of making people laugh.

---

[1] Stig Björkman, ed., *Woody Allen on Woody Allen* (New York: Grove Press, 1993), p. 103.

Rather, Woody's humor is funny in such a way that it vindicates itself as insightful, although, again, the matter and insight are often easy enough to miss.

Case in point: the nature of aesthetic appreciation. I will present a straightforward but, I think, insightful view of aesthetic appreciation that emerges from Woody Allen's work, chiefly, but not exclusively, his films, and among them chiefly, but not exclusively, *Manhattan*, *Hannah and Her Sisters*, and *Crimes and Misdemeanors*. Why these three? Well, I'm a Woody fan, and these are my all-time favorites. They also happen to contain a high concentration of germane source material. By way of support, other works in the Woody *oeuvre* will be used. At the same time, however, I do not pretend that this is an exhaustive work of scholarship. My primary interest is in the *Gestalt*, and in such details from the *oeuvre* as are sufficient to suggest it. Not only will I ignore much of Woody's work, I will also, for the most part, ignore the man himself. With all due respect, it is the significance of the work that interests me, not whether, or to what extent, the man himself intended the work to have such significance. After all, Woody would probably sell himself short.

In a nutshell, my view is that aesthetic appreciation involves a blending of both intellectual and emotional responses. Both are necessary, but neither is sufficient. Over-intellectualization inhibits, or serves as a sham substitute for, the emotional response involved in genuine appreciation, yielding a knowledgeable but ultimately superficial approach to art. By the same token, excessive emotionality inhibits, or serves as a sham substitute for, the requisite intellectual ingredient, yielding a heartfelt but ultimately indiscriminate approach to art. In genuine appreciation, there is a balance between the two kinds of response. Neither predominates, and the usual conflict between the two is resolved. What such "resolution" means deserves to be explored, and the implications of this view for the way we understand art are important.

Word to the wise: In writing this, I am *not* over-intellectualizing my aesthetic appreciation of Woody's work. That is another matter, falling within another domain. This is an exercise, not in aesthetic appreciation, but in philosophical extrusion. In the spirit of the view to follow, I would not presume to substitute the latter for the former, although the latter may abet the former in interesting ways.

A Marvelous Negative Capability

Much contemporary art is baffling. The art world is permeated with what Arthur Danto calls an "atmosphere of theory," ignorance of which leaves many artworks difficult if not impossible to grasp.[2] It seems that if one is to appreciate theory-driven work, one needs to be conversant with the relevant theory. To some extent this may be true. If an artist's intentions are theoretically couched or sensitive, and if one seeks to understand art in terms of what the artist intended, then such an approach makes perfect sense. It also makes sense if one seeks to interpret art according to established critical procedures, irrespective of whether they pay heed to the artist's intentions. Where theory is needed, let theory reign.

But these are not the only legitimate interests one may have in approaching art. One may, and often should, approach art for the sake of one's own aesthetic pleasure. Even if such gratification falls short of what some authority deems "understanding," it does not fall short of, but rather *constitutes*, genuine appreciation. Let Woody's humor guide us. Woody is arguably at his funniest when he lampoons over-intellectualized approaches to art. Inhaling the "atmosphere of theory" too deeply is seen as inhibiting genuine appreciation, serving as a sham substitute for it, and worse, delegitimating the genuine appreciation of others. Such a stance is overly critical, and at the same time, overly generous. It's pedantic, jargonized, designed to impress, which leads, in some cases, to outright contradiction, which is a theoretical defeater if anything is.

Let's take some examples. Sally (Judy Davis) in *Husbands and Wives* illustrates how over-intellectualization can make one hyper-critical, inhibiting one's appreciation, and delegitimating that of others. Notice how this plays out with Michael (Liam Neeson) in their discussion of Mahler's *Ninth*:

MICHAEL: That music was fantastic.
SALLY: I usually hate Mahler, but it was good. The last movement was too long. I think he should have cut it down.

---

[2] See Arthur Danto, *The Transfiguration of the Commonplace* (Cambridge, Massachusetts: Harvard University Press, 1981), p. 135.

> The second movement was good. Well, it *began* well.
> Then it gets sentimental, don't you think?[3]

She goes on, in hyper-critical mode, to berate his driving, her own *décor*, and the alfredo sauce at dinner. The last is an oh-so-subtle echo of Woody's short "Fabrizio's: Criticism and Response."[4]

Hyper-criticality is also evident in the famous Marshall McLuhan scene in *Annie Hall*. Before the McLuhanese of "hot" and "cool" media is bandied about, much to the irritation of Alvy (Woody), the Professor (Russell Horton), standing behind him in line, gives a mini seminar on Fellini, also to Alvy's great irritation:

> PROFESSOR: We saw the Fellini film last Tuesday. It is *not* one of his best. It lacks a cohesive structure, you know? You get the feeling that he's not absolutely sure what it is he wants to *say*. Of course, I've always felt that he was essentially a—a *technical* film-maker. Granted, *La Strada* was a great film, great in its use of negative imagery more than anything else. But that simple, cohesive core . . . Like all that *Juliet of the Spirits* or *Satyricon*, I found it incredibly *indulgent*, you know? He really is. He's one of the most *indulgent* film-makers. He really is.[5]

One can also see, here, shades of jargonization—yes, I intend the irony—not to mention outright contradiction. To impress his listener, obviously, the professor dismisses Fellini first as a merely technical film-maker, then as a supremely indulgent one. In *Hannah and Her Sisters*, a similar phenomenon is at work when David (Sam Waterston) shows Holly (Dianne Wiest) and April (Carrie Fisher) one of his buildings:

> DAVID: The design's deliberately non-contextual, but I wanted to keep the atmosphere of the street, you know, and in the proportions, and in the material, that's—that's unpolished red granite.

---

[3] *Husbands and Wives* (1992).
[4] *Side Effects* (1981).
[5] *Annie Hall* (1977).

APRIL: It has an organic quality, you know? It's almost—
almost—uh—entirely wholly interdependent, if you know
what I mean. I can't put it into words. The important thing
is that it—it *breathes*.[6]

April jargonizes, putting into vague terms what she says can't be
put in any terms, while David's idea of non-contextual architecture involves paying attention to the atmosphere, proportions,
and material of the surrounding buildings.

A different but related case is Lester (Alan Alda) in *Crimes
and Misdemeanors*. His language, in talking about art, is not
pedantic or self-contradictory, nor is it hyper-critical, at least not
explicitly. He is, however, somewhat dismissive. Of Chekov stories he says, off the cuff, "The guy wrote a *million* of them."
When Emily Dickinson comes up in conversation over drinks,
Halley (Mia Farrow) begins quoting from "The Chariot," and the
ensuing dynamic between her, Cliff (Woody) and Lester is quite
telling:

HALLEY: "Because I could not stop for death—"
CLIFF: "—He kindly stopped for me." The word *kindly*, right?[7]

It's out of appreciation that Halley begins the quotation, and it's
a shared appreciation that prompts Cliff to continue, stressing
the adverb that makes the couplet work. Lester ignores this, and
continues to quote the stanza in its entirety, as if rote memo-
rization is what really counts. By implication, appreciating the
way words are used in the poem—appreciating the poem itself
itself—is dismissed as a side-issue, or worse, a non-issue.

The character that perhaps best exhibits over-intellectualization is Mary (Diane Keaton) in *Manhattan*. Witness the variety
of symptoms in the following exchange with Isaac (Woody):

ISAAC: The photographs downstairs—great, absolutely great.
Did you like it?
MARY: No. I felt it was very derivative. To me it looked like it
was straight out of Diane Arbus, but it had none of the wit.

---

[6] *Hannah and Her Sisters* (1986).
[7] *Crimes and Misdemeanors* (1989).

ISAAC: Well, we didn't like it as much as we liked the plexiglass sculpture, that I will admit.

MARY: Really. You liked the plexiglass?

ISAAC: You didn't like the plexiglass sculpture either?

MARY: Interesting. No, um, uh-uh.

ISAAC: It was a hell of a lot better than that steel cube. Did you see the steel cube?

MARY: Now that was brilliant to me, absolutely brilliant.

ISAAC: The steel cube was brilliant?

MARY: Yes. To me it was very textural, you know what I mean? It was perfectly integrated, and it had a marvelous kind of negative capability. The rest of the stuff downstairs was bullshit.[8]

Isaac dismisses this as "pseudo-intellectual garbage," which perhaps it is, although the underlying problem, again, is that art is being approached in an overly rational fashion. Later, in reference to a piece of sculpture, Isaac pokes fun at this attitude:

ISAAC: This I think has a—a kind of wonderful *otherness* to it, you know? It's kind of got a marvelous *negative capability*, a kind of wonderful *energy*, don't you think?[9]

Mary's hyper-criticality is also exhibited in her role as co-founder of the Academy of the Over-Rated, the ironic counterpoint of which is that, while she's happy to berate Mahler, Fitzgerald, van Gogh, and Bergman, she insists that many of her friends deserve the title of genius, to say nothing of her ex-husband Jeremiah (Wallace Shawn).

I Love Songs about Extra-Terrestrial Life, Don't You?

Just as over-intellectualizing art is a problem, so too is *under*-intellectualizing it. In such cases, the culprit is excessive emotionality, which inhibits, or serves as a sham substitute for, the intellectual component of genuine appreciation. The result here

---

[8] *Manhattan* (1979).
[9] *Ibid.*

is a heart-felt but ultimately indiscriminate approach to art, as when Holly takes Mickey (Woody) to a rock concert in *Hannah and Her Sisters*:

> HOLLY: I love songs about extra-terrestrial life, don't you?
> MICKEY: Not when they're sung by extra-terrestrials.[10]

Similarly, notice what happens in the exchange between Frederick (Max von Sydow) the artist and Dusty (Daniel Stern) the rock star:

> DUSTY: I got an Andy Warhol, and I got a Frank Stella too. Oh, it's very beautiful, *big*, *weird*. If you stare at that Stella too long, the colors just seem to float. It's—kind of weird. . . .
> FREDERICK: Do you appreciate drawings?
> DUSTY: Yeah. Oh, hey, wow. She's beautiful. But, uh, I really need something—I'm looking for something *big*. . . . I got a lot of wall space there. . . .
> FREDERICK: I—*don't*—sell my work by the yard.[11]

The indiscriminate emotionality of Holly is complemented, here, by Dusty's confusion. In Frederick's drawings, he mistakes the beauty of the woman depicted for the beauty of the depiction. (Think of Magritte's infamous *Çeci n'est pas une pipe*.) More amusingly, his criterion as "art collector" is not the beauty, piquancy, or value of a piece, but rather, of all things, its *size*, and its ability to blend in with his sofa—er, sorry—his ottoman.

Other characters in Woody's films exhibit similar tendencies, but the examples above are, to my mind, the most memorable. Still, one may wonder whether there are other sorts of evidence that, on the Allenesque view, aesthetic appreciation involves a significant intellectual ingredient. There are, one of which comes from the man himself, specifically, Woody's definition of art as "entertainment for intellectuals."[12] I have to admit, this is a pretty good definition. Few philosophers could do better. The

---

[10] *Hannah and Her Sisters* (1986).
[11] *Ibid.*
[12] Björkman (1995), p. 103.

point, though, is that if this is what art is conceived to be, then aesthetic appreciation must be likewise conceived as involving a certain intellectual sensitivity, cultivation, and, in the moment, engagement. Otherwise it wouldn't be *for* intellectuals.

The Brain Is My Second Favorite Organ

It's time now to put the pieces together. Aesthetic appreciation involves both the intellect and the emotions. It's not overly intellectual, in the sense that one lacks the requisite emotionality. Nor is it overly emotional, in the sense that one lacks intellectual refinement and discrimination. The two are rather in balance. What would otherwise be base pleasure is distinctively elevated, and what would otherwise be detached abstraction is distinctively grounded. Quality art affects us in both ways, moving us in thought as well as in feeling. A Lester-like way of putting this is to say that Piquancy = Profundity + Poignancy.

In art, profundity engages the intellect, poignancy the emotions, and the experience as a whole is aesthetically piquant. Of course, one can encounter art without being moved to thought or feeling, but in such cases, one fails to appreciate it, or one has a merely intellectual or merely emotional appreciation, and while such appreciation is of aesthetic objects, neither is genuinely aesthetic.

What is the value of such experiences? Woody gives us a clue. In *Manhattan*, artworks and artists dominate Isaac's list of what makes life worth living: "the second movement of the *'Jupiter' Symphony*, Louis Armstrong's recording of 'Potato Head Blues', Swedish movies [read: 'the films of Ingmar Bergman'], naturally, *Sentimental Education* by Flaubert, Marlon Brando, Frank Sinatra," and of course, "those incredible apples and pears by Cézanne."[13]

Fair enough. But why should experiencing such things *aesthetically* be so crucially important? Again, Woody gives us a clue. The characters he portrays are almost invariably in *conflict*—between what they want to do and think they ought to do, between their sense of justice and the recognition of injustice, between their desires and the knowledge that many of them

---

[13] *Manhattan* (1979).

can't be satisfied, and so on. These, if you notice, are conflicts between intellect and emotion. Reason and passion are at odds, and their being at odds is typical of mental life, all too typical.[14] As Cliff puts it: "My heart says one thing, my head says something else. It's very difficult to get your heart and your head together in life."[15] One needs relief from such conflict, and one finds relief in art.

To appreciate art, to experience it aesthetically, amounts to a *resolution* of conflict between intellect and emotion.[16] Although such resolution is often, and perhaps characteristically, pleasurable, it need not have a sedative, calming effect, because aesthetic experience, so conceived, is not a quelling of the faculties, as in sleep, but a coherent engagement of both. Indeed, aesthetic experience is often quite exciting, inspiring thought and action in a way which, arguably, the conflicted mind simply can't equal.

It is a virtue of this view that it provides such a straightforward account of the value of aesthetic experience. Another virtue is this. Some philosophers are skeptics about aesthetic experience.[17] That is, they doubt that there is anything distinctive about it, that there is anything that all, and only, such experiences share. While the motives for such skepticism vary, the best justification for it seems to be that art can and often does have a huge variety of psychological effects.[18] First, some aesthetic experiences appear to be not so much cognitive as *sensuous*. Think, for instance, of appreciating instrumental music, an appreciation which, plausibly enough, seems more purely experiential, more basely pleasurable, than a marriage of intellect and emotion. Even in the cognitive realm, intellectual and

---

[14] See A.T.W. Simeons, *Man's Presumptuous Brain* (New York: Dutton, 1961), especially pp. 31–59.

[15] *Crimes and Misdemeanors* (1989).

[16] In some respects, this is rooted in I.A. Richards, *Principles of Literary Criticism* (London: Routledge, 1925), which is cited with approval in Monroe Beardsley, *Aesthetics* (New York: Harcourt, Brace, 1958), pp. 573–74, and echoed in my "A Comprehensivist Theory of Art," *British Journal of Aesthetics* 36 (1996), pp. 427–28.

[17] For instance, George Dickie, "The Myth of the Aesthetic Attitude," *American Philosophical Quarterly* 1 (1964), pp. 56–65.

[18] Stephen Davies, *Definitions of Art* (Ithaca: Cornell University Press, 1991), pp. 59–60.

emotional content varies widely. What could my laughter at a comedy and my tears at a tragedy possibly have in common? More precisely (if still somewhat simplistically), suppose a tragedy moves me to sad thoughts of terrible fate, while a comedy induces happy thoughts of felicitous coincidence. What could these responses have in common?

Let's tackle these in turn. First, it's not at all obvious that purely sensuous experiences are genuinely aesthetic. As with purely intellectual or purely emotional responses to art, a purely sensuous response may be *of* an aesthetic object without itself being aesthetic in character. Aesthetic pleasure is almost undeniably unlike the sort of base pleasure one enjoys in other domains (although undoubtedly these pleasures may be invested with aesthetic significance). It *feels* different. And even if it didn't, the pleasure of aesthetic experience may simply distract us—as pleasure often does—from distinct, and introspectable, cognitive ingredients. When we find a piece of music piquant, it moves us, stirring up emotions, dredging up thoughts. Where cognitive elements can't be introspected, this suggests that, as the source of aesthetic pleasure, they are not absent but *deep*, emotions one knows not what, an implicit cognitive grasp of the piece's melodic patterns, harmonic structures, and so on. That aesthetic pleasure is so often sought, yet comparatively difficult to come by, suggests that it is altogether different in kind from its purely sensuous counterpart.

This leaves us with the problem of cognitive variance, that is, the problem of how two different experiences could count as aesthetic when they share neither intellectual nor emotional content. Suppose that my emotional response to a tragedy is sadness, while my emotional response to a comedy is happiness; and where the tragedy suggests the thought that even heroes are doomed, that life is most grave indeed, the comedy suggests that even fools will prosper, that life is anything but serious. In each case I am responding to an artwork, but—and this is the key question—in what sense is it plausible to say that the two experiences have the *same* aesthetic character? After all, the sadness of my tragedy-response is contrary to the happiness of my comedy-response. My respective thoughts are likewise incompatible. But on the Allenesque view, it's the balance that matters, reason and passion united, not the particular emotional or intellectual content of the experience. My sad tragic thoughts exhibit this harmony. My happy comic thoughts do too. In the first case, my sadness is not in conflict, but rather coheres, with the tragic thought, and as such does not move me to seek means of alleviation. Likewise, my happiness coheres *in the same way* with my intellectual response to the comedy. The two responses, again, are in consort, mutually supportive. Variety notwithstanding, then, there is something that all, and only, aesthetic experiences share. They're *resolutive*.[19] Thus does Woody score, in my view, a hit, a very palpable hit.

Don't Speak

Ludwig Wittgenstein concludes his famous *Tractatus* with: "Whereof one cannot speak, thereof one must be silent."[20] As Wittgenstein pictures it, we can't speak of matters in the realm of value, which includes, of course, the aesthetic. The aesthetic is one of those things that can be *shown*, and so, in a sense, shared. But the aesthetic can't be captured in language. It can't be so reduced. The Allenesque view is similar. Notice the dynamic of shared appreciation between Isaac and Tracy (Mariel Hemingway) in *Manhattan*, between Elliot (Michael Caine) and Lee (Barbara Hershey) in *Hannah and Her Sisters*, between Cliff and Halley in *Crimes and Misdemeanors*. In character, Woody almost invariably expresses aesthetic approbation in the form of simple, positive statements: "Great," "Terrific," "Fantastic," "Wonderful," and so on. Woody's riff on Wittgenstein, then, is: "Whereof one cannot speak, thereof one must say little." To say more than a little, it seems, is not only to miss the point, it is to over-intellectualize art and thereby preclude genuine appreciation of it.

It's here that Woody and I part ways, and here's why. An overly intellectual or emotional approach to art precludes genuine appreciation, yes. But what determines the excessiveness of either is that it is "all out of proportion" to, and thus has the danger of inhibiting, the other. But proportionality is relative.

---

[19] A term from Holt (1996), pp. 427–28 meaning "exhibits, and consists in, resolution" in the special sense of 'resolution' intended. The usual adjectival forms 'resolved', 'resolving', and the like, did not seem apt.

[20] Ludwig Wittgenstein, *Tractatus Logico-Philosophicus* (New York: Harcourt, Brace, 1933), Proposition 7.

What would otherwise be an excess of thought can be matched by what would otherwise be an excess of feeling, and slight excesses of one, deliberate or otherwise, in the privacy of thought or in discussion with others, may augment the other into a higher, more insightful, more moving resolution. If genuine appreciation is a seesaw balance between intellect and emotion, this does not by itself determine how low, or high, the fulcrum should be set.[21]

---

[21] My thanks to Mark Conard, Aeon Skoble, and Elana Geller for comments on an earlier draft.

7

Art and Voyeurism in the Films of Woody Allen

JEROLD ABRAMS

It began with slapstick and farcical stoogery, but in short order Woody Allen was producing the highly philosophical films he wanted and by which today he is largely defined, films like *The Purple Rose of Cairo, Another Woman, Annie Hall, Crimes and Misdemeanors, Interiors*, and *Play It Again, Sam*. These films are masterpiece fusions of philosophy and film, which share two dominant philosophical themes. The first is an unveiling of social reality as unlimited voyeurism, and the second is an ethical response to that "reality."

No longer conceived as something good, or even reasonable—the world of human relations, in the hands of Allen, is a labyrinthine simulacrum of images, distorted lenses, two-way mirrors, and hidden cameras. No one is safe from the omnipresent voyeuristic glare of film, including we the viewers, who are equally caught in the headlights of the hard Apollonian gaze which stares back at us. It is a nihilistic world, where "to be" means "to be watched," and to watch others—and this world is revealed through the most voyeuristic artistic medium of all, film. Indeed, more than the works of any other filmmaker, Allen's films take as their primary subject matter the very medium of film itself, constituting a kind of "theater of theater." In such a world of voyeurism, there would seem little room for any kind of ethics. Yet an ethics is carved out, one which accepts the Death of Man, his "soul-lessness" in the Modern world, and makes him into "living art."

The Problem of Surveillance in Philosophy

Postmodernism has many definitions, but is typically characterized by a skeptical attitude toward Ethical Truth, a skeptical attitude toward the idea that humanity can be improved, and a
creeping sense of a spreading moral void. It stems mainly from
the German philosopher Friedrich Nietzsche (1844–1900) and
his worldview that "God is Dead." In an age of doubt, beliefs in
God are no longer so reasonable, just as beliefs in any eternal
moral law, or any deepest core of humanity, are also ruled out
of hand—there simply is nothing left to guide us any more. After
the rise of modernity, we have lost our way and fallen into a
vortex of nihilism, ethical fragmentation, and cultural disorder.

Among those contemporary thinkers typically associated
with postmodernity is the French philosopher Michel Foucault
(1926–84), whose work is greatly indebted to Nietzsche.
Foucault explains that the nihilism, voyeurism, and paranoia of
contemporary society should be understood by way of an anal-
ogy to a nineteenth-century prison structure called the "panopticon."[1] In this prison, a circle of isolated cells faces inward
toward a blinding light, which shines all day and all night, making each prisoner feel as though he is always being watched by
others he can't see. It functions as an absolute superego, and is
intended to rip down the barriers of privacy, indeed, to force the
prisoner to internalize the light and survey his own behavior full
time, as he imagines others are doing as well.

The same prison model, Foucault claims, may now be used
to study society at large. Surveillance has become the dominant
cultural ethos—and it is mediated through society's basic institutions, such as schools, hospitals, and especially the social sciences, which give each the power to diagnose every other. And
all of this watching and evaluating is kept in our permanent
records: genomic transcripts, grade reports, medical files, credit
trails, and therapy sessions. There is no private life and the individual is forced always to see herself through the eyes of others. Indeed, with the continual rise of technology, this
surveillance has become even more extreme and very fine-

---

[1] Michel Foucault, *Power/Knowledge: Selected Interviews and Other Writings*
[1972–1977] (New York: Pantheon, 1980), p. 147.

tuned. Legal and illegal, hidden and exposed, from the very small "hand-held" to the very large satellite, film cameras are anywhere and everywhere to record and dissolve the private sphere whenever possible.

According to Foucault, this massive "surveillance society" results in an atmosphere of total exposure, paranoia, and ultimately a "confessing society." And here, with regard to confession, Foucault's vision is not so far from the medieval worldview of divine omniscience: one always confesses as one is always being watched, always feeling guilty and exposed, but without any of the forgiving love of the Christian God. Such anxiety strongly recalls Nietzsche's conception of "slave morality," where we are all psychologically berating ourselves, confessing, exposing, and living according to the dim lights of the Herd— certainly a dark view of humanity, and the future stands to get much worse.

Later in his career, Foucault tried to find a way to live an ethical life within the confessing society of the panopticon. Here, rather than terrible accounts of the loss of internal, private space, Foucault advances a Nietzschean approach to self-creation and enhancement through physical and linguistic experiments with the self (self-narration or self-redescription,[2] subversive thinking, hard drugs, and S&M). These are extreme exercises in fighting back the oppressive public and scientific light of the panopticon, in order to take control of one's own process of subjectification, and thus to create one's own private self-image. One must self-consciously accept the self as mere material for self-sculpture, for molding one's own private experience within and against the fully illumined panopticon.

And this is also precisely what Woody Allen does so well. Allen and Foucault share the same philosophical equation: ontology (or the world) is essentially voyeurism, and ethics is aesthetic self-fashioning. The re-construction of the subject through self-redescription is the only way out of the unending labyrinth of cameras, mirrors, and everyday psychoanalysts. In other words,

---

[2] See Foucault, *The Care of the Self: History of Sexuality.* Volume 3 (New York: Random House, 1986); *Ethics: Subjectivity and Truth,* Volume 1 of *The Essential Works of Michel Foucault* [1954–1984] (New York: The New Press, 1994), and, in particular, within that volume, "Technologies of the Self" (pp. 223–251).

the only way *out* of the labyrinth is, paradoxically, to *remain within it.* One must stoically accept the modern institutional house of mirrors for what it is, but equally attempt to give style to one's constructed character within its millionfold reflections.

The Problem of Surveillance in Woody Allen: The 'Eyes of Film' Are On Us Always

Crimes and Misdemeanors

In *Crimes and Misdemeanors,* the ophthalmologist, Judah (Martin Landau), has his mistress killed, rather than confess the affair as suggested by his friend Rabbi Ben (Sam Waterston). Feeling guilty, Judah searches through his past, and recalls his father's dictum that "The eyes of God are on us always."[3] Morality to Judah's father is a medieval watcher's reward-punishment scheme, dished out by a divine voyeur and judge. The vision haunts Judah, and he nearly confesses, but ultimately snaps out of it—he is a modern man, a skeptic, a scientist, and an aesthete, someone like Nietzsche, for whom "God is dead." The generational transition from Judah's father to Judah mirrors the paradigm shift from the religious Middle Ages to modern rationalism. The medieval God has disappeared, or, simply "gone blind" with the progression of modernity, just as Rabbi Ben steadily goes absolutely blind from beginning to end of the film.

But with this modern Death of God, a new god has come onto the scene. This is the new God of Film, which appears in the second story-line of the film (intertwined with the first). The second story is that of Cliff Stern (Woody Allen). Cliff makes films about the philosophical meaning of life, and ethical causes like the environment and disease—yet he is poor, unsuccessful, and unrecognized. Here with Cliff's character, we see how Film begins to take the place of Judah's God. This new God of Film is still an omniscient surveyor, and still a moral judge, but is entirely in Man's control.

---

[3] Richard A. Blake, in *Woody Allen: Profane and Sacred* (Lanham: Scarecrow Press, 1995), offers an excellent religious perspective on Allen's films, as alternating between sacred ritual and profanation. Here, however, the religious focus is more on the dark side of divine and cinematic voyeurism, control, and confession.

Its power of surveillance is most evident in the relation Cliff has with his brother-in-law Lester. Lester is Cliff's opposite—he makes films too, but they are lowbrow crowd-pleasers, and he ends up rich and very successful. Lester has commissioned Cliff to do a film on Lester, a study in the "Creative Mind" of a film genius. But the finished product is not what Lester expects. In fact, it is just the opposite—not a study of his public success, but a sharp critique of his moral shortcomings. Alone in a private viewing room, Cliff (holier than thou and without apology) sits next to Lester and reveals to Lester his own life on the finished film. Lester is parodied as a fascist, is shown berating his employees, and distastefully seducing one of his actresses. All of it is exposed to Lester on film, as though Cliff as God were "replaying the tape" on a newly arrived soul after death.

Closing in on one another, at the end, the two story-lines of Judah and Cliff finally converge at a wedding party. After learning that Cliff makes movies, Judah wants to tell his own crime story as a pitch for a new film—this is, in fact, Judah's own story of the murderer who gets away clean and lives without guilt. Judah is so proud of the authenticity and quality of his story that, in response to Cliff's doubts about the believability of the plot, Judah almost gives the truth away, strongly asserting, "I'm talking about reality!" But Judah hesitates—this will not be a total confession: he backs away from the precipice of the guilty need to be judged. Judah will not, unlike Rodia Raskolnikov in Fyodor Dostoevsky's *Crime and Punishment*, succumb to the urge to confess his murder.

The difference between the two titles *Crime and Punishment* and *Crimes and Misdemeanors* reveals a difference between the plots as well (and Allen appears to use the Russian novel self-consciously). In the novel, there is a "crime" of murder, a confession, and then a "punishment." In Allen's film, there is also the "crime" of murder, but no confession, and "no punishment." Rather than confession and punishment, Judah attempts to overcome his guilt, to become, in Nietzsche's sense, an Overman, someone who lives beyond the Rule of God or the Rule of Man. He lives beyond all rules, save his own—he lives "beyond good and evil,"[4] and attempts to transform his crimes

---

[4] See Nietzsche's title, *Beyond Good and Evil: Prelude to a Philosophy of the*

into art. This kind of figure is precisely what Raskolnikov believed he would become and failed to become, and what Judah doubted he could ever become, and ultimately succeeded in becoming.[5]

The Purple Rose of Cairo

A similar equation of divine voyeurism and life as art is given in the surreal tragedy, *The Purple Rose of Cairo*. In the middle of the Depression, Cecilia (Mia Farrow) escapes her terrible life and abusive husband, Monk (Danny Aiello), by going to the same film repeatedly—and its title is *The Purple Rose of Cairo* (the film within the film). Little does she know, however, that while she is watching the film, the film is also watching her, in the form of Tom Baxter (Jeff Daniels), the star of the film. And just as Cecilia wants to escape into the object of her own voyeurism, so too does Tom want to escape into the object of his, to venture out of Film into Reality, so he can be with Cecilia.

Their voyeuristic objects are simply reversed. She's watching the screen, wholly unaware that she is being watched. And he is watching out, voyeuristically enjoying her voyeurism, knowing she does not suspect his glance. By way of this technique, Allen sets up yet an additional metaphysical layer of voyeurism between his own film and the viewer-voyeur at home (or in the real-life theater). We too, the watchers watching the film, are made aware of our own position, and our own desire to fuse with the object of our attention.

The optical gaze seems so powerful as to be virtually unlimited and omniscient, and clearly of a kind with *Crimes and Misdemeanors*. Indeed, the equation of God and Film is also repeated here, and made very explicit: Tom can't understand the things of the real world, but when Cecilia tries to explain God to him, Tom equates the definition of God with the filmmakers who made the film *The Purple Rose of Cairo*. After all, the film-

---

Future, (New York: Vintage, 1966). Nietzsche's Overman emerges in the future as an individual who lives beyond Man's rule of Good and Evil. He forms his own moral rules, which apply only to himself. He lives without guilt as a self-creating superhuman.

[5] An interesting contrast of perspective might be found in the 1998 film *A Simple Plan*, in which a small act of vice snowballs into a great tragedy

makers created him as a character. They determine the plot of his reality, and they are the ultimate optical judges of his being.

In addition to this conception of unlimited voyeurism, one also finds in *The Purple Rose of Cairo* elements of Allen's constructive and aestheticist ethics. At the end of the film, Cecilia is forced to choose between her actual life and going into the film forever: she must choose between reality and illusion. Ultimately, she chooses reality, and is punished for it severely.

In the closing moments she refuses to walk into the screen to join Tom (rather than to join the actor playing Tom), and be lost forever inside the self-consciously aestheticist world of illusion, where she can become what she wants, live her dreams, and control her destiny. Even experimenting with re-writing the script of a set film, she feels the wondrous power of the Shakespearean mask, but ultimately gives it up. Instead, she chooses an actor—a liar, who does not want her at all—over the persona staged, and ultimately is stuck only with her husband Monk, terrible poverty, and eternal pain. The film is, indeed, a tragedy which punishes Cecilia; although, because it is a tragedy, Woody Allen's own ethics is revealed as one in which Film *ought* to win over Reality.

Annie Hall

Similar themes of voyeurism and the triumph of illusion over reality are repeated in Allen's film, *Annie Hall*. The story of Alvy Singer (Woody Allen) alternates between third and second person perspectives, the latter of which is very jarring: Alvy will often turn to the viewers in the theater and tell us he knows we are watching him.

A key example arises when Alvy and Annie Hall (Diane Keaton) go out to "watch" a film.[6] Standing in line waiting, Alvy becomes irritated with an academic show-off who is waxing theoretical on the cultural semiotics of Marshall McLuhan. Having had enough, Alvy breaks into second person toward the viewer, and explains his irritation. The academic follows him and complains to us, and Alvy, that he has a right to be heard too. And then, brilliantly, Alvy produces McLuhan from behind a screen (analogously to what Allan does to us). Having eavesdropped

---

[6] Woody Allen, *Annie Hall*, DVD, Chapter 7.

on their conversation, McLuhan chides the academic, to say he is totally wrong about his work, and that he doesn't deserve an academic chair at all. Alvy, pleased with himself, again in the second person, addresses the camera to say, "Boy, if life were only like this!"

And, in fact, most of Alvy's life *is* like that, at least as we see it: he is a character half in and half out of fantasy, half in reality and half in his own film (which he desperately tries to control). The theme continually reappears, notably in his discussions of psychoanalysis, which is a technique for handling the patient's own psychological schism between reality and illusion. Alvy is in therapy, and has convinced Annie to get into therapy too, in addition to buying her books on death, and getting her into adult education. Clearly he wants to remold her reality according to his own illusions, perhaps to make her into someone in whom he can lose himself completely. Her subconscious resistance, however, comes to a head after she returns from therapy, greets Alvy, and starts to mix up her words.

> ALVY (*thinking*): ". . . What'd the doctor say?
>
> ANNIE (*putting away some groceries*): "Well she said that I should probably come five times a week. And you know something? I don't think I mind analysis at all. The only question is, Will it change my wife?"
>
> ALVY: "Will it change your wife?"
>
> ANNIE: "Will it change my life?"
>
> ALVY: "Yeah, but you said, 'Will it change my wife'!"
>
> ANNIE: "No, I didn't. (Laughing) I said, 'Will it change my life,' Alvy."
>
> ALVY: "You said, 'Will it change . . .' Wife. Will it change . . ."
>
> ANNIE (*yelling out, angry*): "Life. I said, 'life.' "
>
> ALVY: (*to the audience*) "She said, 'Will it change my wife.' You heard that because you were there so I'm not crazy."
>
> ANNIE: "And, Alvy . . . and then I told her about how I didn't think you'd ever really take me seriously, because you don't think that I'm smart enough."
>
> *She walks out of the room.*[7]

---

[7] Woody Allen, *Annie Hall*, Complete Script, http://corky.net/scripts/annieHall.html.

It's a "Freudian slip," which slips out in the course of an attempt to articulate what she is thinking about her Freudian subconscious. Annie meant to say "life," but she says what her subconscious is thinking: she says "wife." Annie secretly believes that Alvy wants to change her, that he's using school and therapy to make her something different, a reflection of Alvy. With the obvious slip, Alvy, frustrated, turns to the camera, again in the second person, and logs his complaint. Though, in fact, we the voyeurs, from whom he seeks verification of reality, can't really help him in this. For we know all too well that he is culpable, and that Annie's subconscious has spoken the truth: he really does want to change his "wife" (his girlfriend)—and beyond that, he also really wants to change his *own* life.

Alvy wants to escape from himself, and from the entirety of reality, which he sees as terribly voyeuristic and psychoanalytic. The only solution Alvy seems to accept is simply to live self-consciously in his own world of illusion. The point is made explicitly at the end of the film, in a joke he tells (to us) about the value of illusion over reality. Paraphrasing, it works like this: A man tells a therapist his brother thinks of himself as a chicken. The therapist asks the man why he does not confront his brother, and get him help, so he can feel human. To this, Alvy responds, "I would, but I need the eggs."

Alvy then explains that this is how he sees human relationships. He lives in his own world, which is not entirely real, but he can't leave it. Why? Because he needs the eggs (meaning that he needs the illusion). All of this is done in the second person to the viewer. And it is not entirely clear whether Alvy is on the couch, whether we the viewers really function as Woody Allen's own countless voyeuristic therapists, or, in fact, we are invited as participants to the grand, fantastical, epistemological orgy of therapists, quasi-persons, voyeurs, and alter egos.

Another Woman

The strong equation between psychoanalysis and voyeurism is again developed in *Another Woman*. Mary Nichols, in her book *Reconstructing Woody: Art, Love, and Life in the Films of Woody Allen*, develops the point very well, and the present discussion takes a point of departure from hers. A woman ("*another woman*"), Hope (Mia Farrow) is divulging her private thoughts to a therapist. But in the next room, Marion (Gena Rowlands), a philosophy professor, can't help listening in on the private session. And in the next room, our room, we are also watching Marion listen in. And it is here, as Nichols points out, that, in addition to our constituting a separate layer of voyeurism, we are also forced into an even further layer, in which we are caught in the act of enjoying ourselves as voyeurs. That is, we are caught as voyeurs *on ourselves* as voyeurs: "We too, perhaps unawares, are eavesdropping on ourselves."[8] These aesthetic distances constitute an elaborate study in cinematic recapitulation. To be sure, "a room of one's own" is altogether an illusion—for all rooms here are made of glass, all with cameras behind them, and libraries of videotape behind those. And this goes for our own rooms as well.

Indeed, Nichols is correct to recognize additional layers of voyeurism at work here, but there are perhaps even more. And here it will be helpful to count them up, all the way to infinity. Voyeur Relationship (1) is the therapist watching (and listening in on) Hope. Voyeur Relationship (2) is Marion listening in on Hope (and the therapist). Voyeur Relationship (3) is the viewer's relationship to the film. Voyeur Relationship (4) is the viewer to the viewer (Nichols, above: we eavesdrop on ourselves). And, in addition to these, Voyeur Relationship (5) is constituted by a structure of unlimited voyeurism set up by the medium of film itself.

Just as we catch ourselves watching ourselves watching ourselves through the cinematic medium—simultaneously there arises the realization of an unlimited voyeurism (voyeurism 5 which is cinematically extended *ad infinitum*). This layer of

---

[8] Mary Nichols, *Reconstructing Woody: Art, Love, and Life in the Films of Woody Allen* (Lanham: Rowman and Littlefield, 1998), p. 146. Nichols also draws on Roger Ebert's analysis of the film. Nichols writes, "Together with Marion we violate Hope; together with Allen, we violate Marion. It is no accident that this movie, which is about eavesdropping makes us feel like eavesdroppers. Roger Ebert's reaction to this movie, I believe, is what ours should also be. 'Film is the most voyeuristic medium,' he writes, 'but rarely have I experienced this fact more sharply than while watching Woody Allen's *Another Woman*. This is a film almost entirely composed of moments that should be private.' Ebert points out that not only is privacy violated by characters in the film, Marion's eavesdropping on Hope being the prime example, but 'at times we invade the privacy of the characters'" (Nichols, p. 146; Ebert, "Another Woman," *Go Ebert*, compuserve, cited in Nichols, p. 237, fn. 9).

unlimited voyeurism arises precisely from the voyeuristic medium of film itself, which is a mode of what the philosopher of art Noël Carroll calls "Mass Art." Part of the definition of mass art is that it is made for massive consumption through technological reproduction. Film is made for unlimited numbers of people across all spaces, and infinitely into the future.

As a study in voyeurism, in a voyeuristic medium, which is also made for mass levels of voyeurism, the ultimate achievement of *Another Woman* (and any self-consciously voyeuristic film, in general), is the exposure of society as intensely and unlimitedly voyeuristic. And this is precisely the early Foucault's point about modern institutions. Not one or two or even three layers of voyeurism, but the radical exposure of the mass art of film as voyeuristic, of the masses as voyeurs, each as voyeur on every other and herself—this is the ultimate effect of the film.

Interiors

In *Interiors* the theme of visual objectification is repeated. It is the story of a woman named Eve (Geraldine Page), and her artist daughters, Flyn (Kristin Griffith), Renata (Diane Keaton), and Joey (Mary Beth Hurt). Eve is an artistic interior decorator, but her real material is people, their "interiors," their psyches. The name of Eve recalls another "Eve," the original mother of the Garden of Eden. Like the original, Allen's "Eve" creates people as originals too, but her intention is High Art, and has nothing to do with "humanity." Moreover, in addition to artist, she is also the audience, as she imprisons her living sculptures in a museum, which she watches over like an absolute panoptical light. Her interior adornment of the familial sphere is a museum (or mausoleum) of Still Lifes on display, prisoners in an open-air prison, under the pressure of High Art's hard Apollonian gaze. Her daughters are slaves biologically embedded in one woman's manic will to form.

Indeed, even Eve herself is equally a prisoner, as her supposed self-mastery is too unreflective to realize that it slavishly depends on objects of her own creation. As the German philosopher G.W.F. Hegel (1770–1883) argues, in *The Phenomenology of Spirit* (in the section on the "Master-Slave Dialectic"), the master does not realize that her own self-consciousness is actually somewhat slavish. The master's personal identity is, in fact, intrinsically intertwined with what her slaves think of her, how they respect her, how they perform, even as static objects. Without her Art/Children/Slaves, the Master Eve would be entirely helpless, a master of nothing—and there would be no one around to recognize her as Master. She is not at all free, since she depends on her slaves for her own self-identity. The master is "needy," slavish to attention and recognition, not at all autonomous, as she thinks she is.

And here again, in *Interiors*, the only possible "escape" for Eve (or her children/*oeuvre*) is to accept the soul-lessness of the world, to accept herself as a work of art in progress, and fuse her very life with art of her own control. Although here, the only person of the film who comes close to achieving this goal is Flyn. Renata is a well-received poet; and Joey is a photographer; but Flyn is a Hollywood actress. Rather than "making" art, or being in the service of art, Flyn has, instead, fused her art with her own personal identity. She has not left Eve's garden absolutely, as she is still *involved* in "art"; but she has gone to the absolute opposite end of the spectrum of art, from the highest art to the lowest art, from art for the elite, to made for mass-consumption art. Flyn has self-consciously accepted herself as a living work of mass art, and in so doing, she has achieved a sense of identity and freedom through the reconstruction of her identity within the cinematic medium.

On this point, one may also agree with Nichols's interpretation: Flyn "may have sold herself to Hollywood, but at least Hollywood has bought her." And further: "Flyn has a certain self-knowledge that her sisters lack. She knows what she is . . ."[9] Flyn has found herself in another world, having chosen Film as her God, over Eve (the Divine Mother): and here in Film she may fuse her life with art, living within characters of her own making. Indeed, she escapes Eve's Artificial Garden of Eden and becomes her own demigod in another voyeuristic world of her own control. This is precisely Allen's ethics, and, as such, should not be mistaken for a virtue ethics. Yet this is the primary mistake in Nichols's otherwise excellent study. For, rather than perfecting the human form, the way to freedom from unlimited voyeurism is absolute self-creation.

---

[9] Nichols, p. 50.

Unlimited Voyeurism and Aesthetic Self-Fashioning

Nichols thinks of Allen's work as a study in the relation between art and life, ultimately culminating in a rich virtue ethics.[10] But, in fact, Allen's ethics is *not* a virtue ethics, since it is not a matter of flourishing, or the achievement of a state of pure contemplation. Moreover, a virtue ethics implies continuity with a community (if not continuity with nature), in which co-members take seriously the enhancement of virtue.

It is only within a community that the virtues can be learned, acquired, and developed. And ultimately such a community must also aim at a distant, collective, and normative goal, embodied in a certain form of ethical life. But Allen's extreme paranoia can find no comfort in society; there is simply no community-based virtue-type intersubjectivity available. Rather, his work is situated squarely in New York City, a city of fragmentation, differentiation, market forces, malaise, alienation, and unlimited Social Darwinism. New York—for all its greatness—is *not* a virtue-based community.

Nichols's conclusion of virtue is only partially right: Allen's ethics is *like* a virtue ethics insofar as it is perfectionistic—but that's where the link ends. For it is neither a virtue ethics based in dynamic embodied form as in Aristotle, nor one based in a coherent cultural narrative;[11] in fact, it is not really one based in *any* ethical continuity with nature *or* community. Rather Allen's ethics is based in *isolation* from the community, indeed, in skepticism toward the very idea of community. In a word, contrary to the conditions for virtue, ontology for Allen is

---

[10] Nichols writes as follows: "Although Allen's films begin with contemporary assumptions, nihilistic and existential, they move from them to reveal the potential of the human soul for fulfillment in deeds of virtue and love. The world in which this potential can be actualized is a moral one. Allen's work is evidence that the American mind is open to questions of truth and virtue and shows how a popular art form such as the film might provide society moral and intellectual education" (p. xiv).

[11] Alasdair MacIntyre uses a narrative-oriented virtue ethics in *After Virtue* (Notre Dame: University of Notre Dame Press, 1981). And Martha Nussbaum's is more naturalistically based; see, for example, "Non-Relative Virtues: An Aristotelian Approach," in Martha Nussbaum and Amartya Sen, eds., *The Quality of Life* (Oxford: Oxford University Press, 1993).

voyeurism. "To be" is "to be *watched*," to be voyeuristically violated, to violate the privacy of others, to live in a world made of lenses, mirrors, satellites, and miles and miles of videotape.

Instead, Allen's aesthetic ethics mirrors Foucault's. The goal of the later Foucault is to stare headlong into the nihilistic machine of one's own subjectivity and appropriate it as one's own. Such a "goal" is perfectionistic as in a virtue ethics, but *detached*, and with no universal goal, no community-based goal, and no goal, really, other than one's own. The method is to take one's own details, one's own inherited contingencies, and attempt to give them style, knowing full well that this style is completely conditioned by one's accidents. It is to give birth to a dancing star, in Nietzsche's sense, a persona who dances his own style amidst the chaos of the world, and recognizes that this chaos of mirrors, and this absence of souls, is the condition for the possibility of becoming a subject of one's own making. And this solution is precisely what Woody Allen proposes for an ethics within the theater of theater, perfectly evident in *Play It Again, Sam*.

Play It Again, Sam

Allan Felix (Woody Allen) in *Play It Again, Sam* is a film critic whose wife, Nancy (Susan Anspach), leaves him so she can "live," in contrast to Allan, whom she calls "one of life's great watchers." Allan's *alter ego* is Humphrey Bogart (Jerry Lacy), who walks off the screen and into Allan's life (to watch him as well). The voyeurism is everywhere apparent, but ultimately it gets to Allan, and he needs release, which comes in the form of an ethics of self-fashioning. At the end of the film, Allan has decided to let go of Linda (Diane Keaton), and tell his best friend (Linda's husband), Dick (Tony Roberts), about their affair. The scene takes place at night on an airport runway, and mimics the ending of *Casablanca*.

Here the letting go, however, is really two-fold: for, in addition to letting Linda go, Allan is equally letting go of his *alter ego*, Bogart. We watch as Allan is actually speaking to himself in front of his *alter ego*, but having also absorbed the perspective of Bogart (in an entirely illusory *Casablanca* setting). Allan speaks to Bogart about himself, but he does so in the second person. He explains *to himself* that he's short and ugly, but that somehow he's managed amidst, and surely *because of*, these accidents to give birth to his own style. And thus ends Allan's own story, a detachment from the mirrors as best he can, and a commitment to live as a self-stylizing character amidst them. The position is very Foucauldian, and, in fact, goes back to Nietzsche. In *The Gay Science*, Nietzsche writes,

> *One thing is needful.*—To "give style" to one's character—a great and rare art! It is practiced by those who survey all the strengths and weaknesses of their nature and then fit them into an artistic plan until every one of them appears as art and reason and even weaknesses delight the eye. Here a large mass of second nature has been added; there a piece of original nature has been removed— both times through long practice and daily work at it. Here the ugly that could not be removed is concealed; there it has been reinter- preted and made sublime. . . . For one thing is needful: that a human being should *attain* satisfaction with himself, whether it be by means of this or that poetry or art.[12]

In Allan's character, one can see precisely this recognition— only, it occurs in the context of being a watcher and being watched, which is precisely one of Foucault's important addi- tions to Nietzsche:

DICK [*to Linda*]: We better be going.
DICK [*to Allan*]: I'll call you, Allan.
BOGART [*to Allan*]: That was great. You've uh—you've really developed yourself a little style.
ALLAN: Yeah, I do have a certain amount of style, don't I?
BOGART: Well, I guess you won't be needing me any more There's nothing I can tell you now that you don't already know.
ALLAN: I guess that's so. I guess the secret's not being you— it's being me.
ALLAN:—True, you're—you're not too tall and kinda ugly but—
ALLAN:—what th'hell, I'm short enough and ugly enough to succeed on my own.

---

[12] Friedrich Nietzsche, *The Gay Science* (New York: Vintage, 1974), pp. 232–33.

BOGART: Hmmm.
BOGART: Here's looking at *you*, kid.[13]

Allan no longer needs Bogart because he has fused his life with art. He no longer watches himself through Bogart because Bogart is no longer outside of him. Allan is finished "*looking* at you, kid," through his *alter ego*. And his paranoia subsides as he accepts himself, and no longer seeks for an ideal outside himself. He has begun to pursue his own individualized ethics, begun to pursue the "one thing which is needful," according to Nietzsche, "to give style" to his own postmodern character.

Similarly, in *Interiors* the Hollywood actress achieves freedom by living self-consciously under the godlike medium of film, stylizing herself as her many characters. And likewise *The Purple Rose of Cairo* is a tragedy which punishes Cecilia for choosing life over art. In *Crimes and Misdemeanors* Judah attempts to transform his crime into film. And with *Annie Hall*, Alvy Singer rejects reality in favor of illusion, because he simply "needs the eggs."

These films, taken together (and joined with the strong voyeurism of *Another Woman*), evidence the same equation found in Foucault: surveillance is juxtaposed against art's fusion with life. As life is placed under film's omniscient gaze, and each individual's most private psyche is surveyed, recorded, and judged, the ensuing anxiety allows for only a few solutions. Among them are self-destruction through death or insanity, absolute submission to one's confessor, or to live as a self-sculpting shade in a fully transparent Postmodern Hades.

Allen too, within the panopticon, has marshaled the very lights of surveillance, has within his films commandeered his own cinematographic chariot, inserting himself into screens of his own control, and thus creating his own moral universe. In this sense, his is a rather complex study in self-fashioning, and, simultaneously, an exposition of the terrorized grimace within the panopticon. Allen self-consciously fuses the ideas of art and life, and then injects his own being into the mix. His films are

---

[13] The text here is taken from *Woody Allen's Play It Again, Sam*, edited by Richard J. Anobile (New York: Grosset and Dunlap, 1977), pp. 184–190. The book is essentially a copy of the film script, but with frames, and dialogue running under each frame.

notably a *theoretical* study in the fusion of art and life, but equally a *performative* exercise in making oneself a work of art through film.

And There Is No Escape

Allen's work stands alongside the great filmmakers, but not for "farce" as some may think[14]—that is much too simple an interpretation. Of course, there are farcical elements in Allen, especially the early Allen, but the mature works develop a much more critical approach to film, surveillance, voyeurism, and social science.

As Fellini's thought penetrates surrealism and the spirit of Carnival, and Hitchcock's evokes suspense, Allen's is decidedly elsewhere.[15] Rather than a theater of horror, the absurd, the surreal, suspense, or of pain, his is a specifically *meta*-theatrical study of the camera itself, best conceived as a "theater of theater." It is a theater of infinite surveillance. This theater of theater, moreover, does not fade downward into a Hitchcockian vertigo, nor upward into a verticalized and centralized Leviathan, but is spread everywhere at once, without edges, and without center. Once in the Middle Ages, such a light was God, all good, moral, and loving—but now the light is a panopticon, absolutely leveled and fully nihilized. Within the panopticon, we have become the watchers *and* the controllers, everyday superegos, common-man psychoanalysts, visual prisoners, and confessors alike. There can be no absolute escape from this unlimited cinematic voyeurism—for the Eyes of Film are on us all.[16]

---

[14] Albert Bermel, *Farce: A History from Aristophanes to Woody Allen* (New York: Simon and Schuster, 1982).

[15] Hitchcock is not limited to that label, and, indeed, Allen appears to draw heavily on the multiply layered voyeurism of *Rear Window*.

[16] I am very grateful to Elizabeth F. Cooke, Aeon Skoble, and Mark Conard, for very helpful comments on an earlier draft of this essay—of course, any mistakes which remain are my own.

8

"You Don't Deserve Cole Porter": Love and Music According to Woody Allen

JAMES B. SOUTH

There are many features typical of a Woody Allen movie: the use of New York as a kind of character; the hyper-intellectual conversation; the neurotic behavior of central characters; and the distinctive and remarkably consistent appearance of the credit sequences. Any such list would be incomplete, though, unless it included mention of music. Founded on what is usually called "the great American songbook," Allen's soundtracks blend older popular music and jazz to original effect. In this chapter, I want to explore one reason why the use of music in Allen's films is so consistent, and why it takes the form and content it does.[1]

Philosophical assessments of Allen come in two broad types. There is the familiar and popular view that Allen is a quintessential product of the modern mind, that is, the product of Nietzsche, Sartre, and a scientific world-view that points to a world that is meaningless.[2] On this reading, Allen provides us

---

[1] This is a generalization, and several of Allen's films use other musical forms to great effect. Most obviously, the adoption of Prokofiev's music in *Love and Death* (1975) is intrinsic to the evocation of Czarist Russia, while Mendelssohn provides the perfect backdrop for the countryside atmosphere of *A Midsummer Night's Sex Comedy* (1982). More recently, *Shadows and Fog* (1992) has a soundtrack that is exclusively devoted to the music of Kurt Weill.

[2] Readings of Allen's movies that suggest that his primary aim is to expose the fact that life is meaningless include: Nancy Pogel, *Woody Allen* (Boston: Twayne, 1987) and Sam B. Girgus, *The Films of Woody Allen* (New York: Cambridge University Press, 1993).

with a filmic view of the nihilism at the root of all our lives, and he tries to strip away the illusions that values are anything other than prejudices and preferences. By contrast, other critics see in Allen's work a much different perspective, one in which Allen affirms moral value, whether by making an irrational Kierkegaardian "leap of faith"[3] or by revealing "the potential of the human soul for fulfillment in deeds of virtue and love."[4]

I find myself persuaded by the latter camp: Allen's movies do reveal a set of moral values, values that stand in contrast to much of the contemporary world. In addition, I think that this set of values springs from a theme that is repeatedly visited by Allen, namely, the human capacity for love, as well as the very fickleness of that capacity. It is precisely the centrality of issues of love that makes his use of music so telling. After all, the music he most often uses evokes an earlier time and place. Rarely, even, does he use contemporary versions of the "American Songbook," choosing instead to use older recordings that sound like they are from an earlier age, thereby reminding us of the past as past. Now, Allen is too good a filmmaker to flag the importance of music directly.[5] Nonetheless, in what follows, I will argue that an important philosophical lesson emerges from a consideration of Allen's use of music.

"He Loves and She Loves"

Manhattan is a prolonged exercise in the union of music and emotion. It starts with the opening clarinet passage from *Rhapsody in Blue* playing behind a voice-over and close-up scenes of daily New York life. As Isaac (Woody Allen) tries to describe a character, the music continues to build until he gets

---

[3] For such a reading, see Sander Lee, *Woody Allen's Angst: Philosophical Commentaries on His Serious Films* (Jefferson: McFarland, 1997).

[4] Mary P. Nichols, *Reconstructing Woody* (Lanham: Rowman and Littlefield, 1998), p. xiv.. In my too brief reconstruction of the philosophical attitudes, I am indebted to Nichols's masterful discussion of the main approaches in the "Introduction" of her book.

[5] In Stig Bjorkman, ed., *Woody Allen on Woody Allen* (New York: Grove Press, 1993), p. 34, Allen has described his typical use of music as follows: "I like the sound of the records. I can control it, I can do the music myself, right here in this room [the editing room] . . . I just pick up the world's great music and melodies, and I can choose whatever I want."

it just right: "He was as tough and romantic as the city he loved. Behind his black-rimmed glasses was the coiled sexual power of a jungle cat." "I love this," Isaac interjects, before continuing: "New York was his town. And it always would be."[6] At that moment, we see a long panoramic shot of New York City as the crescendo of Gershwin's *Rhapsody* unfolds. After the panoramic shot, there is another series of shots of New York buildings, streets, and the like culminating in the outside sign of Elaine's restaurant. Inside, we join a conversation, clearly in progress, between Isaac and his friend Yale (Michael Murphy):

> YALE: I think the essence of art is to provide a kind of work-
> ing through the situation for people, you know, so you
> can get in touch with feelings you didn't know you had.
> ISAAC: Talent is luck. The important thing in life is courage.[7]

With this opening exchange, Allen has neatly set up the issue of the emotions that will play such a large role in the movie.

Later in the movie, there is a scene in a planetarium. Isaac and Mary (Diane Keaton) are walking along a desolate plane-tary landscape, whispering. Mary starts to name the moons of Saturn. Isaac is nonplussed and admits he can't name any of them, adding that, "fortunately, they never come up in conver-sation." He goes on to point out that knowing facts of that sort is useless, since "nothing worth knowing can be understood with the mind. Everything really valuable has to enter you through a different opening."[8] A little later in the conversation, Isaac notes that the brain is the most over-rated organ. The con-trast Isaac makes here is one between reason and emotion, and it is not difficult to see the "different opening" as the heart, the metaphorical location of the emotions.

Sander Lee takes this scene as confirmation that Allen rejects the intellect in favor of "nonrational intuition."[9] However, I think Lee is a little too quick here. Although we typically contrast emotion with reason, there is no need to assume that the pic-ture is so simple. In fact, Allen suggests as much at the end of

---

[6] *Manhattan* (1979).
[7] *Ibid.*
[8] *Ibid.*
[9] Lee, *Woody Allen's Angst*, pp. 98–99.

Manhattan. Isaac has run across town to talk to Tracy (Mariel Hemingway), only to find her about to leave for a six-month stay in London. The conversation that follows rehearses the attitudes he expressed when he and Tracy were together. She asks if he loves her, and Isaac, for the first time, says that he does. She points out that she is now eighteen years old, legal but still a kid. When they were first together, Isaac had constantly used Tracy's youth as a reason not to commit to the relationship, but now he avers that she isn't "such a kid." With her customary emotional honesty, she tells him that his breaking up with her really hurt. He replies that he didn't mean to hurt her, and explains: "It was just the way I was looking at things then."[10]

This last claim needs to be examined. "Looking at things" in different ways doesn't just happen. The change in attitude Isaac undergoes is both cognitive (he sees things differently) and affective (there is more to his change than a purely cognitive change). Isaac's statement points out the way in which emotion and cognition are interconnected. But this interconnection between cognition and emotion is complex. Is it because Isaac has a new belief about Tracy (for example, she isn't so young) that he now wants to re-involve himself with her? Or would it make more sense to say that because he now feels differently about her that his belief about her age changes?

One way of getting at the complexity of this interaction is to think about what can cause such a change of belief. In the scene just prior to the one in which Isaac admits he now views his relationship with Tracy differently, he had been making notes for a short story about New Yorkers who neurotically created emotional problems for themselves in order to avoid the "terrifying" problems about the universe. At the same time he wants to make the story optimistic, so he asks the "big" question: what makes life worth living? He proceeds to construct a list of items that make life worth living for him. The inference that is implicit here is that Isaac *is* one of those New Yorkers who neurotically make problems for themselves. The list he provides for himself is varied, beginning, notably, with Groucho Marx (about whom, more below), running through Willie Mays, Louis Armstrong's "Potatohead Blues," Frank Sinatra, the First Movement of

---

[10] *Manhattan.*

Mozart's "Jupiter" Symphony, and ending with Tracy's face. At the mention of Tracy's face, the realization hits home for him that, indeed, that's a reason to avoid the self-imposed neurotic problems. At that very moment of realization, the soundtrack music begins playing a lush rendition of the Gershwin classic "He Loves and She Loves." The lesson is straightforward: at the moment that Isaac realizes he loves Tracy, that she is one of the reasons life is worth living, the set of beliefs he has about Tracy changes.

"I'm in Love Again"

The picture of emotional change that Allen presents in *Manhattan* is a filmic counterpart to Aristotle's theory of the emotions. Aristotle, rejecting an overly simplistic view of the relation of emotion and reason, argues that, "the emotions are all those feelings that so change men as to affect their judgments, and that also are attended by pain or pleasure."[11] In other words, Aristotle claims that it is a mistake to see emotion and reason as if they were in conflict; rather emotions carry with them a certain cognitive orientation to the world. There is no such thing as a purely rational mind or a non-rational emotion:

> When people are feeling friendly and placable, they think one sort of thing; when they are feeling angry or hostile, they think something totally different. Or the same thing with a different intensity: when they feel friendly to the man who comes before them for judgment, they regard him as having done little wrong, if any; when they feel hostile, they take the opposite view.[12]

Philosophers influenced by this treatment of the emotions tend to speak of emotions as providing frameworks or orientations towards the world.[13] This orientation to the world not only affects our beliefs about the world, but even our sensory connection to the world: how we see the world, how we hear the

---

[11] Aristotle, *Rhetoric* II.1, 1378a21, in *The Complete Works of Aristotle*, ed. Jonathan Barnes (Princeton: Princeton University Press, 1984). All translations of Aristotle are taken from this edition unless otherwise noted.

[12] *Rhetoric* II, 4, 1377b30–1378a4

[13] The most extensive discussion of this language of "emotional orientation to the world" can be found in Jonathan Lear, *Love and Its Place in Nature* (New York: Farrar, Straus, and Giroux, 1990), pp. 29–68.

world, is connected with the emotional orientation we have towards the world.[14]

Now, if we accept the Aristotelian lesson that emotion influences our judgments and sensations, that emotional orientations towards the world involve internal justifications (for example, it is because I believe someone slighted me that I feel anger towards him), we must recognize that there is not always a lot that reason by itself can do to sway emotions. In other words, we need to resist making the following sort of easy inference: if emotions are cognitive in the way Aristotle thinks, then changing beliefs ought to be sufficient for changing emotions. In brief, if I believe that flying is safe, I ought not to fear flying. But, obviously, the matter is not that simple. It might not be the case that I can provide an argument to change my emotion, since my emotion already comes with its own argument. In much the same way, Aristotle is insistent that arguments alone can't make people good who were brought up in such a way that the virtues did not become habituated in them.[15]

The issue, consequently, is how we can change emotions, if the emotions will not always listen to reason, or, more precisely, an alternative reason. For Aristotle, habituation is key to effecting a unity between proper belief and proper emotion, yet the time for habituation is childhood. The problem lurking here is that it is hard to see how an adult can be responsible for the habituation that took place in her childhood. As Maud Chaplin has nicely stated the problem, "By the time we are capable of deliberative choice, our characters have already been decisively shaped, and we are stuck with certain emotional and cognitive responses, insofar as they can be separated, that we cannot always account for."[16] How might emotional change come about if we can't look to help from reason?

---

[14] The role of emotion in our sensing has been highlighted by S. Leighton, "Aristotle and the Emotions," in Amélie Oksenberg Rorty, ed., *Essays on Aristotle's Rhetoric* (Berkeley: University of California Press, 1996), pp. 206–237.

[15] Aristotle, *Nicomachean Ethics*, X, 9, 1179b3–20, in *The Complete Works of Aristotle*, ed. Jonathan Barnes (Princeton: Princeton University Press, 1984).

[16] Maud Chaplin, "Commentary on Sherman," in John J. Cleary and Gary M. Gurtler, S.J., eds., *Proceedings of the Boston Area Colloquium in Ancient Philosophy* (Leiden: Brill, 2000), p. 85. My discussion here owes much to Chaplin's essay, which nicely sets out the basic Aristotelian view.

Aristotle makes an interesting, though frequently overlooked, suggestion in his *Politics*. Discussing the proper education of citizens in a good city, he argues that such an education should be directed not only at reason, but also at the character and emotions of the citizens. Crucially, he claims that music has the power of forming our characters.[17] Just how this happens is a bit mysterious, but Aristotle holds that "everyone who listens to representations comes to have the corresponding emotions, even when the rhythms and melodies these representations contain are taken in isolation"[18]

There can be no doubt that Allen uses both "rhythms and melodies taken in isolation" and music with lyrics to good effect in his films. Instances of the former include Bach's Double Violin Concerto, which is woven throughout *Hannah and Her Sisters* to express Elliot's desire for Lee, and Schubert's "Quartet No. 15 in G Major" used in *Crimes and Misdemeanors* to express "tension" and "portent."[19] While these uses of pure music occur in several films, nonetheless Allen more frequently makes use of music that has a lyrical component. Frequently the music to the songs is used by itself, but, as I hope to show, the music by itself does not do all the work, since Allen relies on the viewer knowing the lyrics to the songs he's using in order to fully understand the point he's making.

A couple of brief examples should clarify how central music and lyrics are to appreciating key themes in Allen's movies. *Husbands and Wives* (1992) makes use of Cole Porter's "What is this Thing Called Love?" at the beginning of the film and throughout. Surely no more apposite song is available for expressing the way that relationships start and fall apart in the

[17] Aristotle, *Politics* VIII, 5, 1340b11. Of course, "music" for Aristotle did not refer to just the instrumental sounds, but incorporated the lyrics as well. Thus while he claims that the pure music of a song plays a crucial role in fostering emotions, at the same time, like Plato before him, he is well aware that the lyrics of a song tell a story that has an emotional impact.

[18] *Politics* VIII, 5, 1340a12–13. Translated by C.D.C. Reeve in his "Aristotelian Education," in Amélie Oksenberg Rorty, ed., *Philosophers on Education* (New York: Routledge, 1998), pp. 51–65. Reeve's is the best brief discussion of the role of music in moral education. A more extensive discussion can be found in David J. Depew, "Politics, Music, and Contemplation in Aristotle's Ideal State," in David Keyt and Fred. D. Miller, Jr., eds., *A Companion to Aristotle's Politics* (Oxford: Blackwell, 1991), pp. 346–380

[19] Bjorkman, *Woody Allen on Woody Allen*, p. 219.

movie: "Love flew in through my window / I was so happy then. / But after love had stayed a little while / Love flew out again." The lyric captures perfectly the mystery of the "ins and outs" of love, suggesting in its use of the image of flying that we have little or no control over it, or ways to understand it. So, too, in *Stardust Memories* (1980), the "Stardust" of the title has its origins in the song of the same name—a song that recounts a memory of love: "Tho' I dream in vain, / In my heart it will remain / My stardust melody, / The memory of love's refrain." In the movie, Sandy Bates (Woody Allen) looks for something to "hang on to" just before an operation. The "stardust memory" he has is one in which "everything seemed to come together perfectly." Yet it is quickly revealed that this memory is a memory of a scene from a movie, not from Sandy's real life. Thus, even his memory of a perfect moment is only a dream, only an imaginary moment that has what reality it has due to its preservation on film. The song perfectly captures the elusiveness of attachment and the precarious relation between reality and memory that are at the center of the movie.

Given the distinctive sound associated with so many of Allen's works, there can be little doubt that he thinks music provides a way of helping us to orient ourselves to his movies and that it can aid us in understanding some of their broader themes. Music works both to help us in evaluating the actions of various characters, as well as helping us to understand the broader themes present. While many different emotions could be used to support this approach, I will focus on love. After all, love and its vicissitudes are central to many of Allen's finest works.

"You Made Me Love You"

A good example of the interplay between music and love occurs in *Hannah and Her Sisters*. Indeed, this is an especially interesting case because it is one of Allen's most popular movies, while also being one that he sees as something of a failure. He has expressed concern over its ending, stating that he "copped out" by tying things together too much.[20] I think that exploring his use of music will help us see simultaneously why the movie

---

[20] Bjorkman, *Woody Allen on Woody Allen*, p. 156.

succeeds and why he might be right in stating that he copped out.

The movie begins with "You Made Me Love You" playing over the opening credits. In the context of the movie, as we shall see, this song is a signal that emotional life is something over which we have limited control. After the credits, the first shot of the movie is Lee (Barbara Hershey) from the perspective of Elliot (Michael Caine). His voiceover communicates the degree to which he has fallen in love with Lee, though he is married to Hannah (Mia Farrow) and Lee is with Frederick (Max von Sydow). Elliot recounts all Lee's characteristics that fascinate him and claims that "I can't help it, I'm consumed by her."[21] At the first sight of Lee as seen through the eyes of Elliot, the music changes to "I've Heard that Song Before." This latter song's lyrics, which we don't hear, point to the inconstancy of love and the way that love is dependent on a dream.[22]

Helplessness in the face of love, first signaled by the use of "You Made Me Love You," is underscored later in the same scene when we see Hannah's parents at the piano singing "Bewitched, Bothered, and Bewildered." This unfolding musical score mirrors the plot that we are about to see play out between Elliot and Lee. Elliot thinks he is in love with Lee and pursues her. They try to establish a relationship, but it fails. It is noteworthy that Elliot's subsequent actions in pursuing Lee are accompanied by "I've Heard that Song Before" and "Bewitched, Bothered, and Bewildered." In using these same songs repeatedly, Allen provides the movie with a musical consistency and coherence that effectively underscores its plot. Nonetheless, Elliot and Lee do not end up together. Although Lee leaves Frederick, Elliot can't bring himself to leave Hannah. Eventually Lee finds someone else and Elliot rediscovers his love for Hannah. What we see play out in the story of Elliot and Lee is the inconstancy of romantic love. The decisive moment for Elliot occurs when he realizes that Hannah needs him to take care of

---

[21] *Hannah and Her Sisters* (1986)
[22] The lyrics include the following: "It seems to me I've heard that song before. / It's from an old familiar score. / I know it well, that melody. / It's funny how a theme / Recalls a favorite dream, / A dream that brought you so close to me. / I know each word, because I've heard that song before. / The lyrics said: 'for evermore.' / For evermore's a memory."

her, when she admits that she feels lost. As Elliot realizes his love for Hannah, we hear "Bewitched, Bothered, and Bewildered."

"I'm in Love Again"

The counterpart to the Elliot and Lee story is that of Holly (Dianne Wiest) and Mickey (Woody Allen). They had once tried dating, but their date together had been comically disastrous. Holly had taken Mickey to hear a rock band, horrifying Mickey, while Mickey had taken her to hear Bobby Short playing Cole Porter. In the scene we witness, he is playing "I'm in Love Again." Even more horrifying to Mickey than the rock band was the fact that Holly had been bored by Cole Porter. In Mickey's eyes, this represented a major character flaw, akin to her cocaine dependency. He makes this moral judgment clear when he tells Holly, "You don't deserve Cole Porter."[23] Throughout the movie, we see Holly searching for a place in the world, trying out a series of jobs while trying to make it as an actress. Mickey's search is the more philosophical: after a health scare, he tries to discover the meaning of life, trying out a series of religions in the same way that Holly tries out jobs.

Holly finally finds her way by taking up writing, while Mickey has to go through a particularly dark phase in which he contemplates, and even begins an attempt at, suicide. After his attempt goes comically awry, he walks around for hours, happening at last on a movie theater. He enters and starts watching a movie, the Marx Brothers' *Duck Soup*. As he watches the movie, his attitude noticeably changes. His reaction to the movie is striking: "It's not all a drag. Geez, I should stop ruining my life searching for answers I'm never going to get and just enjoy it while it lasts."[24] When Mickey and Holly meet again, after Holly has written a script and Mickey has come out of his depression, the meeting is due to his seeing Holly in record store. As he walks down the street, we hear "Bewitched, Bothered, and Bewildered" playing on the soundtrack. He sees her through the window of the record shop. Of course, he could have kept

---

[23] *Hannah and Her Sisters.*
[24] *Ibid.*

walking; there's no particular reason for him to walk into the store and start talking to her. Yet he does. The next day they get together. She reads him her script, which he likes. As they leave to go to lunch, the soundtrack plays "You Made Me Love You." We see them eating lunch and walking through the park. It is then that he recounts, and we see, his hitting "rock bottom." When he's through with the story, the same song is playing.

At the end of the movie a year has passed since Holly and Mickey have reunited and since Elliot and Lee have called it off. Lee has married someone else. The scene begins just like the opening scene of the movie: we hear Elliot's voiceover talking about Lee while "I've Heard That Song Before" plays in the background. Elliot wonders "what came over me" in his previous infatuation, since he now knows that he loved Hannah "more than he realized." We then see Holly arrive while Elliot and Hannah watch the scene around them. Hannah's parents are again at the piano, this time playing "Isn't it Romantic." Mickey shows up and we discover that he and Holly are now married. He asks how she can top their story together, and she replies by telling him that she is pregnant. By this time the music has segued into "I'm in Love Again," the very song that marked their first disastrous date. They kiss and the closing credits start.

Applying the Aristotelian account of the emotions, we see that Allen is fully aware of the fact that emotions bring with them an orientation to the world, and he uses music effectively to bring out that point. A complex emotion such as love makes us see the world differently by shaping our beliefs. And, while the music used throughout the film underscores the contingency of love, its ability to reshape the way we think about ourselves, and others, Allen additionally makes a point about the way that music can shape our character. The example is Holly, and her progress throughout the movie is signaled by her appreciation of music. From her initial rejection of opera and Cole Porter, she chooses to sing "I'm Old Fashioned," a song by Jerome Kern, at an audition. When she and Mickey meet again at the record store, she is in the jazz section. She is holding two albums of opera music, and the stability of her life is mirrored by her new-found musical taste, proving that she has the ethical character to succeed in love.

We are now in position to see why Allen thinks *Hannah and Her Sisters* to be something of a failure as a film. There is the very obvious fact that everyone ends up happy in satisfying relationships, along with Mickey finding some meaning in life. In fact, the twin storylines of the movie work against the message of its music. The music's message consists of reminders that love does not last, that love is not something within human control, that it is a kind of enchantment. The parallel with Mickey's epiphany concerning the meaning of life is clear. Mickey realizes, on the basis of his emotional enjoyment of the Marx Brothers, that life might be worth living. So too, by ending the movie with the characters in love, Allen has suggested that love might be achievable and within our control. However, he has not given us any reason to believe him. Of course, we would like to believe that such happy endings are possible, but Allen is aware that the movie is itself a kind of enchantment.

"I'm Thru with Love"

In *Everyone Says I Love You*, Allen reconnects with the Marx brothers while attempting to blend a traditional musical with the central theme of love and its importance for emotional orientation. However, unlike the "cop out" of *Hannah and Her Sisters*, this time Allen presents a rather darker view of love. Through a series of stories connected by a very large extended family, Allen portrays the vicissitudes of love with a striking realism unusual in a traditional musical. Three songs recur throughout the movie and set the tone and themes of the movie: "Everyone Says I Love You," "My Baby Just Cares for Me," and "I'm Thru with Love." It's obvious enough that the use of these three songs suggests a natural movement in the origin and progression of love. First, someone falls in love, the relationship proceeds well for a while, and then, for some reason, it ends. The lover is then "thru with love," but the story doesn't end there because "everyone says, I love you." Even after a devastating breakup, the impulse to fall in love again is there. In the words of Mickey at the end of *Hannah and Her Sisters*, "the heart is a very, very resilient little muscle."

More significantly, *Everyone Says I Love You* provides us with an account of why such a pattern recurs. The key is to be found in the human desire to dream, to fantasize. This theme is repeated throughout the movie. At the beginning of the movie, Skyler (Drew Barrymore) appears to be in love with Holden

(Edward Norton), but is really in love with a fantasy, a fact made explicit in her singing "I'm a Dreamer, Aren't We All?" This dream causes her to fall in love with the ex-con Charles Ferry (Tim Roth). When she finally realizes her mistake, she goes back to Holden, with a renewed appreciation for his virtues and a genuine, but less idealistic version of love. So too, Von (Julia Roberts), who is married, has managed to construct a fantasy about her perfect man. When she thinks she has met him, she falls madly in love, leaving her husband and moving to Paris. However, it turns out that realizing this fantasy does not satisfy her, and she breaks up with her "ideal" lover, Joe (Woody Allen), and returns to her husband. In explaining why she is leaving Joe, she sets out the problem clearly:

> VON: I have seen my dream come true, and my fantasy no longer tortures me. I can deal with it.
> JOE: But that's so neurotic!
> VON: I Know. I'm crazy.[25]

A bit later, Joe's extended family, his ex-wife Steffi (Goldie Hawn), his daughter and his ex-wife's family, are all trying to convince him that he ought to go to a party that he had planned to go to, but is now too depressed to attend after the break-up with Von. He resists, claiming that he's "not in the mood for Groucho." The clinching counter-argument is given by Skyler, when she says, "It's later than you think." The scene then cuts to a group of French singers performing "Hurray for Captain Spaulding" in French, recalling the crucial use of the Marx Brothers in *Hannah and Her Sisters*. Joe and his ex-wife then reminisce about their early history, failed marriage, and their child together. The ex-wife then sings "I'm Thru with Love," although she clearly isn't since she is happily married to Bob (Alan Alda).

I think that what is particularly interesting in this exchange is the phrase "It's later than you think." This echoes the use of the song earlier in the movie when Steffi's father has died. At the funeral, the grandfather's ghost, accompanied by a group of other ghosts sing the song, trying to get the lesson across that

---

[25] *Everyone Says I Love You* (1996).

death is an ever present pressure factor in life. As if to under-
score the idea that the insistent pressure of impending death is
a factor in emotional orientation, especially in relation to affairs
of the heart, Allen includes "It's Later Than You Think" as the
last song in the closing credits. So, completing the circle, we
arrive at the following cycle—a) falling in love; b) enjoying
mutual love within a relationship; c) becoming dissatisfied in
love because of unrealistic expectations; and d) recognizing the
finitude of life and returning back to falling in love.

"Just What They Say It for I Never Knew"

In the discussion above, I have done little more than scratch the
surface of the complex relation between music and emotions,
especially love, in Allen's work. What I have tried to provide is
a framework that allows the viewer a way to appreciate the centrality of music in his films, while recognizing the way that
music and emotion, especially love, are connected in them. One
way to note the significance of this view for Allen is to recognize that at the end of *Everyone Says I Love You*, when Allen runs
the titular song over the closing credits, he omits a central verse
from the song. In the original version of the song, as performed
by Groucho Marx in *Horse Feathers* (1932), Groucho sings
"Everyone says I love you / but just what they say it for I never
knew / it's just inviting trouble for the poor sucker who / says
I love you." For Allen, love may invite trouble, but he knows
exactly why people say "I love you." They have no choice.[26]

---

[26] I would like to thank Mark Conard and Aeon Skoble for their very helpful
comments on earlier drafts of this chapter.

9

Dead Sharks and Dynamite Ham: The Philosophical Use of Humor in *Annie Hall*

LOU ASCIONE

If we can say anything about Woody Allen with certainty, it is that he has a deep understanding of humor and knows how to use it, not merely as a means for entertainment, but also as a means for philosophical commentary. Indeed, Woody Allen uses humor for philosophical ends as often as he does for mere entertainment, and it is this application of humor that gives his work its distinctive, intellectual tone. In this chapter, we will take a look at just how Woody Allen uses humor as a means for philosophical commentary and specifically, we will study his use of humor for social and cultural analysis. To accomplish this, we will focus on Woody Allen's classic film *Annie Hall*, as this film exhibits some of Woody Allen's purest uses of humor to achieve philosophical ends.[1]

We begin our task with a brief introduction to the philosophy of humor, so that we can understand how humor can be used as an effective means for both criticism and analysis, thus revealing its philosophical value. We will then use this theory as a framework for examining *Annie Hall*, and in doing so we will hopefully develop an understanding as to exactly how Woody

---

[1] Indeed, *Annie Hall* begins and ends with jokes, told in monologue form, by Alvy Singer (Woody Allen), and these jokes are used, not to make the audience laugh, but as means for giving the audience a philosophical context in which to better understand the film.

Allen uses humor for both entertainment and philosophical commentary. Although there are several theories of humor in the history of philosophy, the clearest and most coherent view of humor was outlined by Arthur Schopenhauer, who was one of the first philosophers to undertake a rigorous analysis of humor, and thus provide a conceptual means for understanding its nature.

Schopenhauer's Theory of Humor

Schopenhauer begins his theory of humor by telling us that laughter is a response to something called "the ludicrous," which is a suddenly perceived incongruity that emerges between our conceptual representations of reality and reality itself. More specifically, Schopenhauer tells us that this form of incongruity is best understood as a conceptual shift. In his famous work *The World as Will and Representation*, Schopenhauer summarizes his understanding of humor in the following manner:

> [T]he origin of the ludicrous is always the paradoxical, and thus unexpected, subsumption of an object under a concept that is in other respects heterogeneous to it. Accordingly, the phenomenon of laughter always signifies the sudden apprehension of an incongruity between such a concept and the real object thought through it, and hence between what is abstract and what is perceptive. The greater and more unexpected this incongruity in the apprehension of the person laughing, the more violent will be his laugher.[2]

According to Schopenhauer, our understanding of events in the world is an activity of representation, which involves locating events within a conceptual framework. As we develop our understanding of an event, we simply enrich this representation by associating it with more and more concepts within this framework. However, when it comes to the ludicrous, this process of developing a representation becomes problematic as we suddenly realize that some of the concepts that we associate with an event are in direct, logical conflict with the rest of the

---

[2] Arthur Schopenhauer, *The World as Will and Representation*, Volume 2 (New York: Dover, 1966), p. 91.

conceptual representation. It is this representational conflict caused by conceptual incongruities that stimulates laughter.

For example, the classic "pie in the face" is funny (in theory) because of the abrupt conceptual shift it causes. At first we view a person in a perfectly normal setting, in which nothing is particularly unusual, and we begin building a conceptual representation of this normal event. However, when a pie is unexpectedly thrown into that person's face, we are forced to suddenly shift our conceptual representation of the event from a completely normal situation to a wholly unusual situation, and this causes us to laugh.

In this particular instance, the normal associations, which make up our original understanding of the event, include the concept of dignity, and it is the sudden loss of this concept that makes the situation become instantly ridiculous. That is, the dignified (pre-pie) conception of the event is unexpectedly shattered by the sudden introduction of the pie in the face, and the ridiculous (post-pie) conception now becomes an integral, yet conflicting representational aspect of the event. In fact, the more dignified the person believes him or herself to be "pre-pie," the more ridiculous the "post-pie" result, and hence the more humorous the event.

Essentially, there are two basic requirements for an event to be humorous, according to Schopenhauer: a preliminary understanding of a situation, and then a secondary understanding of the same situation which results from the addition of further information about the situation. In either case, it is a peculiar shift from one understanding to another that causes a situation to be humorous, and it is the speed and degree of this shift in understanding that ultimately determines the specific impact of the humor.

For example, we are all familiar with the distinction between people who know how to tell jokes and others who can't. Given Schopenhauer's theory of humor, we can now view this difference as either having or lacking the skills to present a shift from preliminary to secondary understandings of situations in the appropriate amount of detail, and at the proper tempo to maximize the humorous impact of the conceptual shift. Any lack of salient details to a joke precludes an effective conceptual shift from taking place, and likewise, an overabundance of information often might conceal the salient details of a joke which also prevents an effective conceptual shift from taking place. Similarly, if the pace at which information is transmitted in a joke is too slow, the conceptual shift in understanding is not sudden enough to evoke laughter, and if the information is given too quickly, the intended conceptual shift may turn out incomplete, or may not occur at all.

Therefore, people ruin jokes by giving too much or too little information that gives us our understanding of the event in question, or by either rushing or dragging out the pace of the information delivery. Successful humor requires a keen awareness of a situation, including subtle details about the mood and expectations of an audience, and then making the audience suddenly aware of an unexpected change in the situation, such that some preliminary concepts about the situation are changed in a harmless and unique way. This is why humor is much more an art than a science, and it requires conceptual craftsmanship and intimate knowledge of an audience to succeed in making them laugh.

The Philosophical Value of Humor

One subject, regarding humor, which Schopenhauer did not address, is its philosophical value. Although Schopenhauer was keenly interested in the structure and nature of humor, he seemed to be either unaware or uninterested in its application as a means for philosophical commentary. This is where Woody Allen comes into play. Through an analysis of Allen's works, we learn that humor can be implemented as a powerful medium for communicating philosophically important ideas. There are, essentially, two reasons for this.

First, as expressed by Schopenhauer, humor emphasizes unexpected incongruities in a situation, and these incongruities can be used to gain new insight into a subject matter. Second, humor is not subject to the same levels of criticism as other forms of communication, and this makes it possible to induce the audience to reflect upon philosophical matters that are normally avoided.[3] Humor can only be appreciated when judgment

---

[3] For more discussion on this issue, see Kelly Dean Jolley's "Wittgenstein and *Seinfeld* on the Commonplace," in William Irwin, ed., *Seinfeld and Philosophy* (Chicago: Open Court, 2000).

is temporarily suspended regarding the content of the information presented, and it therefore allows information to pass into our consciousness which might otherwise be filtered out. Information presented in a humorous context is, therefore, immune to certain types of criticism to which the same information would be subject if presented through any other medium.

Because of this critical immunity, humor can be used to present philosophical ideas and/or to raise important questions that many people would simply reject outright because they are not part of accepted culture. Some important philosophical ideas and questions are superficially unattractive to the general public, and therefore are unlikely to even be considered for intelligent reflection if presented in a non-humorous context. In *Annie Hall*, Allen illustrates this use of humor by presenting specific ideas and raising interesting questions regarding social and cultural behavior, and in doing so, he leads the audience to reflect upon philosophical matters that would probably be avoided in a non-humorous format.

Woody Allen and Social Analysis

We can begin with a scene from *Annie Hall*, which is not necessarily the funniest part of the movie, but is nonetheless an excellent example of using humor as a means for social analysis. In this scene, Annie (Diane Keaton) invites Alvy (Woody Allen) up to her apartment for the first time, and they have a drink on the balcony while they converse. During the conversation, subtitles are used to tell us what each person is thinking throughout the conversation, and we see that what Alvy and Annie are saying is not what they are thinking. More specifically, because they are mainly concerned with impressing each other and forging a new romantic relationship, we witness a dialogue in which both Alvy and Annie are too preoccupied with evaluating their own performance within the conversation to fully participate in it. They criticize what they are saying as they are saying it, and as a result, their actual communication becomes virtually meaningless.

What makes this scene humorous is the incongruity between what both people are saying and what they are actually thinking. Ordinarily, we do not get such a privileged vantage point on a conversation, but the philosophical value of presenting this conversation in such a manner is evident. When watching this scene, we become aware of the fact that these incongruities between thought and speech emerged along with the possibility of romance. The deeper implication is that romantic relationships are somehow very different from merely friendly relationships, and that romantic relationships typically involve deception at some level. This scene is therefore a good example of how humor can be used as a medium for social criticism, and it is as interesting as it is amusing.

There are, however, other scenes in *Annie Hall* that are entertaining, but not quite so enlightening. In such scenes, Allen uses humor simply to raise interesting philosophical questions, and he then gets the audience to reflect upon these questions. In fact, it is often the case that the raising of such questions is an integral part of the film's theme. For instance, at the end of *Annie Hall*, we are left with more questions about subjects like love and romance than we had at the beginning of the film. It seems to be Allen's intention to illustrate that there are no easy answers to certain important questions about life, and to foster the audience's appreciation for the difficulties involved in trying to understand such complex topics.

As a clear example of this, in an unusual scene at the beginning of *Annie Hall*, in which Alvy reflects upon his grammar school days, there is a bizarre mixing of the present with the past. We hear Alvy narrate about his grammar school class as we observe the action. At some point, however, the adult Alvy steps into the scene and interacts with the children and the teacher of his past, who then act as if they were living in the present along with Alvy:

As adult Alvy talks, the camera shows young Alvy move from his seat and kiss a young girl. She jumps from her seat in disgust, rubbing her cheek, as young Alvy moves back to his seat.

1ST GIRL: Ugh, he kissed me, he kissed me.
TEACHER: That's the second time this month! Step up here!

As the teacher, really glaring now, speaks, young Alvy rises from his seat and moves over to her. Angry, she points with her hand while the students turn their heads to watch what will happen next.

YOUNG ALVY: What'd I do?
TEACHER: Step up here!
YOUNG ALVY: What'd I do?
TEACHER: You should be ashamed of yourself.

The students, their heads still turned, look back at Alvy, now an adult, sitting in the last seat of the second row.

ADULT ALVY: I was just expressing a healthy sexual curiosity.
TEACHER (*the young Alvy standing next to her*): Six-year-old boys don't have girls on their minds.
ADULT ALVY (still sitting in the back of the classroom): I did.

The girl the young Alvy kissed turns to the older Alvy, she gestures and speaks.

1ST GIRL: For God's sakes, Alvy, even Freud speaks of a latency period.
ADULT ALVY: Well, I never had a latency period. I can't help it.
TEACHER (*with young Alvy still at her side*): Why couldn't you have been more like Donald? (*The camera pans over to Donald, sitting up tall in his seat, then back to the teacher.*) Now, there was a model boy!
YOUNG ALVY (*still standing next to the teacher*): Tell the folks where you are today, Donald.
DONALD: I run a profitable dress company.
ADULT ALVY'S VOICE: Right. Sometimes I wonder where my classmates are today.

The camera shows the full classroom, the students sitting behind their desks, the teacher standing in the front of the room. One at a time, the young students rise up from their desks and speak.

1ST BOY: I'm president of the Pinkus Plumbing Company.
2ND BOY: I sell tallises.
3RD BOY: I used to be a heroin addict. Now I'm a methadone addict.
2ND GIRL: I'm into leather.

The humor in this scene is embedded in the strange temporal incongruities regarding Alvy and his classmates, who are at once children and adults. What these incongruities do, philosophically, is to raise important questions about the relationship between our childhood and our adult behaviors. This includes the perennial questions regarding the relationship between genetics and culture in determining behavior. For instance, when we hear children talking about what they have become as adults, we immediately begin to wonder how they got from point A to point B. How do innocent seven-year old children, with similar cultural backgrounds, grow up to be so different from each other? What mixture of events in their lives and inherent dispositions led to such varied identities?

Allen offers us no answers for these questions, but he certainly implants these questions in our minds; and these questions comprise the background atmosphere for the remainder of the film. Indeed, one of the major themes of *Annie Hall* is our inability to ever get a complete understanding of how and why people change. At times, we are offered interesting theories regarding this complex question, but never are we given a direct answer, and the implication is that we may never have a complete answer.

The Nature of Romantic Love

To illustrate the above point further, there is another humorous scene in *Annie Hall* in which Allen raises specific philosophical questions regarding the nature of romantic love. This scene involves Alvy interacting with individual passers-by on the streets of New York, who are all willing and able to answer any of his questions about relationships in general, sex, and even his personal problems with Annie. Prior to this scene, we see Alvy and Annie at the end of their relationship. Annie has fallen out of love with Alvy, and he is desperately trying to find some simple explanation for this and figure out what he could have done differently.

The scene begins when Annie finally breaks up with Alvy as they are walking down the street and having yet another argument. Annie gets in a cab, and an extremely frustrated and confused Alvy starts randomly questioning people on the street in search of answers:

ALVY: That's fine. That's fine. That's great! (*He turns toward the camera as the cab drives away.*) Well, I don't know what I did wrong. I mean, I can't believe this. Somewhere she cooled off to me! (*He walks up to an older woman walking down the street carrying groceries.*) Is it-is it something that I did?

WOMAN ON THE STREET: It's never something you do. That's how people are. Love fades. (*She moves on down the street.*)

The humor in this scene is generated entirely by the incongruities regarding the behavior of this lady passing by. On the one hand, she is supposed to be just a lady walking down the street, on the other hand, she is somehow aware of Alvy's predicament and has a well thought out response to his apparently impromptu question. In other words, the lady passing by appears to be following the story not as an insignificant participant but as part of the audience as well. It is this existential incongruity that creates the humor in this scene, but it also introduces an interesting thesis regarding romantic relationships, namely "love fades." If this thesis is true, then many of the traditional claims about love are false, and common ideals such as finding the "right" person in one's life, may turn out to be mythical.

The humorous nature of this scene is what created the opportunity for a philosophically unpopular idea regarding romantic love to be presented to the audience. Through the character incongruities, Allen is able to bring our attention to a viewpoint that is opposed to the standard thesis that true love lasts forever. This non-standard theory of romantic love, introduced by Allen, is that there is no such thing as true love, but that all romantic relationships have a beginning, a middle, and an end, and although some romances last longer than others, all eventually fade. Allen uses an indirect approach to present this thesis because any direct approach would most likely be rejected outright by the audience. Most audience members accept the standard beliefs about true love as a matter of course, and are therefore not likely to genuinely consider the new thesis as a competing theory of romantic love. A development of this competing thesis then occurs as we witness Alvy refusing to accept this unorthodox conclusion. He therefore continues to interview people as he moves down the street, hoping to learn some secret which would explain Annie's behavior and possibly get her back. He approaches an older man and then a young couple.

ALVY (*scratching his head*): Love fades. God, that's a depressing thought. I have to ask you a question. (*He stops another passer-by, a man.*) Don't go any further. Now, with your wife in bed, d-d-does she need some kind of artificial stimulation like like marijuana?

MAN ON THE STREET: We use a large vibrating egg. (*He walks on.*)

ALVY (*continuing to walk*): Large vibrating egg. Well, I ask a psychopath, I get that kind of an answer. Jesus, I-I, uh, here . . . (*He moves up the sidewalk to a young trendy-looking couple, arms wrapped around each other.*) You-you look like a really happy couple. Uh, uh . . . are you?

YOUNG WOMAN: Yeah.

ALVY: Yeah! So . . . so h-h-how do you account for it?

YOUNG WOMAN: Uh, I'm very shallow and empty and I have no ideas and nothing interesting to say.

YOUNG MAN: And I'm exactly the same way.

ALVY: I see. Well, that's very interesting. So you've managed to work out something, huh?

YOUNG MAN: Right.

YOUNG WOMAN: Yeah.

ALVY: Oh, well, thanks very much for talking to me.

Although these responses to Alvy's questions seem more humorous and less insightful than "love fades," they are indirectly supporting the same claim, the truth of which Alvy (along with the audience) does not want to admit, namely, that long-term romantic love is mythical. For example, when Alvy stops the man to ask him about his sex life, Alvy intentionally chooses an older, conservative looking man who has most likely been "happily married" for a long time. Alvy is looking to the man for some wisdom and hoping to find out the secret to his success. As it turns out, the man has no secret, and he and his wife do rely on some external form of stimulation to keep their sex life going.

When he does not get the answer he wants, Alvy then disregards the man as a crackpot and finds an obviously happy young couple who may help him find the secret to romantic success. Unfortunately, their response is no better. With this couple, we only learn that romantic compatibility might only be possible if neither person has any personality to express. The implication is that couples may be happy together provided their relationships are not built on any intellectual interaction, which continually requires growth and learning to remain strong.

In fact, we may infer from this that the desire or need for intellectual growth may preclude long-term romantic relationships because both people would eventually require external relationships to maintain their individual growth. If this is so, love does fade, and Alvy and Annie have simply run the course of their relationship. This idea is even made explicit by Alvy later in the film, when he and Annie are seated in an airplane returning from California and both realize that their relationship is about over.

> ANNIE (*looking back at Alvy*): Alvy, uh, let's face it. You know something, I don't think our relationship is working.
> ALVY: Tsch, I know. A relationship, I think, is-is like a shark, you know? It has to constantly move forward or it dies. (*He sighs.*) And I think what we got on our hands (*clearing his throat*) is a dead shark.

Woody Allen and Cultural Analysis

One complex philosophical problem, humorously explored by Allen in *Annie Hall*, is the relationship between culture and the individual. More specifically, Allen seems to be concerned with a problem sometimes referred to as "provincialism." Provincialism is a common social problem in which individuals identify themselves so closely with a particular culture that they are unable to effectively communicate with individuals from other cultures, and often have a tremendous difficulty even understanding their behavior. In *Annie Hall*, Allen illustrates the debilitating effect provincialism can have on human relationships, and he uses humor to present this uncomfortable picture to the audience.

Right from the beginning of *Annie Hall*, we see that both Annie and Alvy grew up in very different family cultures. Annie comes from a conservative, Protestant family in Wisconsin, and Alvy grew up in a Jewish-American family in Brooklyn. The incongruities between their cultures are a constant source of humor for Annie and Alvy because they both view these cultural differences as mere idiosyncrasies that are amusing but not to be taken seriously. They do not identify themselves with their cultural upbringing enough to exhibit provincial attitudes, and therefore their cultural differences do not interfere with their relationship. However, we soon see that Annie's family is, in fact, provincial to the point that they are incapable of having any meaningful communication with Alvy, and this failed communication exemplifies the problem of provincialism. In this scene, we therefore get a deeper understanding of the nature of provincialism and how it affects human relationships.

The scene begins with Alvy sitting at the family table with Annie, her mother and father (Collen Dewhurst and Donald Symington), her brother, Duane (Christopher Walken), and her "Grammy" (Helen Ludlam), whom we already know to be an anti-Semite. The lack of cultural appreciation (and perhaps straightforward disdain) for Alvy's Jewish heritage is made blatantly explicit by the fact that the meal being served is ham. Alvy is obviously uncomfortable as he tries to join in the conversation, including an awkward attempt to compliment Annie's Grandmother on the ham.

> MOM HALL (*holding her wine glass*): It's a nice ham this year, Mom. (*Grammy Hall takes a sip of her wine and nods.*)
> ANNIE (*smiling at Duane*): Oh, yeah. Grammy always does such a good job.
> DAD HALL (*chewing*): A great sauce.
> ALVY: It is (*smacking his lips*). It's dynamite ham.
>
> (*Grammy Hall stares down the table at Alvy; a look of utter dislike. Alvy tries not to notice.*)

After this, Annie's Mom tries to break the tension a bit by starting a conversation with Alvy, who in turn responds with a joke to lighten things up. Unfortunately, the cultural gap between the two suddenly becomes painfully clear as Alvy's attempts at humor are rejected outright:

> (*Grammy continues to stare at Alvy; he is now dressed in the long black coat and hat of the Orthodox Jew, complete with mustache and beard.*)

MOM HALL (*lighting a cigarette and turning to Alvy*): Ann tells us
   that you've been seeing a psychiatrist for fifteen years.
ALVY (*setting down his glass and coughing*): Yes. I'm making excellent progress. Pretty soon when I lie down on his couch, I
   won't have to wear the lobster bib.

(*Mom Hall reacts by sipping from her glass and frowning. Grammy
continues to stare.*)

The Provincial New Yorker

The irony in *Annie Hall*, however, regarding the theme of
provincialism, is that Alvy is also an extremely provincial New
Yorker in that he refuses to even consider the virtues of any way
of life other than that of New York. Indeed, the root of Alvy's
provincialism seems to be a deep-seated fear of ever leaving
New York. We see this right from the start of the film when Alvy
refuses to entertain the possibility of leaving New York and
moving to California as his best friend, Rob (Tony Roberts), constantly suggests. In such discussions, the incongruities between
Alvy and Rob regarding their opinions about leaving New York
show us that Alvy is much more provincial than most New
Yorkers. Although Alvy and Rob grew up together in Brooklyn,
we see that they have completely opposing ideas about the
virtues of living in New York. We also notice that they have
decided to call each other "Max."

ROB: Right, Max. California, Max.
ALVY: Ah.
ROB: Let's get the hell outta this crazy city.
ALVY: Forget it, Max.
ROB: We move to sunny L.A. All of show business is out
   there, Max.
ALVY: No, I cannot. You keep bringing it up, but I don't
   wanna live in a city where the only cultural advantage is
   that you can make a right turn on a red light.

A few scenes later, Alvy's provincialism is again reinforced
when he and Annie eat lunch in a typical New York
Delicatessen. Alvy orders "a corned beef" and Annie then orders
"a pastrami"; however, she asks for it to be served on white

bread with mayonnaise, lettuce, and tomato. This is humorous because of the incongruity between the way Annie ordered her pastrami and the typical way in which it is ordered, namely, on Rye with mustard. To a provincial New Yorker, such as Alvy, Annie's order is virtually a form of "food sacrilege," and Alvy clearly expresses his feelings in the form of a silent gesture that is both subtle and judgmental. As the waiter leaves, Alvy's facial expression clearly indicates his embarrassment regarding Annie's lack of appreciation and respect for such cultural matters. The fact that he does not say anything to Annie (not even in the form of a joke) indicates that he takes this matter seriously, and we can almost sense that he views such behavior as a minor character flaw in Annie. The irony of this situation, however, is that Alvy's response only exemplifies his own character flaw, namely his New York provincialism.

After this, we eventually see just how profoundly provincial Alvy is when he and Annie go to California to visit Rob, who has since moved to Beverly Hills. Both Rob and Annie appreciate California for what it is, but Alvy fights desperately to maintain his provincial stance and simply refuses to admit that there is anything good about California:

(*It's a warm, beautiful day. Rob, Annie and Alvy in Rob's convertible are moving past the spacious houses, the palm trees. The sunlight reflects off the car. Annie, excited, is taking the whole place in. Background voices sing Christmas carols.*)

VOICES (*singing*): We wish you a Merry Christmas, We wish you a Merry Christmas, We wish you a Merry Christmas, And a Happy New Year.

ROB (*over the singing*): I've never been so relaxed as I have been since I moved out here, Max. I want you to see my house. I live right next to Hugh Hefner's house, Max. He lets me use the Jacuzzi. And the women, Max, they're like the women in *Playboy* magazine, only they can move their arms and legs.

ANNIE (*laughing*): You know, I can't get over that this is really Beverly Hills.

VOICES (*singing*): We wish you a Merry Christmas, And a Happy New Year.

ALVY: Yeah, the architecture is really consistent, isn't it?

French next to-

VOICES (*singing over the dialogue*): Oh, Christmas . . . tree,
   Oh, Christmas tree, How bright and green Our . . .

ALVY: Spanish, next to Tudor, next to Japanese.

ANNIE: God, it's so clean out here.

ALVY: It's that they don't throw their garbage away. They
   make it into television shows.

ROB: Aw, come on, Max, give us a break, will yuh? It's
   Christmas.

(*Annie starts snapping pictures of the view.*)

ALVY: Can you believe this is Christmas here?

VOICES (*singing*): Oh Christmas tree, Oh Christmas tree . . .

(*They pass a large house with spacious lawn. Sitting on the lawn is
a Santa Claus complete with sleigh and reindeer. Voices continue to
sing Christmas carols; Annie continues to take pictures.*)

ANNIE: You know, it was snowing-it was snowing and really
   gray in New York yesterday.

ROB: No kidding?

ALVY: Right, well, Santa Claus will have sunstroke.

ROB: Max, there's no crime, there's no mugging.

ALVY: There's no economic crime, you know, but there's—
   there's ritual, religious-cult murders, you know, there's
   wheat-germ killers out here.

The irrationality of Alvy's provincialism is apparent in this
scene because neither Annie nor Rob reciprocate his criticisms.
In fact, both Annie and Rob do their best to ignore Alvy and
try to get him to stop being so negative. The incongruity
between the attitudes of Annie and Rob, and that of Alvy, is
the source of the humor in this scene. However, this humor
also has a rather pathetic feel to it as it indicates the distance
that Alvy is creating between himself and his best friends, due
to his provincialism. Both Annie and Rob are expanding their
cultural range and appreciating new and different social set-
tings, while Alvy's provincialism prevents him from joining
them in this adventure. This will eventually take its toll on
Alvy's friendship with both Annie and Rob, as we see at the

end of the film when Alvy visits Annie, after she eventually moved to California, and he also gets to see Rob. On this trip Alvy finally realizes that two of his closest friendships are over after he experiences, and perhaps better understands, the cultural limitations created by his provincialism.

In this scene, Annie and Alvy arrange to meet at an outdoor health food café in Los Angeles, and we see that Alvy is way out of his element. Alvy arrives before Annie, and while he is waiting, we witness Alvy awkwardly trying to order from a menu with which he is clearly unfamiliar. He nonetheless disingenuously tries to act as if he knows what he is doing, and orders what he believes to be normal: alfalfa sprouts and a plate of mashed yeast. His order seems absurd and ridiculous, and this immediately reminds us of Annie's unusual food order in a New York deli; however, there is an obvious and important difference between the two. While Annie took her unfamiliarity with Jewish delicatessens all in her stride and just ordered whatever she wanted, Alvy was obviously distressed over his inability to understand and control his current situation (a New York trait), and he makes his order intentionally "hyper-normal," in the sense that it is meant to exemplify the typical, ridiculous Californian (lack of) culture. Alvy's provincialism makes him incapable of enjoying unfamiliar environments, whereas Annie enjoys the challenge of learning new cultures, and as a result, continuously grows as a person. This becomes ultimately evident when Annie appears.

Upon Annie's arrival, it becomes instantly apparent that the cultural incongruities between her and Alvy have grown considerably. Annie is not only dressed like a native Californian, but she also acts more like a Californian. She is relaxed, in good spirits, and her confidence and new level of independence are undeniable. Life in California has made Annie happier and stronger than she has ever been as long as Alvy has known her. Annie's appearance clashes noticeably with that of Alvy, who looks and acts like a New Yorker, and makes no attempt to acquiesce to his surroundings. Annie has obviously assimilated the Californian way of life, while Alvy remains an extremely provincial New Yorker.

What happens next is perhaps the most significant scene in the film: Annie and Alvy are unable to communicate effectively. The cultural distance between them has grown to the point that any attempts to establish communication become both uncomfortable and confrontational, and it is as this point that Alvy and the audience simultaneously realize that the combination of Annie's cultural growth and Alvy's provincialism have made it impossible for the two to ever get back together again. This realization then makes the audience reflect on earlier scenes in the film in which Annie and Alvy were a great couple.

For example, we think about the time when Alvy and Annie were laughing hysterically because they accidentally let live lobsters escape in the kitchen and were both too scared of the lobsters to catch them. Their communication was deeply meaningful and, as Alvy tells us in the beginning monologue, they were in love. As the audience, we can't help but wonder along with Alvy, what happened to bring this romance to such an unfortunate end? No answer is given in the film, but this lack of an answer suggests that it may just be the way life is. Relationships simply have a beginning, a middle, and an end, and there is nothing we can do to stop them from running their course. Some grow while others do not, and even the rare occurrence that two people happen to "grow together" seems only the result of dumb luck. Love does indeed fade.

The harshness of this conclusion gets softened, however, by a humorous scene immediately following this conversation between Annie and Alvy, in which Alvy also gets to see Rob before leaving California. What we find out is that Rob has not exactly grown as a person, as Annie clearly has, but has simply fallen into the clichéd rich, indulgent, weird California lifestyle. Rob picks Alvy up from the police station (Alvy was arrested for taking out his frustrations about losing Annie by playing bumper cars with real vehicles), and we notice that the only aspect of Rob's personality that has not changed is that he still calls Alvy "Max." Here is the scene:

ROB: Imagine my surprise when I got your call, Max.
ALVY (*carrying his jacker over his shoulder*): Yeah. I had the feeling that I got you at a bad moment. You know, I heard high-pitched squealing.

(*They walk over to Rob's convertible and get in.*)

ROB (*starting the car*): Twins, Max. Sixteen-year-olds. Can you imagine the mathematical possibilities?

ALVY (*reacting*): You're an actor, Max. You should be doing Shakespeare in the Park.

ROB: Oh, I did Shakespeare in the Park, Max. I got mugged. I was playing Richard the Second, and two guys with leather jackets stole my leotards.

(*He puts on an elaborate helmet and goggles.*)

ALVY (*looking at Rob's helmet*): Max, are we driving through plutonium?

ROB: Keeps out the alpha rays, Max. You don't get old.

Humor and Philosophy

This visit to California finally made Alvy aware of his provincialism and how it affected his relationship with both Annie and Rob. Yet, it also educates the audience regarding the nature of provincialism and makes us reflect on the complex social and cultural factors that change people. Always behind this, however, is the humor created by Allen, who is extremely adept at drawing a fine line between humor and seriousness. By using humor to highlight incongruities in human behavior, he is able to make critical commentaries as well as raise important philosophical questions regarding social and cultural issues. Comments such as "long term romantic relationships may be mythical," questions such as "what factors in life shape human behavior?" and insights into the problems of provincialism are not topics that people are normally eager to reflect upon. This is especially true when people are looking to be entertained.

Only a sophisticated mixture of humor and philosophy, such as Allen's *Annie Hall*, can educate as well as entertain. The fact that humor permits the expression of behavioral incongruities without involving the intellectual resistance to topics that may be distasteful, uncomfortable, or simply uninteresting for many people, gives it great potential to be used for philosophical ends. Of course, humor has no inherent philosophical value, but only has potential philosophical value, and must be crafted properly to realize its full potential. The value of most humor is limited to entertainment, and few people are capable of creating humor that also provides intellectual insight. Woody Allen is one of the few able to produce humor for both entertainment and philosophical ends. By doing so, he pushes humor to its full potential as a medium for communication.

10

Reconstructing Ingmar: The Aesthetic Purging of the Great Model

PER F. BROMAN

> JACOBI: Are you an Artist or a Mouse?
> ROSENBERG: I'm a Mouse, I'm an Artist.
> JACOBI: Art's holy freedom. Art's holy laxness.
>
> —COLONEL JACOBI (GUNNAR BJÖRNSTRAND) and JAN ROSENBERG
> (MAX VON SYDOW) in *The Shame* (1968)[1]

> Aesthetics: Is art the mirror of life, or what?
>
> —WOODY ALLEN[2]

What can Woody Allen possibly like about Ingmar Bergman's films? Allen's lively, joyful comedies seem to have nothing in common with the darkly Swedish, moralistic films of Bergman. Whereas in Allen's work any kind of crisis might serve as fodder for a memorable and amusing anecdote, Bergman's work is almost always utterly serious, dealing with death and emotional misery. After the mid-1950s, when Bergman had reached his prime, very few of his films had any humorous content. Yet, Allen has made numerous references to Bergman in interviews and in his works.

---

[1] [Är Du en konstnär eller en potta? / Jag är väl en potta, jag är väl en konstnär. / Konstens heliga frihet. Konstens heliga slapphet.]
[2] Woody Allen, "Spring Bulletin," *Getting Even* (New York: Random House, 1966), p. 57.

In this chapter I will discuss Allen's allusions to Bergman from an aesthetic point of view. I will discuss the various kinds of allusions found in a couple of movies and the kinds of effects they can have on a viewer, and will position them in a modernist-postmodernist framework. I will also argue that reading Allen through a Bergmanesque filter will contribute to an expanded understanding of Allen's aesthetics.

Comparing Allen and Bergman

The similarities between Allen and Bergman are striking. Both are filmmakers—as opposed to merely directors—as they write and direct their own stories.[3] Both have an extraordinary sense of the film medium: A film is not merely a documentation of a story, it is an artwork with special artistic concerns. For both of them the plots are focused on the dialogue (or more frequently the monologue, in Bergman's case), rather than the action. The narrative past is important for them both, and is often introduced through flashbacks. The past contains happiness and pain, and unveils the source of one's failures.

Many of their stories focus on women, and both filmmakers feature strong casts of actresses. The family is important also: compare the gatherings around the dinner table in *Fanny and Alexander* or *Wild Strawberries* with those in *Annie Hall* or *Hannah and Her Sisters*. Several generations of the families are gathered for a big meal, and often family members perform music. Such scenes make for grand cinematography, and also explain hierarchies within the family structure. In general, the children are important. In *Fanny and Alexander*, they constitute the very center of the narrative. In *Persona* the unbearably shameful feeling of hate towards one's own child is a central topic. In Bergman's world children are sources of emotional concerns, whereas in Allen's films, they are a source of all kinds of practical problems: sharing custody and buying presents. But Allen treats children as adults. He introduces them to his own obsessions in life: he teaches them about women (*Manhattan*, *Deconstructing Harry*) and takes them to movies (*Crimes and*

---

[3] Bergman's autobiography, *Laterna Magica*, for example, is a painful account of his childhood and explains the self-therapeutic character of his film making. The Bergmanesque world on screen is probably a completely real one to him.

Misdemeanors). As in virtually all of Bergman's movies, the main characters in Allen's films are artists. They are writers (authors of fiction or writers for television), film makers, painters, actors, and occasionally musicians and circus artists.

Allusion

> NAT: Hello, Moe? Me. Listen, I don't know if somebody's playing a joke, or what, but Death was just here. We played a little gin. . . . No, *Death*. In person. Or somebody who claims to be Death. But Moe, he's such a *Schlep!*[4]

William Irwin and J.R. Lombardo have argued that allusions provide a special kind of pleasure when used in an artwork: "The comprehension of an allusion combines the pleasure we feel when we recognize something familiar, like a favorite childhood toy, with the pleasure we feel when we know the right answer to the big question on *Jeopardy* or *Who Wants to be a Millionaire?*"[5] They argue that using an allusion can be an effective way to convey an idea or any kind of narrative element. The allusions that Irwin and Lombardo discuss are references to other artworks in *The Simpsons*. These allusions are most often clear: a character quotes a character from elsewhere or the narrative borrows situations from more or less known sources and puts them in a new context to convey new meaning. Allen's references to Bergman are likewise often clear, but take different forms. They involve more than just borrowed images, characters, or plots—they are artistic *recompositions*. I will illustrate this by discussing three examples, each of which represents a different notion of allusion.

Another Woman and *Deconstructing Harry*

Consider Allen's *Another Woman*, for which Bergman's *Wild Strawberries* must have served as one major source of inspiration. In *Wild Strawberries* a physician, Professor Isak Borg

---

[4] Woody Allen, "Death Knocks," in *Getting Even*, p. 53.
[5] William Irwin and J.R. Lombardo, "*The Simpsons* and Allusion: 'Worst Essay Ever'," in William Irwin, Mark T. Conard, and Aeon J. Skoble, eds., *The Simpsons and Philosophy: The D'oh! of Homer* (Chicago: Open Court, 2001), p. 85.

(played by the legendary silent-film director Victor Sjöström) travels to his *alma mater* to be honored on the fiftieth anniversary of his graduation. His daughter-in-law accompanies him in the car, as do three young hitchhikers, one girl and two boys. During the daylong trip the party takes rest stops at places of past importance to Isak. The journey is both a geographical journey and one down memory lane, and the professor gains a great deal of self-understanding at these stops. His daughter-in-law also reveals a number of truths to him: He is and has been a non-empathic, pedantic, self-obsessed, Scroogy, know-it-all in the eyes of his family. The hitchhiking girl, Sara, reminds Isak of his childhood love, his own cousin, and she triggers particularly painful memories (both girls are played by Bibi Andersson). However, as it turns out, his professional life has been very successful. In a town where he had worked as the local physician, he encounters a couple who thank him for everything he did for the community, and announce that they intend to name their child after him. The honorary ceremony goes well, too, and in the end, the professor is redeemed and he goes to bed in peace.

In *Another Woman,* the main character, Marion Post (Gena Rowlands), is confronted with truths about herself, revealed by different people who surround her during a sabbatical from her position as a professor of philosophy. She receives insights into herself from a woman undergoing psychoanalysis in the neighboring apartment, from her sister-in-law, and from a novel written by a former admirer. Marion, too, is accused of being judgmental and cold. And, as in *Wild Strawberries*, she has ended up marrying the wrong person. But Marion has had a very successful professional life, and during a dinner at a restaurant, a former student approaches her, revealing that her classes with Marion had changed her life. Marion "was the inspiration to all the women in the philosophy department." This statement is almost identical to that in the parallel scene in *Wild Strawberries. Another Woman* ends with Marion's reconciliation with life.

Another Woman is one of Allen's few non-comedic movies— probably the best of those—and the allusion to the Bergman film is very direct. *Another Woman* almost constitutes a remake, but one set in a different time and in a different context. In the other Allen film that alludes to *Wild Strawberries, Deconstructing Harry,* the strategy is markedly different. The allusions are distorted to such an extent that the search for them becomes a challenging but rewarding task.

In Allen's version the main character, author Harry Block (Allen), is on a journey to be honored by his *alma mater*, the liberal-arts college in upstate New York that once expelled him (Allen himself was expelled from NYU during his freshman year). Accompanying him in the car are three people: a friend, a prostitute whom he has paid to join him, and his son whom he has had to kidnap, as he was not scheduled to have custody of the boy that day. They travel in the most Swedish of the Swedish cars, a Volvo of the 240 series, a box-like automobile that radiates Swedish safety and quality, but has no style or sophistication whatsoever (Volvos are frequently used in Bergman's films).

As in Bergman's film there is a memory trail to be followed, and Block gets the opportunity to confront both his real and literary pasts. Characters from his novels and short stories appear and bring him insights (and laughs, of course). The ending is happy, although his friend dies in the car, and although Block gets arrested for the kidnapping prior to the ceremony and is brought to jail. In a fantasy, he goes to hell (in Bergman's version, the protagonist has visions of being dead), he encounters his own literary characters, who give him the celebration he did not get at the college, and the whole turn of events inspires him to begin yet another novel. In this film, Allen more dramatically alters the locations of Bergman's original. Whereas Borg is confronted by flashbacks of his wife's affair in beautiful outdoor surroundings and of his cousin having a romantic dinner with his own brother, Block has a pleasant encounter with his rival, the devil, in hell, surrounded by eternal fire (somewhat recalling the images of hell in Bergman's comedy *The Devil's Eye*).

Hannah and Her Sisters

Hannah and Her Sisters is another Allen film that incorporates different kinds of allusions to Bergman's works, including a direct connection to Bergman's filmmaking world. In *Hannah* Allen lets his cinematographic world collide with Bergman's by casting one of the actors most featured in Bergman's films, Max von Sydow, as the rude painter Frederick. Sydow, of course, was part of the most iconographic of Bergman's movies, *The*

Seventh Seal, one used and parodied in popular culture by *Seinfeld, Monty Python's The Meaning of Life,* and the Schwarzenegger movie *The Last Action Hero* alike—not to mention by Allen himself in *Love and Death* and *Deconstructing Harry.* In the most famous scene of *The Seventh Seal* Antonius Block (von Sydow; note the use of the same last name by Allen's character in *Deconstructing Harry*) and Death (Bengt Ekerot) meet and begin a game of chess. (I have met people in North America who can recite the initial dialogue between von Sydow and Death in what is probably the only Swedish they know: "Vem är Du?" "Jag är döden." [Who are you? I am Death.])[6] In *Hannah* von Sydow portrays a character very similar to one of von Sydow's Bergman characters: Johan Borg in *Hour of the Wolf,* a taciturn, unpolished painter. I do not want to imply that a recurring actor will necessarily trigger a significant allusion: An appearance by Bruce Willis in an action movie does not necessarily constitute an allusion to John McClane of *Die Hard.* But in the Allen case, the allusion is intriguing since it crosses two very different traditions of film making, as well as two languages.[7]

In *Hannah,* the significance of von Sydow's appearance is underscored in the soundtrack. Allen abandons his normal musical environment of jazz standards right before our first encounter with Frederick, throughout which we hear the agitated first movement of J.S. Bach's Double Violin Concerto. The scene preceding our next meeting with him is a visit to the opera where Puccini's *Manon Lescaut* is performed. In Frederick's second scene, he refuses to sell his work "by the yard" to a *nouveau riche* rock star who "just bought a huge house in Southampton."[8] The last time we see von Sydow, the scene is preceded by the slow movement of Bach's F-minor Keyboard Concerto.[9] Frederick tells his girlfriend Lee (Barbara Hershey) about a television program he had been watching: "You missed a very dull TV show on Auschwitz. . . ." This is a

---

[6] *The Seventh Seal* (1957).

[7] Max von Sydow is of course a recurring Hollywood actor, who is widely known for his roles as Father Lankester Merrin in *The Exorcist* and Jesus in *The Greatest Story Ever Told.*

[8] *Hannah and her Sisters* (1986).

[9] The piece is also used to emphasize the love between Lee (Barbara Hershey) and Eliot (Michael Caine).

different world: the Bergmanesque world of western art music and depressing entertainment.[10] For Allen, classical music triggers serious narratives, alluding to Bergman.

Bergman uses the music of Bach, in particular, to mark significant events, such as the embrace between Karin (Ingrid Thulin) and Maria (Liv Ullman) in *Cries and Whispers*—almost the sole expression of closeness in the film. The scene follows shortly after the recollection of Karin's self-mutilation, and is accompanied by the Sarabande from the Fifth Suite for Solo Cello. There is no dialogue in the scene, only music, which creates an incredibly powerful effect. Allen similarly makes isolated use of classical music in *Crimes and Misdemeanors*. The first movement of Schubert's G-major String Quartet is used in the most puissant scene in the movie, when Judah (Martin Landau) leaves a dinner party to see if his former mistress really has been murdered on his orders, and to rescue some belongings that might tie him to the deed. (Allen also used solo cello music by Bach, the Allemande from the Sixth Suite, in *Another Woman*, in a flashback during a romantic encounter between Marion and her first husband.)

Modernism and Irony

If it bends it's funny. If it breaks it's not funny.

Comedy is tragedy plus time.

—LESTER (ALAN ALDA) in *Crimes and Misdemeanors*

In his films from the 1960s, Bergman is thoroughly modernistic in terms of expression and Allen follows this track, but with an ironic twist. However, Allen is not merely a postmodern Bergman. Both are too original and brilliant to be placed in such a simple dichotomy. The modernist-postmodernist thread, although not directly related to allusions, constitutes another way of reading

---

[10] Bergman is particularly attracted to Bach, and used Bach in several films, including *Autumn Sonata*, *Through a Glass Darkly*, *The Silence*, and *Hour of the Wolf*. There is one example of Bergman using big band music. In *The Passion of Anna* it is used in a quasi-romantic dialogue between von Sydow and Bibi Andersson. In his first movie in German exile, *The Serpent's Egg*, Bergman used traditional jazz for the beginning credits.

Allen through Bergman. I will borrow Andreas Huyssen's definitions of the modernistic artwork from his very influential *After
the Great Divide* and position Bergman within Huyssen's framework. I will then contrast this position with Allen's to show a
different kind of connection between Allen and Bergman.

The modernist work is

1. autonomous and totally separate from the realms of mass culture and everyday life.[11]

There is no doubt that Bergman's films are removed from mass
culture and everyday life. The movies are about crises, particularly marital and family crises, death, incest, and insanity.
Although the events may occur in "everyday life," for most people they are once-in-a-lifetime events, at most. This is true for
many of Allen's movies as well. They are mostly set in everyday
life and take place in an environment "contaminated" by mass
culture, but constitute fantasies, rather than realistic depictions.
But most of Bergman's recurring topics are distorted in Allen's
works. Death for example—the process of dying in Bergman—
often takes a self-ironic twist in Allen—death as a hypochondriac's fear of dying.

Modernism, according to Huyssen, is also

2. self-referential, self-conscious, frequently ironic, ambiguous, and
rigorously experimental.

Bergman achieves a high degree of self-reference through his
use of a small pool of actors—Bibi Andersson, Erland Josephson,
Max von Sydow, Liv Ullman, and Gunnar Björnstrand appear
most frequently. Allen also uses a pool of actors, including Mia
Farrow, Diane Keaton, Judy Davis, Dianne Wiest, Tony Roberts,
and Allen himself, of course, who return in movie after movie.
(In contrast to Allen, Bergman hardly ever appears on screen,
and when he does, he makes only brief Hitchcock-like appearances.) Sometimes, after having seen many movies in close prox-
imity, it is hard to recount the story lines of either filmmaker. The

---

[11] Andreas Huyssen, "Mass Culture as Woman," in *After the Great Divide:
Modernism, Mass Culture, Postmodernism* (Bloomington: Indiana University
Press, 1986), pp. 53–54.

films blend together with the familiar faces of the recurring actors. (Allen, for example, is having, has had, or wants to have a romantic encounter with Farrow in the movies in which they both appear.) The two most important actresses for each film-maker somewhat resemble each other: Ullman and Farrow[12] often portray the same kind of characters, devoted and mild-tempered women, while Andersson and Keaton appear in stronger and more independent roles, often as impudent and volatile young women.

Bergman's movies are ambiguous and experimental indeed, and it is often hard to find one clear moral standpoint in a Bergman film. A few movies are incomprehensible from a narrative perspective. Allen's works, on the other hand, have clear story lines and morals with an ironic twist, as in *Crimes and Misdemeanors*. The ironic content in Bergman's works is limited, however, unless we consider unintentional irony: The gloomy images of empty rooms with nothing but ticking clocks on the soundtrack strike most viewers today as nothing but ironic—the beginning of *Cries and Whispers* being the archetypal example. By developing his own clichés of seriousness Bergman has set the stage for ironic interpretations of his works.

Further, Huyssen argues that modernism is

3. the expression of a purely individual consciousness rather than of a *Zeitgeist* or a collective state of mind.

There is no doubt that Bergman's films are autobiographical. They deal with timeless issues of love, death, and the presence or absence of God, issues that preoccupy Allen as well. Often there is no definite reference to a specific time or place within the plot. Even in a time-bound, Ibsen-like costume film such as *Cries and Whispers*, the actual drama has been removed from time and place. The metaphysical sense of time and place is also emphasized by Bergman's locations. His films often take place on a deserted island by the sea, commonly Fårö in the Baltic Sea, whereas Allen's take place on the island of Manhattan.

---

[12] Bergman, too, appreciated Farrow. During the initial stage of *Cries and Whispers*, a film first conceived as a bilingual film, Bergman had Farrow in mind for a role. See Bergman's *Bilder* (Stockholm: Norstedts, 1990), p. 88.

These two locations become symbolic in different ways. Bergman presents a clear, clean timeless stage. Allen, on the other hand, thrives in most cases in the culture of New York of the time of the movie's conception. His movies constitute a cultural critique to a larger extent than do Bergman's.

Huyssen also argues that modernism's

> 4. experimental nature makes it analogous to science, and like science it produces and carries knowledge.

Although this category is applicable to much modernist music and visual art, Bergman's films do not conform to this category very often. His aesthetic consciousness comes out of the theater, particularly out of Scandinavian fin-de-siècle works by Strindberg and Ibsen, works that he directed on stage many times. But both Bergman and Allen take advantage of the film medium in a modernist way. As Huyssen continues,

> Modernist literature since Flaubert is a persistent exploration of and encounter with language. Modernist painting since Manet is an equally persistent elaboration of the medium itself: the flatness of the canvas, the structuring of notation, paint and brushwork, the problem of the frame.

Just consider the beginning and end of *Persona,* featuring fragments of a film running through the projector, accompanied by modernist music by Lars-Johan Werle. The viewer is reminded that this is a film. The language of Bibi Andersson's monologue toward the end points to the limits of language itself. The speech turns into surrealist poetry. The viewer is made even more aware of the work of art as a film in *The Passion of Anna*. Here Bergman lets the four main actors comment on their respective characters outside of the narrative, as if the entire movie were a documentary. Allen occasionally uses experimental forms, in which fantasy segments interrupt the unfolding narrative. *Annie Hall* may be the best example of this technique. He has also included comments made by characters outside of the narrative, as in *Husbands and Wives*. Even more experimental is *What's Up, Tiger Lily?* in which Allen served as a "re-release director" using an existing film, *Kagi No Kag,* and rewrote the dialogue.

Art and Pretension

Allen, of course, is aware of the widespread perception of Bergman as highbrow and laborious. In *Manhattan* there is a brief discussion of Bergman. Mary (Diane Keaton) and Yale (Michael Murphy) have just begun nominating candidates to the Academy of the Overrated (an Academy that includes Gustav Mahler, Heinrich Böll, van Gogh—pronounced in Dutch by Mary to emphasize her pretentiousness—and Norman Mailer[13]). When they nominate Bergman, Isaac Davis (Allen) angrily replies, "Bergman is the only genius in cinema today."[14] Mary's response is "His view is so Scandinavian, it's bleak, my God, I mean all that Kierkegaard, right, real adolescent. You know, fashionable pessimism. I mean, *The Silence*, God's silence. O.K., O.K., O.K., I mean, I loved it when I was at Radcliffe, but, I mean, all right, you outgrow it. You absolutely outgrow it." But Mary herself is of a divided mind regarding the pretension of high culture and art. In the previous scene, she made comments about a sculpture—a steel cube—during a visit to a museum: "that was brilliant . . . it was very textural, you know what I mean, it was perfectly integrated, and it had a marvelous kind of negative capability." Does she deny Bergman's films having "negative capability"? Or, take the wonderful, classic dialogue in *Annie Hall* as Annie (Diane Keaton) and Alvy Singer (Allen) are having a midday glass of wine on Annie's balcony, the day of their first meeting. The stammering dialogue (given in the left column) is subtitled with their real thoughts (given in the right column). Alvy asks, "Did you shoot these photographs in there, or what?"

Yeah. Yeah, I sort of dabble around, you know.	I dabble? Listen to me—what a jerk.
They are wonderful, you know. They have a quality.	You are a great-looking girl.
Well, I would like to take a serious photography course.	He probably thinks I'm a yo-yo.

---

[13] In *Sleeper* Allen's character Miles Monroe describes Mailer as a "great writer" who "donated his ego to Harvard Medical School for study."
[14] *Manhattan* (1979).

Photography is interesting, 'cause, you know, it's a new art form so a set of aesthetic criteria has not emerged yet.	I wonder what she looks like naked?
Aesthetic criteria? You mean whether it's a good photo or not?	I'm not smart enough for him. Hang in there
The medium enters in as a condition of the art form itself.	I don't know what I'm saying—she senses I'm shallow.
Well to me, I mean, it's all instinctive, you know. I just try to feel it, you know. I try to get a sense of it, and I don't think about it so much.	God, I hope he doesn't turn out to be a shmuck like the others.
Still, you need a set of aesthetic guidelines to put it in social perspective, I think.	Christ, I sound like FM radio. Relax.[15]

This dialogue lies at the center of Allen's aesthetics. Art is a serious matter, but pretentious discussions of art should definitely be mocked. And for most Allenesque characters, art is fine, but sex is even more important. The artist is caught in the power field of sexual desire and artistic creativity. The absence of sex creates a flow of creativity. As inventor Andrew (Allen) tells Maxwell (Tony Roberts) in *A Midsummer Night's Sex Comedy,* "Because of my problem in bed with her, I can now fly."[16]

Art and Life

To me, it's a really interesting character, a guy who can't function well in life, but can only function in art. You know, it's sort of sad in a way but also funny.

—HARRY (ALLEN) in *Deconstructing Harry* (1997)

---

[15] *Annie Hall* (1977).
[16] *A Midsummer Night's Sex Comedy* (1982).

MARTIN: Have you written one single true word during your life as an author? Huh? Answer if you can.

DAVID: I don't know.

MARTIN: No, there you see. The incredible fact is that your half-truths are so refined that they resemble truth.

DAVID: I'm trying.

MARTIN: Yes, that's possible. But you can never reach out.

DAVID: I know.

MARTIN: You are empty and skillful.

—MARTIN (MAX VON SYDOW) and DAVID (GUNNAR BJÖRNSTRAND) in *Through a Glass Darkly* (1961)[17]

For Allen, art contains the truth about the world. Not necessarily in a metaphysical sense, but rather in a down-to-earth sense. The creation of art is an important part of life. Art is the mirror of the artist, and of his or her life. But art is never larger-than-life, as in some of Bergman's films, most prominently *The Rite,* in which three actors perform an ancient Greek ritual, killing their accuser, or in *The Magician,* in which the magic trick causes death (or the illusion of death). Virtually every prose work by a main character in an Allen movie is based on the character's own experiences. As Gabe Roth (Allen) tells Rain (Juliette Lewis) in *Husbands and Wives* regarding her imprudent experiences in life at a young age, "God, you've got material for your first novel, and the sequel, and then an opera by Puccini."[18] There is virtually always a struggle, against writer's block or against the demands of the heartless commercial world upon an artist (as in *Annie Hall*). The outcome is rarely any literary masterpiece (from what we can tell), and consists of nothing more than gossip, often to the great embarrassment of the people mentioned in the book.

The reconstruction of *Wild Strawberries* in *Deconstructing Harry* is a compelling one. It is a deformed mirror, with symbolic allusions. It is far more compelling in terms of the effect of the

---

[17] [Har Du skrivit ett enda sant ord under Ditt författarliv? Va? Svara om Du kan. / Jag vet inte. / Nej, där ser Du. Det ohyggliga är att Dina halvlögner är så raffinerade så de liknar sanning. / Jag försöker ju. / Ja det är möjligt. Men Du når aldrig fram. / Jag vet. / Du är tom och skicklig.]

[18] *Husbands and Wives,* (1992).

allusions than the movies that are more commonly associated with Bergman's influence, due to their serious topics and cinematography à la Sven Nykvist: *September* and *Interiors,* or the comedies *A Midsummer Night's Sex Comedy* and *Love and Death* which are spiced with Bergmanesque licks.[19] *Deconstructing Harry* takes such a far-out approach to Bergman that the allusions become almost unrecognizable. Allen's ironic allusions and commentaries purge Bergman, removing the most exuberant pretentiousness, but with a friendly wink. This reading connects very well to Umberto Eco's discussion of modernism and postmodernism:

> I think of the postmodern attitude as that of a man who loves a very cultivated woman and knows he cannot say to her, "I love you madly," because he knows that she knows (and that she knows that he knows) that these words have already been written by Barbara Cartland. Still there is a solution. He can say, "As Barbara Cartland would put it, I love you madly."[20]

It is okay for Allen to make these films, since he finds justification in tradition and in Bergman—the great model.

Watching Allen's works—and particularly *Deconstructing Harry*—with Bergmanesque glasses lends a new dimension to them. In Allen's reconstruction of Bergman, his characters problematize high art and even Allen's own highbrow taste. The artist does not carry the truth, but does carry the key to self-understanding. Writing a novel may be as effective a tool for unlocking self-knowledge as years of sessions on the analyst's couch. But in all this ironic humor, Allen even accomplishes moments of genuine truth, despite being surrounded by an utterly non-serious narrative, in a way that often speaks directly to the viewer. Take the scene in *Deconstructing Harry* when he asks his sister "Wouldn't it be a better world if not every group thought they had a direct line to God?" That statement comes across as the real Woody Allen giving the audience his genuine

---

[19] Nykvist was the cinetomagrapher for a couple of Allen movies, *Another Woman*, "Oedipus Wrecks" of *New York Stories*, and *Crimes and Misdemeanors.*
[20] Umberto Eco, *Postscript to The Name of the Rose* (New York: Harcourt Brace, 1984), p. 67.

conviction. And, as Allen lets Mickey Sachs (Allen) say in *Hannah*, "Millions of books written on every conceivable subject by all these great minds, and in the end none of them knows anything more about the big questions of life than I do." I believe Mickey and I believe it is the voice of Allen himself.[21]

---

[21] I am grateful for comments on earlier drafts of this piece from Nora Engebretsen and Jonathan Kochavi.

Act III

Five Films

11

The Dangers of Hedonism: *A Midsummer Night's Sex Comedy*

SANDER LEE

A Midsummer Night's Sex Comedy (hereafter referred to as *Sex Comedy*) mimics its inspiration, Shakespeare's *A Midsummer Night's Dream,* in its light comic tone and bucolic setting. Like *A Midsummer Night's Dream, Sex Comedy* presents a tale of romantic longing and magical transformations. One of its characters even shares the name Ariel with a character from the original. Yet, despite these similarities, I will contend that *Sex Comedy* explores serious philosophical concerns not present in Shakespeare's whimsical tale.

Philosophical Sources

Professor Leopold Sturgis (José Ferrer) is the first professional philosopher to appear in an Allen film; yet, surprisingly, his theoretical orientation differs dramatically from that of Allen.[1] *Sex Comedy* opens with Sturgis asserting, "Ghosts, little spirits or pixies, I don't believe in them!" He goes on to explain his skepticism to a college class of young men:

> Nothing is real but experience, that which can be touched, tasted, felt, or in some scientific fashion proved. We must never substitute

---

[1] Although it may be difficult to say exactly what Allen's philosophical position is, I would contend that he is clearly not the same sort of philosopher as Leopold Sturgis.

qualitative events which are marked by similar properties and
recurrences for fixed substances . . . As I stated quite clearly in my
latest paper, metaphysical philosophers are simply men who are
too weak to accept the world as it is. Their theories of the so-called
mysteries of life are nothing more than projections of their own
inner uneasiness. Apart from this world, there are no realities.[2]

When a student retorts, "But that leaves many basic human
needs unanswered," he responds, "I'm sorry, I did not create the
cosmos, I merely explain it."

In choosing to set *Sex Comedy* in 1906 and in the United
States, Allen makes it clear that he plans to comment on the
changes wrought by the influence of Sturgis's approach (analytic
philosophy) on American thinking and belief. The beginning of
the twentieth century saw the birth of the two philosophical
movements that have since dominated Western philosophy:
phenomenological existentialism and analytic philosophy.
Allen's concerns have always been most identified with phenomenological existentialism, a movement which has its roots in
European thought. On the other hand, the analytic movement,
which started in England at about the same time, has been the
predominant approach among professional philosophers in the
English-speaking world, even during those periods when, in the
1950s and 1960s, the existential approach became particularly
popular among students and the artistic community.

The analytic approach can be summarized by simply
expanding on Leopold's initial comments. Sounding very much
like Bertrand Russell, Leopold holds an extreme form of the
empiricist position, the view that all we can know to exist is
what we experience through the senses. For Leopold, therefore,
the sciences, as opposed to metaphysics, are our most important
source of knowledge. Leopold thinks that nothing at all can be
known about such things as the soul, and therefore those seriously seeking the truth should not waste their time by pursuing
such topics.

Later followers of this approach, such as the British philosopher A.J. Ayer or those Austrian thinkers collectively known as
the Vienna Circle (Rudolf Carnap, for example), further argued
that all discussion of metaphysical issues should be disre-

---

[2] *A Midsummer Night's Sex Comedy (1982).*

garded as "meaningless gibberish" (the very words used by Leopold).[3]

In his 1936 book *Language, Truth, and Logic*, Ayer uses his "verifiability theory of meaning" in an attempt to prove that all utterances which are neither tautologies nor empirical descriptions are "meaningless." A tautology is a statement which is necessarily true. An example would be "All bachelors are unmarried." It is not necessary to do a survey of bachelors in order to confirm this proposition as it is true by definition. An empirical proposition is one capable of being verified by the senses as either true or false. The sentence "It is snowing today" would be an example of such a proposition because its truth or falsity may be empirically verified on any given day (by looking to see whether it is, in fact, snowing). Even if this statement happened to be false on the day it was uttered, Ayer would still call it "meaningful" because its truth could be tested by observation.

Meaningless utterances, Ayer argued in 1936, make no claims whatsoever. They arise from verbal confusions. Ayer maintained that statements like "God exists" or "God does not exist" are not true or false, but strictly nonsensical, because they cannot be confirmed by any evidence we can observe. Ayer also claimed that ethical statements, like "Murder is wrong," are strictly meaningless. Closed to all forms of verification, they simply express— or, using Ayer's term, "evince"—emotions, as when a person says "Ouch!" upon stubbing a toe. For the Ayer of 1936, many statements concerning morality, art, politics, or religion can be discounted as nonsensical because they cannot be tested by observation.[4]

---

[3] Metaphysics is the branch of philosophy dealing with the fundamental nature of reality, beyond what we can observe with our eyes and ears. It therefore discusses such questions as whether time has a direction, whether numbers really exist independent of human minds, or whether everything that happens can be explained in terms of matter and energy. Some philosophers have tried to get rid of metaphysics, but this is an extreme position which has never caught on.

[4] Following intense discussion of Ayer's *Language, Truth, and Logic*, this position, known as "logical empiricism" or "logical positivism" was quickly abandoned by all philosophers, including Ayer himself, and it had never been accepted by the majority of analytic philosophers. But it became comparatively well-known among non-philosophers, who saw it as typifying a certain approach to philosophy, one which Woody Allen is mocking.

Analytic Philosophy and Hedonism

These analytic philosophers didn't simply devote themselves to the work of science, relinquishing all interest in the pursuit of the pleasures of the senses. In fact, because the experience of the senses is reliable, the pursuit of pleasure is, in their estimation, a meaningful and understandable activity in which to engage. Thus many such philosophers end up supporting empiricist approaches to social concerns, approaches which have their source in the seventeenth-century, social contract theories of Thomas Hobbes or John Locke, especially as these theories have been updated by nineteenth-century utilitarians such as Jeremy Bentham, or by American pragmatists such as William James.

Social contract theorists believe that the laws of society are solely conventions, the results of agreements reached by the majority of people in order to trade a bit of their liberty in exchange for governmental protection of their individual interests. Utilitarian thinkers expand upon this by arguing that all people inherently seek whatever gives them pleasure and avoid whatever is painful. However, as one person's pleasure may cause another's pain, they conclude that the most efficient system, the one that will be of greatest utility, is one in which the laws are engineered to create the greatest amount of pleasure for the greatest number of people while inflicting the least amount of pain on the least number of people. American pragmatists follow a similar line of thought by arguing that the truth is relative to the interests and goals of the individual measuring it. Thus, the best way to act is always the most pragmatic, or practical, way that has the greatest probability of helping a person to reach his or her goals, no matter what those goals happen to be.

Such thinkers often believe that our interests and goals are determined, rather than chosen, by our biological tastes and the effects of our environmental conditioning. Thus, for some such theorists, all systems of morality, obligation, and responsibility, established by society or by religion, are archaic vestiges of a bankrupt system of thought which should be jettisoned because it fails to further either our discovery of verifiable data or the fulfillment of our innermost desires. If one were indiscriminate in applying this standard, one might be led to reject ethics in favor of a hedonistic lifestyle. So it's no surprise to discover that although Woody Allen's Leopold is engaged to be married to a beautiful young woman named Ariel Weymouth (Mia Farrow), he is interested in having a last fling with a young, sexually liberated nurse named Dulcy Ford (Julie Hagerty).

Cinematic Antecedents

The setting for these sexual escapades is the bucolic home owned by Andrew Hobbes (Woody Allen) and his wife, Adrian (Mary Steenburgen). Over a summer weekend, the Hobbeses play host to a gathering including Leopold, Ariel, Dulcy, and Maxwell Jordan (Tony Roberts), a doctor who is Andrew's best friend and Dulcy's employer. Given the film's title, its setting, and its comic plot of romantic misadventures, many critics have noted its allusions to a variety of sources ranging from Shakespeare to the films of Reinhardt, Renoir, and Bergman.

In her chapter on *Sex Comedy*, titled "Capturing Lost Memories," Nancy Pogel traces the film's allusions to Max Reinhardt's 1935 film version of "A Midsummer Night's Dream," as well as to Bergman's *Smiles of a Summer's Night* and a variety of the films of Jean Renoir, including *A Day in the Country* (1936), *The Rules of the Game* (1939), and *Picnic on the Grass* (1960).[5] It's worth our while to briefly examine a few of her insights.

Reinhardt's film, which maintains Shakespeare's light-hearted story of a magical forest, fairy trances, and misguided lovers, is also, in Pogel's view, affected by elements of the surrealism of German expressionism as well as frightening hints of the gathering storms of fascism and war. Pogel argues that Allen shares with Bergman's film "a concern for innocence and experience—naturalness and sophistication, idealized love and compromise, as well as the related issues of change, time's tyranny, and death."[6] The Renoir films deal with similar themes. *Picnic on the Grass* is about a scientist and politician, who, like Leopold, "is to be married to a rigid, sophisticated woman," but who is tempted away from his intended by a magical spell placed in the

---

[5] Nancy Pogel, *Woody Allen* (New York: Twayne, 1987), pp. 153–164.
[6] *Ibid.*, p. 157

wind by a "Pan-like goatherd," and ultimately marries a "sexy, country woman" named Nanette.[7] Pogel points out that André Bazin, the noted film theorist, had this to say about the film:

> It is as if Renoir, annoyed or frightened by the sinister character of technocratic society and its standardized notions of happiness, was seeking through the healthy, vigorous reproach of an almost farcical fantasy to restore a taste for the joys and charms of life. It is not surprising, then, that the veneer of entertainment should cover the most serious of purposes.[8]

The earlier *A Day in the Country* is a turn-of-the-century farce about a young woman who has a romantic fling with an attractive man by the banks of a river before marrying a man chosen by her parents. After many years of unhappy marriage, the woman returns to the river, where she briefly meets her lover before returning to her husband for the last time. Bazin remarks:

> In no other film has Renoir more openly presented . . . the conflict between the Apollonian world and the Dionysian world, between the fixed framework of existence and the irresistible movement of life, between the theater set built once and for all and the changing, forever moving production which animates it; in short, between order and disorder.[9]

Bazin's discussion is an explicit reference to Nietzsche's claim that in Western society we have become so engaged by the Apollonian values of rationality and discipline that we have neglected to nurture the more life-affirming, Dionysian values of creativity and passion Nietzsche believes to be at the core of human existence, what he calls "the will to power."

Finally, Renoir's *Rules of the Game* details the romantic high jinks of a group of French people during a country weekend of hunting just before the outbreak of World War II. Pogel quotes Renoir on the effect of the coming war on the film's characters:

> "I didn't tell myself, 'It's absolutely necessary to express this or that in this film because we are going to have war.' . . . My work was impregnated with it, despite myself . . . [I wanted] to show a rich,

---

[7] *Ibid.*, p. 159.
[8] *Ibid.*, p. 160.
[9] *Ibid.*, p. 160.

complex society where—to use a historical phrase—we are dancing on a volcano."[10]

Pogel points out that the events in *Sex Comedy* are also intended
to illustrate the dangers inherent in the romantic deceptions in
which the characters engage. In fact, each character in the film
attempts to deceive the person to whom he or she is supposedly most committed. Leopold and Ariel are engaged to be married the next day; yet Leopold pursues Dulcy for one last
passionate fling. Ariel is sought by both Andrew (an old flame)
and Maxwell, who originally pursued Dulcy. Adrian is initially
presented as a somewhat restrained woman who is having sexual difficulties with her husband. However, by the film's conclusion, it is revealed that her sexual problems do not stem from
Victorian modesty, but from her guilt at having deceived
Andrew sexually with Maxwell.

Pogel quotes Gavin Lambert's comments about *The Rules of
the Game*, remarking that these comments could just as easily be
made about *Sex Comedy*:

> "[The characters] are a party of lively, easygoing, unprincipled peo-
> ple. They are not vindictive or pathological; if not rich, they are still
> elegant and charming. Their 'sin' is something much less obviously
> abnormal. It consists in having no values at all, of always evading
> the important issues."[11]

Pogel herself concludes that "the film sits on the brink of
modernism, looking backward toward innocence and authenticity and forward toward a sophisticated, fragmented world where
personal integrity and a sense of place within the natural order
are less available."[12]

The Sartrean "Perfect Moment"

The dichotomy between humanity and nature is symbolized in
Sex Comedy, as in other Allen films, by the presence of contemporary mechanized technology. This film, however, takes
place at a time when twentieth century technology was still in

---

[10] *Ibid.*, p. 163.
[11] *Ibid.*, p. 168.
[12] *Ibid.*, 1985, p. 169.

its infancy, so that we can see more clearly the origins of this rupture. Andrew, as an inventor, seems to be at a crossroads between the two. Some of his inventions—the flying bicycle, the apple-corer, the fish deboner—impose human desires upon nature and thus widen the separation. Yet his most important invention, the spirit ball, appears to create a genuine link to an unseen supernatural world of spirits and magic.

The first time we see Andrew, he is attempting to fly, using artificial wings that emulate nature. As a bird looks on, we see this device fail. His flying bicycle, on the other hand, with no relation to nature, works much more successfully. This dichotomy is also reflected in other aspects of Andrew's life. He makes his living as a stockbroker on Wall Street; yet, in his spare time, he explores the unseen, spiritual world. Like other Allen personae, he lives in New York City, but unlike all the others, he also owns a house in the country to which he loves to get away in the summer. He is also divided internally by his romantic desires. He is torn between his feelings for his wife, Adrian, whom he loves, and his lustful longings for his lost romance with Ariel.

It is in this context that the Sartrean theme of lost opportunities, privileged situations, and perfect moments appears. In Sartre's first novel, *Nausea*, the main character, Roquentin, discusses with his former lover, Annie, her attempts to create such "perfect moments" out of "privileged situations" where everything would come together in a victory of romanticism over reality:

> "The privileged situations?"
>
> "The idea I had of them. They were situations which had a rare and precious quality, style, if you like. To be king, for example, when you were eight years old. Or to die. You may laugh, but there were so many people drawn at the moment of their death, and so many who spoke such sublime words that I quite genuinely thought . . . well, I thought that by dying you were transported above yourself . . . I developed all that later on: first I added a new situation, love (I mean the act of love) . . ."
>
> "And the perfect moments? Where do they come in?"
>
> "They came afterwards. First there are annunciatory signs. Then, the privileged situation, slowly, majestically, comes into people's lives. Then the question whether you want to make a perfect moment out of it."

"Yes," I say, "I understand. In each of these privileged situations, there are certain acts which have to be done, certain attitudes to be taken, words which must be said—and other attitudes, other words are strictly prohibited. Is that it" . . . "In fact, it was a sort of work of art."

"You've already said that," she says with irritation. "No, it was . . . a duty. You *had* to transform privileged situations into perfect moments. It was a moral question."[13]

But, Roquentin tells us, these moments would never quite come off; he would be unsure of the script, and Annie would only end up feeling frustrated. Roquentin discovers that both he and Annie have come to realize this independently over the years since they last saw one another: "That's it. There are no adventures—there are no perfect moments . . . we have lost the same illusions, we have followed the same paths."[14]

Both Andrew and Ariel are tortured by the fact that they did not act on their romantic impulses many years ago by the side of the brook on his land. Andrew claims that he did not act because he believed that Ariel, as a diplomat's daughter raised in a convent school, would be offended by such attentions. He tells Ariel of his immense frustration when he learned, only a month later, after she had departed for an extended European stay, that she was in fact a "modern woman" who had slept with "everyone."

Ariel tells him how much she had wanted him to act and how disappointed she had been when he didn't. She even goads him by revealing that he might have been the one who could have halted her promiscuity and replaced it with a more lasting commitment. He is depressed by these revelations, telling her there is nothing sadder than a lost opportunity. She, on the other hand, is disturbed by Andrew's claim that his interest in her was purely physical. She spends the rest of the film raising issues concerning the connection between lust and love.

This nostalgic longing for second chances haunts the film. All of the characters try to capture time in a variety of ways, ranging from the use of a camera to Andrew's spirit box, a way to tap into the world's unseen forces that in some respects resembles an early motion picture apparatus.

---

[13] Jean-Paul Sartre, *Nausea* (New York: New Directions, 1964), pp. 147–48.
[14] *Ibid.*, 1964, p. 150.

Trying to Recapture a Lost Moment

Andrew and Ariel's lost moment is an example of the Sartrean privileged situation, a set of circumstances which have the potential to become especially meaningful. In their view, if Andrew had acted on his desires with Ariel, they would have shared a spontaneous, magical, perfect moment which could have changed their lives. By the time of their accidental reunion, they have become obsessed with what could have been, and it seems inevitable that they will try to recreate their moment by taking advantage of this second chance.

The natural and the unseen worlds act in concert to encourage them to take advantage of this gift from fate. The brook, which symbolizes both the currents of emotion and the passage of time, invites them to relive their moment. The spirit ball even shows them an image which they take to be a recreation of that moment. Ariel shows her willingness to recreate the past by wearing the same dress that she wore that day, while Andrew takes advantage of Maxwell's infatuation with Ariel in order to have an excuse to be alone with her.

Andrew's use of his friend's passion as a way to explore his own romantic feelings suggests the plot of *Cyrano de Bergerac*, a hint reinforced by the presence in the cast of José Ferrer, an actor renowned for his work in that role. Yet, when Andrew and Ariel finally do attempt to recreate their lost moment, they discover that, despite all the omens, they are physically and emotionally incompatible. Their lovemaking is so unsatisfactory that they are forced to "bull their way through it." Let down by the failure of their experiment in time travel, they agree that the effects of time can't be overcome because "we change, we become different people."[15] They also confirm the cliché (repeated throughout the film) that we learn an awful lot about ourselves in the experience of lovemaking. This time, however, it is stated in a decidedly less romantic fashion.

Thus the notion of the perfect moment is revealed, as in *Nausea*, to be a shallow and inauthentic way to view one's life. Perfect moments are worthless fantasies, used in a doomed attempt to create meaning for one's life by ignoring the roles

---

[15] *A Midsummer Night's Sex Comedy.*

necessarily played by freedom, responsibility, and the unceasing passage of time.

A Second Perfect Moment

The point that viewing our lives in this romantic way is inauthentic is reiterated by the revelation that there was a second perfect moment of which Andrew was unaware, namely the moment between Maxwell and Adrian the summer before. This second momentary impulse functions as a kind of negative twin to the first, especially when it is revealed as the source of the Hobbeses' marital problems. In this way, it becomes clear that Andrew and Ariel were wrong to regret their failure to act. While they were correct in thinking that acting on impulse would have changed their lives, they were wrong to assume that such change would necessarily have been for the better.

As Dr. Maxwell Jordan, Tony Roberts plays a character very much like his role of best friend in so many of Allen's earlier films. Like his characters in the films *Play It Again Sam, Annie Hall,* and *Stardust Memories,* Maxwell initially seems to epitomize the superficial lifestyle of the hedonist, a man who lives to seize the moment, to make the most of the pleasures at hand. He repeatedly justifies this attitude by referring to the horrors of illness and death which, as a doctor, he confronts on a regular basis. Given the end to which all life comes, he argues, isn't it best to make the most of time we have? These views also echo Alvy's contention in *Annie Hall* that life can be divided into the horrible and the merely miserable. If one is lucky enough to be just miserable, then one should make the best of it. It is no accident that Roberts's character is named Max, the nickname Rob and Alvy used for one another in *Annie Hall*.

When we first see Maxwell, he is making love to one of his patients in his examining room as she tells him that her husband is getting suspicious. When she declines his invitation to join him for the weekend at Andrew's, we see him walk behind a wall with a chart displaying human anatomy. This chart is reminiscent of the skeleton in the climactic scene of *Manhattan,* and its presence seems to connect Maxwell with the character Yale (Michael Murphy) in their common selfishness and lack of moral values, a similarity to which we will later return.[16]

Maxwell issues the same invitation for the weekend to Dulcy, his new nurse. When he begins his usual seduction lines, telling her that she must have noticed his interest over the past few weeks, she points out that she has only been working there for five days. Despite his transparent inauthenticity, Dulcy quickly agrees to join him and demonstrates her "modern," clinical attitude towards sex by telling him that separate rooms will not be necessary.

However, when Maxwell meets Ariel, it is love at first sight. They recognize each other's perfume and cologne, a coincidence which Maxwell compares to animals recognizing each other's scent. From that point, Maxwell is transformed into the romantic hero, a man willing to sacrifice everything, including his life, to convince a woman of his love. He fakes his own poisoning with a mushroom in order to steal a kiss, a kiss which Leopold manages to see through a telescope. Later Maxwell grazes his temple in an apparent suicide attempt, and, finally, when he is accidentally wounded by Leopold with an arrow (actually meant for Andrew), he reveals his own perfect moment with Adrian.

In fact, Maxwell tells Andrew, the images of the romantic couple displayed by the spirit ball, which Andrew took to be of himself and Ariel, were really a recreation of the scene between Maxwell and Adrian. When Andrew demands to know how he could deceive his best friend in such a way, Maxwell argues that he had no choice because, once again, the moment was so perfect that he just couldn't let it pass.

When Andrew responds by putting a gun to his head, Adrian discovers him and learns that her secret has been revealed. Rather than being dismayed by the revelation that she is as pleasure-seeking and deceitful as everyone else in the film, she says that she feels a great weight has been lifted from her shoulders. Throughout the film, as we have noted, she has been trying to resolve her sexual problems with Andrew, problems which threaten to destroy their marriage.

---

[16] In *Manhattan* (1979), Yale is unfaithful to his wife and betrays his best friend.

On Andrew's suggestion, she has consulted Dulcy for advice, on the theory that, as a modern woman and a practical nurse, Dulcy would understand all the mechanics required to satisfy a man sexually (as though romance could be reduced to its merely physical elements). Dulcy has told Adrian to try to create a perfect moment of her own by spontaneously initiating sex in unconventional places around the house. Adrian's first attempt to follow this advice, in the kitchen as she and Andrew cleaned up after dinner, was a complete disaster because Adrian was unable to overcome her self-consciousness. We had assumed at the time that Adrian's problems emanated from an overly developed sense of modesty or, perhaps, an unconscious realization of Andrew's obsession with his memories of Ariel. When it is revealed that her problems result from her guilt over her fling with Maxwell, we learn the ironic truth, that she is better equipped than Ariel to engage in successful and spontaneous sexual relations with Andrew.

After their lovemaking, we see them coming out of the barn with Andrew still reeling from an experience he describes as "religious." Adrian promises him that this is just the beginning of her penance, and says she can't wait to show him something Dulcy called a "Mexican Cartwheel." He drools in anticipation, saying that it sounds "incredibly filthy." When Adrian asks if he forgives her, he answers, "Forgive you, I could ordain you! You cleared my sinuses for the whole summer."[17] Sensuality has erased all remnants of their deceptions and moral missteps. They can now rebuild their marriage on the only foundation this film offers: pure, hedonistic self-interest. One wonders how long such a relationship will last, although to these characters, it is the intensity of the pleasure which matters, not its duration.

As a result of her botched effort to regain lost love, and Maxwell's melodramatic posings, Ariel is convinced that it was not the theory of the perfect moment which failed her so much as it was the attempt to overcome the passage of time. Perfect moments can still exist, Maxwell argues, so long as one takes advantage of them as they appear. To Ariel's claim that she is a frivolous person who can never decide what she wants, Maxwell replies that she simply made a mistake in pursuing

---

[17] *A Midsummer Night's Sex Comedy.*

Andrew. He tells her, "Andrew was a dream out of the past somewhere. I, however, am the man of the moment! We are going to seize this moment and keep it forever!"[18] While we have no doubts about Maxwell's belief in his own sincerity, we are not convinced that their love is any more than a passing fancy that might dissipate altogether when they leave the enchanted woods for a more mundane setting.

Primitive Passions

Leopold was initially introduced as an arrogant, supercilious exponent of the views of logical positivism who denied the importance and appeal of all that can't be reduced to scientific data. Leopold shows his colleagues pictures of Ariel as though she were a prize he has received in recognition for his work. He plans to take her on a honeymoon trip around the continent, where he can continue to explain Europe's glories both to her and to the inhabitants.

Yet once he arrives at the Hobbeses', Leopold is seduced and overpowered by his own primitive passions. He is consumed by jealousy over Ariel; yet, simultaneously, he is powerfully drawn to the physical attractions of the confident and sexually open Dulcy. For her part, although Dulcy claims to be surprised by men's expression of sexual interest in her (as do all the women in the film), she is always willing and always prepared (she tells Maxwell that she brought contraceptives in case he forgot).

When Leopold reveals his desire to celebrate his last night of bachelorhood by making love with her, Dulcy is flattered and says that it should be "an interesting experience." Leopold is so smitten that he loses to her in chess, a game he is teaching her at the time. He tries to seduce her with the uniqueness of the offer he is making by asking if she has ever made love to a much older man. When she replies in the affirmative, he asks her if she has ever made love to a much older man outdoors and is stymied when she again says yes. In a final attempt to offer her something unusual, he asks if the man was a genius (like himself), to which she replies, "He was a dentist."

---

[18] *Ibid.*

Not only the perfect comedic couple—almost a Burns and Allen—Leopold and Dulcy share other qualities. Both have rejected all moral theories in order to focus their energies, both professionally and personally, on that which can be empirically verified. Despite the supposed dichotomy between Leopold's intellectualism and Dulcy's sensuality, Leopold's philosophical views are in fact, as we have seen, completely compatible with theories of hedonism. Leopold confirms this point when he reveals that he has written a book on pragmatism. Thus it comes as no real surprise when Leopold reveals his erotic dreams to Dulcy:

> LEOPOLD: I was taken with a great erotic fervor. All the terrible thoughts of my whole life that I've been afraid to unleash poured forth.
> DULCY: How did I react?
> LEOPOLD: As we pressed lips, the scene changed. We were two savages in the wilderness. It was a prehistoric era and I was a Neanderthal, hunting my enemies with primitive weapons and loving you uninhibitedly.[19]

When Leopold returns from chasing Andrew and Maxwell with his bow and arrow, dressed only in a sheet, he bounds into the house and announces to Dulcy that he is back from the hunt, as he pounces on her to ravish her like a mythological god in a Dionysian dream. It is there, in the throes of passion, that Leopold dies. When all the characters assemble in response to Dulcy's yell, she tells them:

> We were making love. He was like an animal, he tore off my robe. He was wonderful. We did it all, violently like two savages and he was screaming with pleasure. At the highest moment of ecstasy, he just keeled over with that smile on his face.[20]

As Maxwell comforts Ariel, the spirit ball takes life. A glowing presence flies out of the ball as they hear Leopold's voice explaining:

---

[19] *Ibid.*
[20] *Ibid.*

Don't feel sorry for me, Maxwell. My soul has merely passed over
into another dimension. I feel myself floating, liberated. I am at
long last pure essence . . . I am most delighted to say that Andrew
and Adrian were right. These woods are enchanted, filled with the
spirits of the lucky men and women of passion who have passed
away at the height of lovemaking. Promise me, all of you, to look
for my glowing presence on starlit evenings, in these woods, under
the summer moon, forever.[21]

The characters follow the glowing light outside to see the woods
lit up with other such spirits as the music swells and the film
ends.

The Dangers of Hedonism

Thus Leopold, the deepest thinker among them and in a sense
their intellectual leader, finds a way to achieve their goal, the
creation of the perfect moment. We now have the answers to all
of the characters' questions. In this film, lust and love are sepa-
rable and lust is the more important, for in the most primitive
throes of animalistic passion there is the possibility of an experience so exhilarating that one is transformed into "pure
essence, living forever in the joy of that moment." This philosophy is, of course, not a scientific breakthrough, but a return to
a very old theology, the religion of paganism, with its worship
of hooved gods and the pleasures of the senses. From this belief
system spring Judeo-Christian notions of a hooved and horned
creature named Satan who tempts mortals to give up all hope
for moral and spiritual redemption in exchange for the supreme
satisfaction of the senses and a promise of eternal life.

In drawing out the logical implications of the philosophical
and cultural values expressed by the characters in this film,
Allen demonstrates, yet again, the shallowness of contemporary
society. By showing us the origins of these views, Allen hopes
both to educate and to warn us.

For, as Allen has been preaching since *Annie Hall*, it is the
deterioration of our sense of moral and religious responsibility,
coupled with an ever-growing acceptance of an ethos of hedonism, which is making modern life less and less meaningful, and

---

[21] *Ibid.*

is creating a crisis of conscience which, he believes, will be as least as devastating in its consequences as any war. Earlier, it was noted that the chart displaying human anatomy in Maxwell's office is reminiscent of the skeleton in the denouement of *Manhattan*. Indeed, *Sex Comedy* reiterates the warning given by Allen's character Isaac Davis in *Manhattan*. Standing in front of a skeleton of an ancient man, Isaac argues for our fundamental duty to preserve moral standards for the generations that follow:

> What are future generations going to say about us? My God, you know someday we are going to be like him. You know, I mean, he was probably one of the beautiful people. He was probably dancing and playing tennis and everything! And now! This is what happens to us! You know, it's very important to have some kind of personal integrity. I'll be hanging in a classroom one day and I want to make sure that when I thin out that I'm well thought of.[22]

No similar condemnation of hedonism is given in *Sex Comedy* because there is no character qualified to give it. Where *Manhattan* chronicled the moral evolution of Isaac Davis, the characters in *Sex Comedy* end the film even more committed to hedonism than they were at the beginning. In his portrayal of their philosophical vacuity and hedonistic excesses, Allen emphasizes his rejection of such approaches and his ongoing search for a philosophical system that values a commitment to ethical standards and personal responsibility in the face of the challenges presented by relativistic schools of thought such as those professed by the characters in the film.[23]

---

[22] *Manhattan*.
[23] This essay is a modified version of a chapter that appeared in *Woody Allen's Angst*, © Sander Lee, by permission of McFarland and Company, Inc., Box 611, Jefferson, NC 28640. Sander Lee is also the author of *Eighteen Woody Allen Films Analyzed* (Jefferson: McFarland, 2002).

12

Inauthenticity and Personal Identity in *Zelig*

DAVID DETMER

Woody Allen's *Zelig* presents, in mock documentary style, a fictitious "chameleon man" character from the jazz age—a man who seems to have no personality of his own, but who rather takes on the characteristics of the people around him. Allen takes the idea to ludicrous, but hilarious, extremes. It's not just that Zelig is shy around shy people, gregarious around gregarious people, and pretends to be a doctor around doctors or a musician when around musicians. No, Zelig also becomes black when around blacks, Chinese when around Chinese people, fat when around fat people, and a Nazi when surrounded by Nazis!

In addition to succeeding as a funny and entertaining film, *Zelig* also provocatively explores three fundamental philosophical issues. One is the age-old problem of personal identity. Quite simply, given all of the ways (some of them quite dramatic) in which I am different from the person I was twenty, thirty, and forty years ago, in what sense can it be said that I am the same person as that young man, teenager, and toddler? In *what*, precisely, does my unique identity (if, indeed, I have one) consist? The character of Zelig, since he changes more radically and more frequently than I do, simply raises this question more starkly.

Another philosophical issue of the film is a critique of inauthenticity, similar to that found in the writings of such existentialist philosophers as Kierkegaard, Heidegger, and Sartre. What these philosophers criticize is the tendency to go along passively with the crowd, to do what others do, to believe what others believe, uncritically, rather than thinking for oneself and acting accordingly. There is the suggestion that those who live this way fail to live their own lives, but rather eventually die having lived the lives only of "the others" or of "the crowd."

Finally, Allen's depiction of Zelig as becoming a Nazi when surrounded by Nazis graphically raises the moral and political (as opposed to the existential) criticism of inauthenticity. The point here is that genocidal campaigns do not happen because thousands go mad; rather, they happen because millions will passively and obediently do the bidding of the few who are mad (or perhaps merely venal). One reason why they do so is that they want to fit in, and to escape from the burdens of independent thought and action.

In this chapter I will attempt to explore and develop these philosophical issues, and to point out a few of the ways in which *Zelig* sheds light on them. In doing so my aim is both to introduce these important issues to those who might be unfamiliar with them (and hopefully to say something of interest about them to those who need no introduction) and to make a small contribution to the appreciation and interpretation of Woody Allen's fine film.

Zelig

Let's begin by taking a closer look at the film. The plot is fairly straightforward.[1] It tells the story of Leonard Zelig (played by Woody Allen), a man with the bizarre ability to transform himself into whomever might be near him at any given time. Indeed, during the course of the film we see Zelig as a wealthy Republican Bostonian, a left-winger who prefers to hang out with the kitchen staff, a gangster, a black jazz musician, a baseball player, a psychiatrist, a Hassidic rabbi, a fat man, a Chinese man, a Greek, a boxer, a rabbi, a Frenchman, a bearded, kilted Scot, an opera singer, an American Indian, a surgeon performing an appendectomy, an Irishman, and a Mexican guitarist,

---

[1] Allen's screenplay for *Zelig* is available in *Three Films of Woody Allen* (New York: Vintage, 1987), pp. 1–141. Subsequent quotations from the film will be drawn from this source, with page numbers indicated in parentheses.

among others. This ability eventually comes to the attention of the public, and Zelig, "the chameleon man," becomes a major popular cultural phenomenon of the 1920s. He receives treatment from a psychiatrist, Eudora Fletcher (played by Mia Farrow). At first her efforts are frustrated by Zelig's tendency, when in her presence, to take on the persona of a psychiatrist. But she begins to make a breakthrough when she hits upon the clever scheme of "confessing" to Zelig that she is not a psychiatrist, but merely pretends to be one. Though her therapy is interrupted by an episode in which Zelig's half-sister kidnaps him and exploits him as a sideshow freak, eventually she cures him and they fall in love. They plan to marry, but a problem quickly emerges: it is revealed that Zelig, in his various guises, has already married several women. Consequently, he is sued, not only for bigamy and adultery, but also, as his various personalities have been quite busy, for "automobile accidents, plagiarism, household damages, negligence, property damages, and performing unnecessary dental extractions" (p. 107). The fickle public, which had celebrated Zelig as a hero, turns on him. He suffers a relapse and flees. Eudora frantically and persistently searches for him and finally finds him onstage with Hitler at a gigantic Nazi rally. Since Eudora is a pilot, they try to make their escape from the Nazis by plane. She panics, but Zelig's illness saves the day—he turns into a pilot and flies successfully, albeit upside-down, across the Atlantic. The fickle public once again embraces Zelig as a hero. He and Eudora are finally able to marry. All of his symptoms disappear, and they live happily ever after.

One noteworthy feature of the film is that Zelig's story is told in documentary fashion, with vintage newsreels, new footage (in grainy black and white so as to look like vintage newsreels), old photographs, new photographs made to look like old ones, old recordings, new ones (scratchy and full of static, so as to sound old), interviews with such modern-day intellectuals as Susan Sontag, Irving Howe, Saul Bellow, and Bruno Bettelheim (all of whom play themselves and provide analysis and historical perspective), and extensive narration. The faked film footage, photographs, and recordings are spectacularly successful. Allen's Zelig character is repeatedly and seamlessly integrated into images of figures of the period. He is seen with Hitler, Pope Pius XI, Eugene O'Neill, F. Scott Fitzgerald, Charlie

Chaplin, Calvin Coolidge, Herbert Hoover, Josephine Baker, James Cagney, William Randolph Hearst, Babe Ruth, Jack Dempsey, and Lou Gehrig, among others. This is so well done that only the presence of Allen, Farrow, or other members of the cast enables the viewer to discern that a given photograph or film clip is actually of recent vintage.[2] And Allen is careful never to spoil the illusion that we are watching a documentary about a real historical figure. Much of the story is told by means of narration over still photographs, together with the recently filmed musings of the surviving principals and of the contemporary intellectuals. The "old" film footage is only such as might actually exist had Zelig really been a historical figure—public scenes of Zelig after he had become a celebrity, and private therapy sessions, which Eudora had filmed so as to make a record of the case for future generations.

But it is important to realize that the documentary format and the technical razzle-dazzle required to pull it off convincingly are not offered as ends in themselves. Rather, the style is put to the service of ideas, for the ideas presented in this film are what interest Allen the most. "That's why I wanted to use the documentary form," he explains. "One doesn't want to see this character's private life; one's interested in the phenomenon and how it relates to the culture. Otherwise it would just be the pathetic story of a neurotic."[3] But this point is usually missed, according to Allen: "[T]he content of the film has not even to this day been evaluated properly in the United States, because everyone was so focused on the technical aspects; that was what they talked about all the time. All the nice things they said about the film were in reference to the technique. To me, the technique was

---

[2] Allen explains some of the technical means by which these effects were achieved: "We got old lenses from the 1920s, old cameras and old sound equipment. We tried to get all of that kind of stuff that still existed. And we filmed it in exactly the kind of lighting they would have had at the time. We made flicker-mattes, so that our film would have flickering light like the old films. And we put scratches in the negative... There were also a few trick shots, where I was put into old pictures... [I]t was technically difficult. But Gordon Willis [director of photography] is a genius . . . (*Woody Allen on Woody Allen* [in conversation with Stig Björkman] [New York: Grove Press, 1993], p. 137).

[3] Allen, quoted in Julian Fox, *Woody: Movies from Manhattan* (Woodstock: Overlook Press, 1996), p. 141.

fine. I mean, it was fun to do, and it was a small accomplishment, but it was the content of the film that interested me."[4] So as not to repeat that mistake, let's turn now to the content, or, if you will, the ideas, of *Zelig*.

The Problem of Personal Identity

Philosophers have long been concerned with the question of what it is that constitutes an individual person's unique identity. Suppose I run into a person who claims to be a long lost friend, one I haven't seen for thirty years. Obviously the person will in many ways appear to be different from the one I once knew and now remember. So on what basis do I decide whether or not he or she really is my old friend? After all, people undergo changes all the time, and yet we don't suppose that in doing so they perpetually pass out of existence so as to allow a new person to take their place. Rather, we tend to assume that each person has a unique something—a soul, a personality, an essential feature or set of features—that endures through these changes, preserving his or her identity.

But what is this enduring something? No answer thus far proposed has proved satisfactory, and so the problem is still with us. One classic theory, for example, holds that memory is the criterion of personal identity.[5] On this theory I am the same person today that I was as a child, teenager, and young adult, because I remember many of my experiences from these earlier periods of my life. While this seems plausible enough at first, and perhaps does capture part of the truth of the matter, it faces obvious difficulties. Memory is notoriously unreliable. Most of my past experiences are now hopelessly beyond my powers of recollection. What is worse, some of what I "remember" never happened. It is tempting to try to get around this by ruling out false memories and counting as the criterion of personal identity only the accurate recollections. But this is to argue in a circle. My memories were supposed to serve as the criterion by

---

[4] *Woody Allen on Woody Allen*, p. 141. On this point see also Eric Lax, *Woody Allen: A Biography* (New York: Knopf, 1991), p. 276.
[5] The classic statement of this theory is to be found in John Locke, *An Essay Concerning Human Understanding*, Book II, Chapter 27. This chapter is included in *The Empiricists* (Garden City: Anchor, 1974), pp. 62–75.

which *I* would be identified; but now it looks as though I have to know who *I* am (which experiences were genuinely mine) before I can tell which of my "memories" are properly to be counted as such. Besides, if I were to suffer some horrible injury which wiped out my memories, but otherwise left my personality and temperament very much as it is, it is unclear that I would not still be me. And if an artificial being could be constructed, and programmed so as to have all of my memories (and no one else's), it seems clear that this artificial being would *not* be me.

So much for the memory theory. Another classic theory holds that bodily continuity is the criterion of personal identity. On this view I am the same person that I was as a child because, although my body has changed since then, the changes have been gradual and continuous. It must be conceded that, as a practical matter, we do primarily identify people by their bodies. And yet, as numerous science-fiction stories have firmly established, it is not at all difficult to imagine cases of bodily transfer—that is, instances in which a person comes to exist in a different body than he or she had inhabited previously. To be sure, we are here dealing with the world of fiction, not fact. Nonetheless, the very fact that we find these fictional cases coherent suggests that bodily continuity, while usually a reliable indicator of personal identity in our world, does not constitute its essence. After all, a dead body has often changed only gradually and continuously from a living one, and yet we are not the least tempted to describe a dead body as a "person" at all, let alone as the same person as the one who was just alive. We say, instead, that the unique person in question is "gone," or has "passed" or "expired." The body alone, it would seem, is therefore insufficient for personhood.

Such considerations have led some thinkers to propose that what makes a person a unique individual is his or her distinctive immaterial substance, or soul.[6] This, it is supposed, endures throughout the body's many physical changes and may even survive the body's death. Such a conception appears to be inconsistent with a modern scientific worldview, for at least three interrelated reasons.

---

[6] The classic statement of this theory is to be found in René Descartes, *Meditations on First Philosophy* (Indianapolis: Hackett, 1979). See especially Meditation Two, pp. 17–23.

First, science tends to favor naturalistic and physical explanations over supernatural and non-physical ones. Thus, those favoring a modern scientific outlook are likely, rightly or wrongly, to regard the postulation of an immaterial soul, and the invocation of it as an explanation of personal identity, as suspiciously as they would the postulation and invocation of demon possession as an explanation for epileptic seizures.

Secondly, insofar as a person's mind (and/or personality) is usually thought to be identical to, or perhaps merely an outward expression or manifestation of, his or her immaterial soul, there is reason to doubt the latter's independence of the body. For we know that damage to the brain damages the mind and personality as well, and that destruction of the brain, if the evidence of our experience is to be believed, destroys the mind and personality. That the soul might instead detach itself from the body and continue to live without it, while supported by religious and cultural traditions, therefore seems highly unlikely from a scientific standpoint.

Finally, in contrast to a scientific theory, it seems to be in principle impossible empirically to verify or to falsify the hypothesis that immaterial souls exist, or that persons are individuated by them. This last objection is the most important one, since it should trouble even those who are not concerned to uphold a modern scientific worldview. For the unverifiable and unfalsifiable nature of the soul hypothesis appears to render it useless for practical purposes. That is, it can never be used in any practical situation in which we need to determine the identity of a specific person, or to distinguish him or her from others. To see this, consider the issue of criminal punishment.

Suppose we have clear proof that Joe Smith has committed a murder. But now we need to know whether or not the man standing before us in court is this same Joe Smith. If bodily continuity will do the trick, we have no problem, as we can consult fingerprints, DNA, and other physical markers to establish a match. But if Joe Smith is to be identified by his immaterial soul, we are out of luck. Similarly, you might be able to identify a long lost friend by recognizing his or her body (the face, most likely), or by using the test of memory (e.g. can the person accurately answer questions about past experiences the two of you shared that only your friend would be likely to know?). But you won't be able to identify your friend by examining his or her immaterial soul.

Existentialism

An alternative approach to these issues can be found in the works of such existentialist philosophers as Kierkegaard, Nietzsche, Heidegger, and Sartre, and it seems that Allen's approach in *Zelig* is also to be located within this existentialist tradition.[7]

While the existentialists have written little directly on the problem of personal identity, they have made it clear in their writings on other subjects that they reject the notion that a human being is a substantial subject—the view that there is some permanent thing, some essence, in us that constitutes and individuates us. Thus, on the existentialist view, what makes me me is not my body, my soul, my memory, or anything of that sort, but rather my choices, projects, values, and commitments— what I stand for, what I am about. Such also seems to be the point of view expressed in *Zelig*. For example, after Zelig has been cured of his affliction, the narrator in the film comments: "Zelig, no longer a chameleon, is at last his own man. His point of view on politics, art, life, and love is honest and direct.

---

[7] Even aside from the doctrinal content of his films, there is ample evidence of Allen's familiarity with, and sympathy for, the existentialist tradition. First, several of Allen's comic essays contain satirical treatments of existentialist philosophy and literature. For example, "My Philosophy" makes gentle fun of Kierkegaard, and "Notes from the Overfed" performs the same service for Dostoyevsky's *Notes from Underground*. (Both essays are to be found in Allen's *Getting Even* [New York: Vintage, 1971].) Secondly, in a 1994 interview, Allen offers brief, and largely positive, remarks on the philosophies of Sartre, Heidegger, Buber, Nietzsche, and Kierkegaard ("Appendix: Questions and Answers with Woody Allen," in Sander H. Lee, *Eighteen Woody Allen Films Analyzed* [Jefferson: McFarland, 2002], p. 223). Moreover, as Lee points out (p. 11), at the beginning of Allen's film *Husbands and Wives* the character played by Mia Farrow is shown holding a book with Sartre's name clearly visible on the cover. Indeed, biographer Lax informs us that Allen "has been particularly drawn to" Sartre's writings "since an early age" (p. 351). It is not surprising then, that a collection drawn from the short-lived *Inside Woody Allen* comic strip (written by Allen) was entitled *Non-Being and Something-Ness* (New York: Random House, 1978), an obvious spoof of Sartre's monumental *Being and Nothingness*.

Though his taste is described by many as lowbrow, it is his own. He is finally an individual—a human being. He no longer gives up his own identity to be a safe and invisible part of his surroundings" (p. 96).

To be sure, this may not solve the problem of personal identity. For example, if I commit a crime today, it is not clear that I could escape responsibility for it by becoming a different person tomorrow, even if I (quite genuinely and sincerely) were suddenly to convert to a radically different "point of view on politics, art, life, and love."

However, consider the following three points.[8]

(1) The existentialist view seems to be that the quest for a criterion of personal identity is misguided. If a person changes radically, it is up to us to decide how to describe her. If we are more impressed by the ways in which she remains the same, we are more likely to consider her to be the same person after the changes. If we are more impressed by the ways in which she has changed, we are more likely to think of her as a different person. There is no truth of the matter, in the sense of there being a deep fact about the nature of the self waiting to be discovered. It should be emphasized, however, that such a stance need not entail that the issue is an arbitrary or subjective one, if by that we mean that we can make no mistake, or that one decision would be as good or wise as another. Rather, on this view it is still possible to be simply mistaken (when, for example, one erroneously thinks that a person has changed in some respect when in fact she has not, or when one misestimates the extent of a particular change), and there may well be better reasons, all things considered, for resolving the issue one way rather than another, even when no such mistake has been made.

(2) The existentialists distinguish between a strict, formal sense, on the one hand, and a more momentous, "existentialist" sense, on the other, in which a person is identical with himself. Thus, according to Heidegger, "The *Dasein* [Heidegger's technical term which, for our purposes, approximates to "human being"] is not only... identical with itself in a formal-ontological sense—everything is identical with itself— . . . Instead, the

---

[8] I am very much indebted in my discussion of these three points to David E. Cooper's *Existentialism*, Second Edition (Malden: Blackwell, 1999), pp. 98–101.

Dasein has a peculiar selfsameness with itself in the sense of selfhood. It is in such a way that it is in a certain way *its own*, it *has itself*, and only on that account can it *lose* itself."[9] Thus, a person can remain the same person in a "formal-ontological" sense (the sense in which the pen I'm now holding in my hand is the same thing as itself, since everything is identical with itself), even as he "loses" himself in the sense of selfhood (for example, by becoming estranged from his fundamental projects, values, and commitments, perhaps because of a desire to conform with "the crowd").

> this is the sense at issue in self-reflection, self-understanding, self-integrity, self-constancy, self-creation, and a host of other hyphenated notions, including self-estrangement. Someone seeking to understand himself is hardly concerned with the criteria by which he is 'strictly' the same self as the one he was on the day of his birth. The man who ponders if he is the same person as of yesteryear is not asking if his body is spatio-temporally continuous with the old one. . . . The person . . . who wonders if he has 'lost himself' is not puzzling over whether the law of identity has been suspended.[10]

(3) But still, one might wonder: Just what is this "self" which one might understand, create, or lose, or from which one is in danger of becoming estranged? The existentialists reply that we must not allow language to confuse us into thinking that such expressions as self-understanding or self-estrangement require analysis in terms of the self. After all, it is clear that a "self-monitoring computer is not one with a self that it monitors," and that "when my dog scratches itself, it is not its self which itches."[11] Thus it seems possible that "self" has no independent meaning, but rather derives its meaning from phrases such as self-understanding and self-estrangement that are, on this account, logically more primitive. As Heidegger puts it, "When we say that . . . *Dasein* understands itself, its own self . . . we must not rest this on some fabricated concept of soul, person,

---

[9] Martin Heidegger, *The Basic Problems of Phenomenology* (Bloomington: Indiana University Press, 1982), p. 170.
[10] Cooper, p. 100.
[11] Cooper, p. 100.

or ego but must see in what self-understanding the factical *Dasein* moves in its everyday existence."[12]

Inauthenticity

In the case of *Zelig*, it would appear that the most relevant logically primitive phrase would be "self-estrangement," for Zelig, prior to his recovery, was as self-estranged as a person can get. The reason, from an existentialist point of view, is that he was leading an "inauthentic" life. A thread running through almost all existentialist writings is a critique of the modern tendency to drift through life passively, adopting uncritically the values, attitudes, and behaviors of others—of the "masses" or the "herd"— as opposed to carefully carving out one's own projects, values, and commitments, based on one's own experience, thinking, creativity, interests, and talents.[13] This tendency is perfectly exemplified, of course, by the character of Zelig.

But why would anyone choose to live such a life? Zelig, under hypnosis, explains that he wanted to be like the others because "it's safe," and "I want to be liked" (p. 32). Later, still under hypnosis, he tells us that the first time he pretended to be like those around him was in school when "some very bright people" asked him if he had read *Moby-Dick*, and he "was ashamed to say I never read it" (p. 40).[14]

It's easy to ridicule and condemn such insincere conformity as cowardice, and, indeed, the existentialists do condemn it

---

[12] Heidegger, p. 160.

[13] While there are many differences of emphasis and omission, and a few disagreements on details, such a critique in essence can be found in each of the following works, among others: Søren Kierkegaard, *The Present Age* (New York: Harper and Row, 1962); Friedrich Nietzsche, *The Will to Power* (New York: Random House, 1968), especially sections 287, 361; Gabriel Marcel, *Man Against Mass Society* (Chicago: Regnery, 1962); José Ortega y Gasset, *The Revolt of the Masses* (New York: Norton, 1994); Heidegger, *Being and Time* (New York: Harper and Row, 1962), especially Division One, Chapter Four; and Jean-Paul Sartre, *Being and Nothingness* (New York: Washington Square Press, 1992), especially Part One, Chapter Two.

[14] In a nice touch at the end of the film Allen recalls this scene by having the narrator inform us that Zelig (who had been cured for some time) told his doctors on his deathbed that "he had had a good life and the only annoying thing about dying was that he had just begun reading *Moby-Dick* and wanted to see how it came out" (p. 129).

harshly. It is clear (as we will see) that Allen too rejects it, just as the character Zelig eventually comes around to doing, but Allen nonetheless offers a more sympathetic account of the inauthentic person's motivation than do any of the existentialist philosophers. He does this, primarily, by reminding us that Zelig is right to be concerned about his safety. It truly can be dangerous to be disliked and to be "different" from those around oneself. It is easy to miss this point in the film, since Allen chooses always to present this painful point in a humorous fashion. For example, we learn that the family life in which Zelig grew up was "marked by constant violent quarreling, so much so that although the family lives over a bowling alley, it is the bowling alley that complains of noise" (pp. 19–20). Even worse, Zelig tells us (in a trancelike voice, while under hypnosis) that "[m]y brother beat me. . . . My sister beat my brother. . . . My father beat my sister and my brother and me. . . . My mother beat my father and my sister and me and my brother. . . . The neighbors beat our family. . . . People down the block beat the neighbors and our family. . . ." (p. 77). It is easy to see how a person constantly exposed to such an environment would desperately want to blend in with others, to be invisible (like a chameleon), to be liked, and to be safe. In the same vein, we learn that "[a]s a boy, Leonard is frequently bullied by anti-Semites. His parents, who never take his part and blame him for everything, side with the anti-Semites" (p. 20). Thus, Zelig, who is bullied for being different (Jewish) would of course be motivated to try not to be different.[15] (The strategy backfires, however, for we learn that "[t]o the Ku Klux Klan, Zelig, a Jew who was able to transform himself into a Negro or Indian, was a triple threat" [p. 39].)

While it is understandable that many people would find the inauthentic life attractive, I think it is clear that the existentialists and Allen are right to reject it. They offer at least seven good reasons for doing so:

(1) Because the inauthentic person, like Zelig, tries to be all things to all people, his or her life is condemned to incoherence. Such a life is necessarily scattershot and lacking in direction.

---

[15] For a consideration of anti-Semitism from the standpoint of an existentialist analysis of inauthenticity, see Sartre, *Anti-Semite and Jew* (New York: Schocken, 1974), and Sartre, "The Childhood of a Leader," in his *The Wall and Other Stories* (New York: New Directions, 1948).

(2) Whereas when one chooses his or her projects, values, and commitments carefully and critically, they take on a certain weight and seriousness, leading to a life of intensity and purpose, the uncritical and passive acceptance of the values of those around oneself tends to make those values appear to be trivial.

(3) Such conformity, since it opposes whatever is excellent or distinctive, leads to a leveling and flattening quality of life.

(4) The project of uncritically adopting the views and attitudes of others allows little outlet for personal creativity.

(5) Whereas young children, at least for a time, must accept uncritically the judgments of their parents, a big part of the process of maturing and becoming an independent person has to do with learning to think for oneself. Indeed, as we have seen, the existentialists hold that the self, in its most momentous sense, has to do primarily with one's distinctive and unique choices, projects, values, and commitments. Thus, the inauthentic person "loses" himself or herself in the anonymity of the crowd, and fails to become a mature, independent person.

(6) Inauthenticity renders satisfying interpersonal relationships difficult, if not impossible, to attain. The reason is that it is hard to love, or even to like, someone who is inconsistent and stands for nothing. There can be a rather shallow and tepid getting along with others on this basis (not a thing to be taken lightly, if the alternative is being beaten up or worse), but not much more. Moreover, when Zelig-like characters do manage to get someone else to care for them, surely they must realize that there is something illusory about it. They are not loved for themselves, for there is no self (in the most momentous sense) there to love, but rather only an act, an imitation of others. How can this be satisfactory? Clearly it is better to be loved, liked, and respected for oneself, and by a few others whom one also loves, likes, and respects, than it is to present a false and perpetually shifting image to the masses so as to win the bland approval of everyone indiscriminately. (Indeed, as the narrator in *Zelig* informs us, "[i]n the end, it was, after all, not the approbation of many but the love of one woman that changed his life" [p. 129].)

(7) Finally, the beliefs of the inauthentic person are not justified. He or she simply accepts the opinions of others uncritically, without even bothering to inquire into their justification.

This is enormously dangerous from a moral and political point of view. Indeed, I think Allen's main point in *Zelig* is to point out these dangers. Let's now turn to them.

Inauthenticity and Fascism

How do holocausts happen? How is it that the great numbers of people who must lend their cooperation to a genocidal campaign in order for it to succeed are persuaded to do so? It is not difficult to understand that a few people might be lunatic, or evil, enough to wish to lead us down the path of barbarism. But it is hard to see why, when they do, so many are ready, passively and obediently, to follow.

Zelig sheds a good deal of light on this issue. A desire to be safe and to be liked leads people to the strategy of trying to think and act like those around them. This, in turn, requires a person not to question whether the thoughts and actions in question are really wise, or good, or in any sense justified. Rather, their justification lies in the simple fact that they are the beliefs and practices of those whom one wants to emulate. In this way one easily can, passively and uncritically, become a fascist.

Thus, it is no accident that Allen chooses to depict Zelig, prior to being rescued by Eudora, as a Nazi at a rally with Hitler. Indeed, in commenting on his film to an interviewer Allen remarked, "I thought that desire not to make waves, carried to an extreme, could have traumatic consequences. It could lead to a conformist mentality and, ultimately, fascism."[16] It would be a mistake, however, to think that Allen's point is merely of historical interest, as an explanation of the Nazi holocaust, but with little relevance to our contemporary situation. For when asked by an interviewer whether Zelig's dilemma of wanting to fit in was common at the beginning of the Nazi era, Allen replied: "I think that's eternal and universal. Many people have their integrity, but many many others lack this quality and become who they're with. If they're with people who advocate a certain opinion, they agree."[17]

---

[16] Michiko Kakutani, "How Woody Allen's *Zelig* Was Born in Anxiety and Grew into Comedy," *New York Times* (July 18th, 1983), p. 13.

[17] *Woody Allen on Woody Allen*, p. 139.

A series of brilliant experiments conducted by psychologist Solomon Asch tends to confirm Allen's claim.[18] In Asch's study, groups of six subjects were shown three lines of various lengths and asked to identify which one of them matched a fourth line in length. The correct answer was easy to discern, and individuals in the control groups did so effortlessly and accurately. But in many of the groups Asch secretly instructed all members of the group but one to select one of the incorrect lines. He also arranged it so that these confederates would speak first, and in the presence of the non-confederates, before the latter were called upon to give their opinions. Under these circumstances, in which the claims of the group conflicted with the clearest evidence of one's own experience, a substantial percentage of subjects, about one-third, went along with the group. It is easy to imagine, moreover, that the conformity rate would climb significantly higher in connection with moral or political beliefs. After all, it seems unlikely that one would face much of a social sanction merely for disagreeing with the group on such a bland and inconsequential issue as the assessment of the length of lines.

At this point it might be objected, however, that conformity need not translate to obedience. People might be willing to mouth falsehoods so as to ingratiate themselves with the crowd, but it need not follow that they would therefore be ready to visit harm on others merely because an authority figure tells them to do so.

But consider, in this regard, the famous studies carried out by Stanley Milgram.[19] Milgram informed his subjects that he was conducting an experiment on the nature of human learning. The theory to be tested by the experiment held that people learn correctly and effectively when they get punished for making a mistake. Subjects were then asked to administer electric shocks to a learner whenever he made a mistake, with the shocks become progressively more intense, to the tune of fifteen volts, with each mistake. This was to be done by moving from one switch to the next, proceeding from left to right. The switches were labeled: "Slight Shock," "Moderate Shock," "Strong Shock,"

---

[18] S.E. Asch, "Effects of Group Pressure Upon the Modification and Distortion of Judgments," in Eleanor E. Maccoby, et al., *Readings in Social Psychology*, Third Edition (New York: Holt, Rinehart, and Winston, 1958), pp. 174–183.

[19] Stanley Milgram, *Obedience to Authority* (New York: Harper and Row, 1974).

"Very Strong Shock," "Intense Shock," "Extreme Intensity Shock," and "Danger: Severe Shock." The last two switches were simply marked "XXX." The "victim" of these shocks (he was an actor who was not really receiving shocks) was kept out of sight of the subjects and instructed, at first, to give them no feedback during the experiment. Under these conditions virtually all of the subjects went all the way to the end of the board, perfectly willing to administer 450-volt "dangerous" and "severe" shocks to an anonymous victim. Then, on later trials (with different subjects), the victim issued mild protests. This effected little change. Finally, trials were conducted (again, with new subjects) in which the victim would, upon receiving a 150-volt shock (after having, at lower voltage levels, grunted, shouted at the experimenter that the shocks were becoming painful, and groaning), cry out, "Experimenter, get me out of here! I won't be in the experiment any more! I refuse to go on!" And at 180 volts: "I can't stand the pain." And at 270 volts: agonized screams. Nonetheless, even on these conditions, 26 out of 40 subjects obeyed the experimenter to the end, repeatedly punishing the victim with the most potent shock available until the experimenter finally called a halt to the proceedings.

In the light of such studies, not to mention our recent genocidal history, it is difficult to disagree with Allen's contention that

> The ultimate result of giving up one's own personality and feeling to be able to blend in for protective reasons, as a chameleon does with its background, is that you're perfect material to be led by fascist persuasive powers. And that's exactly what they counted on. . . . I wanted to make a comment with the film on the specific danger of abandoning one's own true self, in an effort to be liked, not to make trouble, to fit in, and where that leads one in life in every aspect and where that leads on a political level. It leads to utter conformity and utter submission to the will and requirements and needs of a strong personality.[20]

It is therefore vitally important, as the existentialists and Allen argue,[21] to choose authenticity over conformity, integrity over

---

[20] *Woody Allen on Woody Allen*, p. 141.

[21] Needless to say, the existentialists, unfortunately, did not always follow their own advice. The most notorious example is that of Heidegger's Nazism; for

popularity, even though the personal price to be paid for doing so is sometimes high. For, as Zelig himself puts it, "[y]ou have to be your own person…and make your own moral choices even when they require real coverage. Otherwise . . . you're like a robot, or a lizard" (p. 83).

the only way to avoid concluding that he was just going along with the crowd is to affirm that he was an *authentic* Nazi. And this latter possibility, in turn, illustrates that authenticity, while necessary for a good life, is by no means sufficient for it. One can be an authentic creep.

13

It's All Darkness: Plato, The Ring of Gyges, and *Crimes and Misdemeanors*

JOHN G. PAPPAS

Living well, being just, and dying courageously occupy a great deal of ancient Greek thought, especially in the dialogues of the fifth- and fourth-century B.C. philosopher Plato. In comparison, the all-too-apparent comedic-tragic absurdity of contemporary life and death obsesses the paradoxical mind of Woody Allen.

Allen's *Crimes and Misdemeanors* is a dark, comedic-dramatic story of a "regular" guy and an evil ophthalmologist, which examines questions about justice, along with related issues of wealth, prestige, power, and happiness. The film looks at the separation of the theoretical or ideal from "the real world," and contains two intertwined stories of truth and justice gone awry, one of which is comedic, the other dramatic.

In the first story, Dr. Judah Rosenthal (Martin Landau), a prominent, successful and charitable ophthalmologist with a loving family has been having a clandestine affair with a woman named Dolores Paley (Anjelica Huston). However, his wonderful reputation within his circle of wealth and prestige is being threatened by her irrational demands that he divorce his unsuspecting, loving wife and marry her. Dolores also threatens to disclose Judah's financial shenanigans. Fearful of this exposure, Judah initially seeks confidential advice from his religious friend and soon to be blind patient, Rabbi Ben (Sam Waterston). Then, when that advice—to reason with Dolores and to ask his wife for forgiveness—falls short, he slyly seeks "relief" from his notorious black sheep, gangster brother, Jack (Jerry Orbach).

In the second plot, Clifford Stern (Woody Allen), a basically good-hearted, but down on his luck filmmaker, is working on a documentary about a contemporary philosopher. Since Clifford has no income, his wife persuades her famous and successful brother (who's also brother to Rabbi Ben), Lester (Alan Alda) to hire him to make a public television documentary about Lester's life. Reluctantly, Clifford agrees. By the end of the film, however, Clifford not only blows his opportunity to ingratiate himself with Lester and further his own career, but his documentary on the philosopher, Louis Levy (Martin Bergmann), is halted due to the latter's inexplicable suicide. Adding insult to injury, his failing marriage soon ends and his "worst fear" is realized when an assistant producer with whom he has fallen in love, Halley Reed (Mia Farrow), becomes engaged to Lester.

The Issues

There are two sorts of related questions about justice that both Allen and Plato deal with. The first set concerns what *appears* to happen in life. Why is it that people wish to be unjust, or are unjust, or evil? Why is it that many of these people have power over us? Why is it that they seem to be able to get away with anything, or if caught, are able to buy or talk their way out of trouble? When unjust people take advantage of us or others— get away with their crimes, without punishment, and not just live, but live well, and seem happy—are we not puzzled and outraged by it all? Doesn't it make us pause, and reflect that the just life might not be so great after all, or that it might *not* be the happier life, especially when we suffer at the hands of the evil individual and to his benefit?

The second set of questions is a corollary to the first set: If we could "get even," obtain revenge, recover our honor, our wealth, or dignity, by unjust means, would we? If we *knew* we could get away with murder, would we be able to rationalize it? Could we, if we needed to, momentarily set aside conscience, morality, and faith in God, stoop to the level of the evil person, and recover what we have lost? Before you say "No!", think about it. Don't you sometimes wish that you possessed power, that is, the real power to overcome all your financial or personal problems? Or, say, the power to right wrongs or requite evil, and here is the key phrase—*with impunity?*

In order to provide some answers to these questions, I want to first discuss Plato's ring of Gyges story and his understanding of justice, and then see how it applies to Allen's remarkable film.

Plato's Gyges Story

In the *Republic*, the search for justice begins with an examination of what most citizens believe about living well. Using Socrates as a spokesman for the ideal good life, Plato, through the voices of his real life brothers, Glaucon and Adeimantus, reports the apparently extraordinary but popular view that injustice is to be preferred and that the unjust, evil man is really happier than the just man and better off in life. Glaucon claims that, according to the majority of citizens, first, to do injustice is *naturally* good and to suffer injustice bad, but suffering it oneself is, of course, far worse than inflicting suffering upon others. And, second, if someone lacks the power to inflict suffering, then it is in his best interest—and is more profitable to him—to come to terms with those in power neither to do injustice nor suffer it. Everyone then declares those laws and covenants that command this behavior to be lawful and just.[1]

Arguing for the popular view, Glaucon thus proposes a primitive type of social contract theory of justice, in which if I don't torment you, you don't torment me. It is a middle ground between a best and worse condition in life. The best situation, according to most people, is to practice injustice with impunity. For example, and to take a mundane case, if they could do so undetected, many people might intentionally harm a colleague's chance at getting a promotion, while deceptively making themselves look good. In a worst-case scenario, most people would think it awful to endure unjust suffering or harm without being able to seek revenge (for instance, having one's own chances at promotion undermined, without being able to get even with one's underhanded competitor).

In Glaucon's eyes, most people value justice, not as some great personal or civic virtue, but because in life, most of the time, we are too powerless to practice injustice, either surreptitiously or in the open. And—even worse—if we try our hands

---

[1] Plato, *Republic* (Indianapolis: Hackett, 1992), 359a.

at being unjust, we usually get caught and suffer even more. So we very reluctantly make contracts with others to mitigate our suffering and promote our own pleasure.

In order to make his argument about the pervasiveness and desirability of injustice, Glaucon uses the myth of the ring of Gyges. As the story goes, after a raging thunderstorm and earthquake, Gyges, a shepherd in the king's service, discovers, along with many other wonders, a hollow bronze horse bearing within it a giant, naked dead man wearing on one finger a gold ring. Removing this ring, Gyges wears it to his usual monthly meeting with his king and other shepherds. While sitting at the meeting, he happens to turn the ring inward and not only does he find himself immediately invisible to all present, but the others act as if he were not even attending the meeting! Then, turning the ring back outward, he reappears in the meeting as if he had never disappeared. Puzzled by this happenstance, he tests the ring several times and discovers that it always works. Almost at once, he seizes upon the ring's diabolical power. Using his new magic, he seduces the queen, and with her cooperation murders the king and seizes the kingdom.[2]

Now, suppose there were two such rings—one worn by a just and the other by an unjust person. What kind of behavior could we expect from each? Glaucon argues the majority's cynical position that all men are morally corruptible, including the supposedly just man. That is, even the just man would discover no advantage in being moral: he could and would steal with impunity and have sex with anyone, or release anyone from prison, "and do all the other things that would make him a god among humans."[3] In actuality, then, a just and an unjust man would be equally corruptible. Proof of this view, Glaucon believes, is that if a just man had the ring, but did not employ its all-powerful magic, most citizens aware of his situation would privately consider him stupid and miserable. Publicly,

---

[2] Many nuances can and have been read into this story, but we'll just stick to our main point of comparison with Woody Allen's film. See for example, Bernard Suzanne's very interesting discussion of the Ring of Gyges at http://phd.evansville.edu/tetra_4/republic/gyges.html. There is also a detailed and fascinating discussion by David Gauthier in his book *Morals By Agreement* (Oxford: Clarendon, 1986), Chapter 10.

[3] Plato, *Republic*, 360c, 36.

though, they would loudly praise his restraint, engaging in protective deception, for fear the ring might used against them![4]

Virtue Its Own Reward?

In stark contrast to Glaucon's description of what most people believe, Socrates argues that being just (and also courageous, moderate, and wise—in other words, possessing virtue) really does have important intrinsic value; we really need goodness. And no matter what happens we ought never to relinquish our virtue for vice. This is because the just soul is in complete harmony, each part—reason, emotion, appetite—acting in a division of labor, doing its natural job but guided by the "smaller," superior part, reason.

So virtue *is* its own reward. Injustice, on the other hand, is a corruption of one's own soul—the "bigger" appetitive part ruling over reason. One ought never to succumb to unjust ways, because doing evil harms you. This is why the openly or secretly unjust man, possessing all good things, living a hedonistic, selfish and free lifestyle is really living the *worst* life—a really unhappy existence! And no matter how the virtuous man suffers in life, such as through dishonor, poverty, and even a horrible death, it is this truly good man who always leads the healthier, happier existence.

Given Plato's ideas about justice and the good life, *Crimes and Misdemeanors* makes a very nice Platonic example: Suppose that by cloaking their injustice, men such as Lester and Judah are seen and understood by most people to be good, wholesome, honest, hardworking men. And suppose further

---

[4] Plato's inspiration for his Gyges myth comes from the fifth-century B.C. Greek historian, Herodotus. In the latter's version of the story, the king, Candaules, a proud and vain ruler, persuaded his reluctant bodyguard, Gyges, to sneak into the queen's bedroom and observe her nude. Candaules guaranteed Gyges success against the unsuspecting, beautiful queen. Gyges obeyed the king, but the plan backfired. The queen spotted Gyges leaving her bedroom, and, later summoned Gyges to her boudoir and immediately confronted him with a terrible dilemma: be immediately executed, or quietly assassinate Candaules, and become the king. Gyges's choice here might be a self-evident one—despicable, but realistic. Of course, he assassinated the king, seized power and married the queen. Herodutus, *The Histories*. Loeb Classical Library, Volume 1 (Cambridge, Massachusetts: Harvard University Press, 1920).

that the good-natured man, Clifford, is seen and thought by most people to be completely unjust, or, perhaps in our case, a born loser. Given these various lives, Judah's, Lester's or Clifford's, which one would you choose to live?

Possibly we should study as a moral thought experiment what would happen if Clifford, Lester, and Judah—the main characters—were all given rings which magically offered invisibility and invincibility.[5] How might they act? Would Glaucon's report of the attitude and position of the majority of citizens prove to be true, that no one would willingly act justly if given invincibility?

Crime Does Pay

Judah, you said it yourself a million times, 'You only go around once'.

—JUDAH'S "REAL WORLD" EVIL BROTHER, JACK[6]

Again, Lester and Judah are seen and understood by most people to be good people, whereas Clifford is thought to be a "poor loser," yet this is a misperception. How does Plato's ring device illuminate this? Let's begin with Lester and then Clifford.

As Lester's name literally implies, he is "the shining" role-model for confidence, success and happiness. By working hard and being very ambitious, he has become a successful film-maker. He is adored and admired by almost everyone, both fans and family. To his family, friends and other associates who tolerate his views and work ethic, he is generous and loving. Like the legendary king Midas, everything he touches seems to turn to gold. In the entertainment world, his television shows have garnered for him "a closet full of Emmys."

Clifford, Lester's brother in law, is one of the few outsiders who sees through the façade of Lester's persona: he is a *yutz*—a louse. Lester acquires at any price what he desires, manipulates workers and family, womanizes, mispronounces both

---

[5] Allen's film *Alice* does invoke magical herbs which render Alice and others invisible for the purpose of spying on each other. *Alice*, however, is a story of a woman's "awakening," and so the use of magic isn't malicious.

[6] *Crimes and Misdemeanors* (1989). All other quotes from Woody Allen in this essay are from this film.

"nuclear," and "foliage," and spouts clichés like "comedy is tragedy plus time," and "if it bends, it's funny; if it breaks it's not!" If all that isn't convincing enough for Clifford, Lester wears no socks with his loafers—a clear sign of tastelessness.

Investigating Lester's paradoxical personality is not easy. We might begin, though, with how the twentieth-century French philosopher Henri Bergson interestingly conceives the comic:

> The comic person is unconscious. As though wearing the ring of Gyges with the reverse effect, he becomes invisible to himself while remaining visible to all the world. A character in a tragedy will make no change in his conduct because he will know how it is judged by us; he may continue therein, even though fully conscious of what he is and feeling keenly the horror he inspires in us. But a defect that is ridiculous, as soon as it feels itself to be so, endeavors to modify itself, or at least to appear as though it did. . . . Indeed, it is in this sense only that laughter "corrects men's manners." It makes us at once endeavor to appear to what we ought to be, what some day we shall perhaps end in being.[7]

It is a good bet that Lester's personality or behavior would not change if he somehow acquired a magical ring. Success in the television industry creates his wealth and prestige, and these provide him with the means and ability to do almost anything he desires at will. Initially in the film, he does not see himself as who he is. But how many of us do? Appeasing his sister Wendy (Joanna Gleason), Lester reluctantly turns some of his omniscient power over to Clifford, allowing him to direct a public television documentary on "creative minds." But he angrily fires Clifford after the latter gleefully edits the film to depict Lester's true nature as an egotistical, asinine, pompous, Mussolini-like dictator.

Near the end of *Crimes and Misdemeanors*, at the expensive wedding of his niece which he has graciously funded, Lester (stunned by Clifford's representation of his character) does momentarily "see" himself. When he asks his sister, Wendy, "Am I a phony?", her response, that some people are obviously jealous, soothes and calms his conscience. Then, comforted by her

---

[7] Henri Bergson, *Laughter: An Essay on the Meaning of the Comic* (Los Angeles: Green Integer, 1999), pp. 20–21.

facile response, as Bergson describes the comic, Lester once again becomes invisible to himself.

Sporadically, Lester does attempt to comprehend the human condition, via Emily Dickinson's gloomier poems or when he has "some good stuff on tragedy," or when he wants to incorporate "existential motifs in comedy" into his sitcoms. But do we really believe he is genuine and honest? As far as his religious beliefs are concerned, his love for his brother Ben is his superficial link to anything divine. Nevertheless, Lester's reputation amongst his public—as a decent, honest, hard-working, and charitable man— would seem to be what many people from all walks of life believe to be the best character, and the formula for happiness.

Cliff

Lester and Clifford are diametrically opposed in life. Clifford is a basket of insecurities. He lives on a precipice of anxiety.[8] Generally, he appears to us as what might be characterized by Jews as a *luftmensch*, a dreamer, or worse, a *shlimazl*, a born loser—the "if I sold candles, the sun would never set"—type of person.[9] His own marriage has been slowly decaying: the last time he and Wendy slept together was on Hitler's birthday the previous year. Within his family circle, his sister, Barbara (Caroline Aaron), is a recent widow, and her ten year-old daughter, Jenny (Jenny Nichols), is now fatherless, with Clifford her only male role-model. When Clifford momentarily hesitates at accepting Lester's job offer, the latter's face to face depiction of the difference between them speaks for a majority of people: "Idea for a farce: a poor loser agrees to do the story of a great man's life and in the process comes to learn deep values."

However, Clifford seems likeable and occasionally mischievous, without being malicious. He is not particularly religious. An ex-newsreel editor, he abandoned that career because tornadoes, earthquakes, and the like were too depressing. He has also created documentaries about acid rain, starvation, and poverty. And, as mentioned earlier, his documentary of the

---

[8] Literally Clifford means "Of the cliff." See Evelyn Wells, *What to Name the Baby*, (Garden City: Garden City Books, 1953).

[9] Arthur Naiman, *Every Goy's Guide to Common Jewish Expressions* (New York: Ballantine, 1983).

philosopher, Louis Levy, will result in another film failure, when the latter, a man who survived the horrors of World War II and the Holocaust, and who had always been very life-affirming, commits suicide.

As a critic, Clifford can only angrily remark about Lester's successful television shows, "I can't watch his stuff. It's sub-mental." But Clifford and his documentaries are shunned by critics and public alike, making him neither honored nor wealthy. Consumed with desire to reveal Lester's dark side in the PBS biography, Clifford destroys his one chance at fame, power, and fortune—all that Lester possesses—when, mischievously, he splices moments of Lester's womanizing with images of the arms-folded, jaw-protruded Mussolini, and Francis, a 'talking' jackass. Would anyone trade places with the hapless and possibly envious Clifford?

Even under these conditions, though, we might briefly speculate about what a magical ring would do for the good-natured, but hapless, Clifford. In a similar manner in which we used Bergson to understand Lester, we might examine the reflections of the eighteenth-century French romantic philosopher of the Enlightenment, Jean-Jacques Rousseau, and compare him to Clifford:

> If I had remained free, unknown, and isolated, as nature meant me to be, I should have done nothing but good, for my heart does not contain the seeds of harmful passion. If I had been invisible and powerful like God, I should have been good and beneficent like him. It is strength and freedom which make men good: weakness and slavery have never produced anything but evildoers. If I had possessed the ring of Gyges, it would have made me independent of men and made them dependent on me. I have often wondered, in my castles of the air, how I would have used this ring, for in such a case power must be closely followed by the temptation to abuse it. Able to satisfy my desires, capable of doing anything without being deceived by anyone, what might I have desired at all consistently? One thing only: to see every heart contented; the sight of general happiness is the only thing that could have given me lasting satisfaction, and the ardent desire to contribute to it would have been my most constant passion.[10]

---

[10] Jean-Jacques Rousseau, *Reveries of The Solitary Walker* (Harmondsworth: Penguin, 1979), pp. 101–03. Nonetheless, Rousseau eventually admits that with endless temptations, he would throw away the magic ring!

To summarize, we ought to believe that Clifford, bequeathed the wealth and power that Lester possesses, would use his "ring" in a decent, fair, and honest manner. Again, evidence of Clifford's good-nature is that, handed the vast power to further craft Lester's phony image to demi-god status and simultaneously garner wealth and prestige for himself, Clifford actually exposes the truth about Lester. But truth begets ruin for Clifford. Any other individual handed that sort of power and control would attempt to glorify himself as well by portraying Lester as the god he is not. Clifford's mischievous, but not malicious, honesty actually works against him. So is honesty the best policy?

Judah and Aunt May

What good is the law if it prevents me from receiving justice? . . . Is what she doing to me just? Is this what I deserve?

—JUDAH ROSENTHAL

Judah, the Law, without the Law it's all darkness.

—RABBI BEN

Judah, a prestigious and wealthy ophthalmologist, is philanthropic and well-respected. As a man of science, he is skeptical of religion. Like Lester, he possesses wealth, prestige, adoration of family and friends. As his name literally implies, he is *praised* by all.[11] But, unlike Lester, he seems to us more of an enigma and self-contradiction. Not a womanizer like Lester, he nevertheless currently finds himself in an imbroglio of a collapsing adulterous affair with a very neurotic woman, Dolores. We also notice that, although philanthropic, he illegally manipulates funds. Dolores' grieving and painful nature openly covets Judah.[12] She threatens to reveal Judah's financial scams, and she writes to his wife, Miriam (Claire Bloom), about their affair (though Judah "miraculously" intercepts the letter). Judah is beside himself. If exposed now, his "ring" of wealth and prestige would "go up in smoke." Interestingly, his "ring" is useless to him under these conditions. Dolores refuses to be bought off.

---

[11] Wells, 254.
[12] Wells, 68.

His prestige in the community and love of family mean nothing to her.

At first, Judah seeks confidential aid from his patient and friend, Rabbi Ben. Ben kindly counsels him to exercise "reason," and, then, if unsuccessful, to confess to and trust in his wife, Miriam, asking for her forgiveness. Ben lives in the "kingdom of Heaven" and has faith in the goodness of human nature and God. Judah apparently has no such illusions; he does not possess faith in either his wife or God.

This distrust of and disbelief in God is apparent in flash-backs. Visiting his childhood home, Judah recalls a bygone Passover Seder. At that Passover, he and his brother discovered that some of their relatives, notably the remarkable Aunt May (Anna Berger), were atheists. Stunned by this revelation, the boys were deeply affected. Aunt May's influence on Judah is outwardly acknowledged by family members. Based on her reaction to the Holocaust, Aunt May's atheism ultimately triggered in Judah and Jack a feeling that all religious beliefs, prayers and supplications before God, were merely superstitions. The prayers voiced by Jews and others did not prevent the slaughter of six million of God's chosen people. Aunt May's tergiversation from her Judaism derives from her inability to understand an apparent contradiction between the Holocaust and God's all-powerful and all-loving, merciful nature.

Attempts to solve this mystery by Jews and Christians alike still abound.[13] But it's not a mystery for Aunt May. Her understanding of any conflict is a powerful and ancient argument: "Might Makes Right." This ancient realism is based on nature: the larger, stronger animal devours the smaller, weaker one. Nature appears to subject the weaker to the stronger; it "favors" the stronger. This view applies to humans as well. Justice exists only by virtue of agreements, by which the weaker compel the stronger, by whatever means, to leave them in peace. Otherwise it is supposedly of no interest for the stronger not to take advantage of those weaker. This is the "nature argument." But where is God in all this?

---

[13] See David Novak's excellent apologetic article from *First Things*: "Arguing Israel and the Holocaust," 109 (January 2001), pp. 11–14. Available on line at www.leaderu.com/ftissues/ft0101/opinion/novak.html.

Like many people, Aunt May believed that had there not been U.S. intervention, the Nazis would have conquered all of Europe and possibly Russia and eventually Asia. Only U.S. military power was able eventually to cut short further genocide and Nazi atrocities. Realistically, the Jews could not defend themselves. And God—for whatever divine inscrutable reasons—did not intervene and prevent this genocide. Ultimately, Hitler was accountable for forty-four million dead. Military power signified to Aunt May a Gyges ring. Only our military power, funded by billions of dollars, stopped both Germany and Japan from their slaughter and enslavement of other, weaker nations.

Entirely unconvincing to Judah's father (David S. Howard) is Aunt May's argument from evil, which says that, because of (an event like) the Holocaust, God does not exist, for if such an all powerful, all benevolent being did exist, he would have prevented it. "If it's a choice between God and Truth," he adamantly declares to May, "I will always choose God." For Judah, though, "God is a luxury I cannot afford." If one has wealth, honor, only a few troubles in life, then God is desirable, affordable, a luxury. But, if certain stressful, uncertain, dangerous moral dilemmas arise, such as the Holocaust; or if financial and moral crises occur (due to a neurotic mistress, for example), He is not indispensable.[14] "For those that want morality, there's morality," declares Aunt May. Then, obviously referring to God, Moses, and the Ten Commandments, she professes, "Nothing is handed down in stone." So, for Aunt May, if a person like Judah gets away with murder and is "not bothered by the ethics," then that person walks free.

Pushing the Button

Survival and preservation of the status quo is everything to Judah. Interestingly, his friend, a pious Rabbi, is going blind. Does a rabbi's slow blindness indicate divine displeasure, God's inability to protect righteous men, or neither? So, even Ben's

---

[14] *The Oxford English Dictionary* carries the sense here: "In particular sense: Something which conduces to enjoyment or comfort in addition to what are accounted the necessities of life. Hence in recent use, something which is desirable but not indispensable." But even here, Judah is non-committal about his faith.

faithful efforts to persuade Judah, that "without the Law, it's all darkness," ultimately leave no moral impression on the latter.

For Judah, the brutal reality is that power and relief come from "pushing a button"—he calls Jack, and all his grief concerning Dolores ends. Jack lacks any conscience, any "spark of goodness." Jack's uncomplicated recommendations are that for money she can be "threatened" or "gotten rid of." Jack only requires money—Judah's "ring," to perform the evil deed.

For a long time after Dolores's murder, Judah wrestles with his conscience. Assertions by Judah such as, "She's not an insect! You don't just step on her!" "It's pure evil, Jack! A man kills for money and he doesn't even know his victims!" and "There is a God, Miriam. Otherwise the world is a cesspool!" reveal a confused state of mind. But does he believe? Does this "man of science" have a conscience?

Another doctor of medicine in the sixteenth century, Rabelais, had warned, "Science without conscience is but the ruin of the soul," [15] and this seems so for Judah. But Hitler had avowed, "I am liberating man from the degrading chimera known as conscience."[16] Slowly, ever so slowly, we see this Judah "liberated" from his conscience. The Ring of Gyges (his wealth and privilege) in Judah's hands only promotes and enables his egoistic, nihilistic tendencies.

By himself, he can't murder her. He is desperate, but lacks the personal will to do the bloody deed himself. Jack, however, represents his much needed physical will. When Judah agonizes over the murder, Jack emphatically avows that he will *never* go to jail, and we recognize what that means: if a man lacks conscience, even his own brother is not safe. This does not go unnoticed by Judah. But there seems no alternative for him. Paradoxically, his ring—his wealth—could not buy Judah's freedom from the lovelorn, grief-stricken Dolores, and it wouldn't save him from his own ruthless brother, were he to decide to turn himself in and confess.

After the murder, when Ben politely queries about the adultery, Judah lies to his friend and rabbi, "She listened to reason!"

---

[15] François Rabelais, *Pantagruel*, Book II, Chapter 8, in Samuel Putnam, ed., *The Portable Rabelais* (New York: Viking, 1968), p. 266.

[16] Lewis Henry, ed., *Best Quotations for All Occasions* (New York: Permabooks, 1945).

The End: Is It All Darkness?

Aware as we are of the lives of the various characters in *Crimes and Misdemeanors*, their material successes and failures, if given Gyges's magical power or wealth, how many of us would truly behave morally like Socrates or Clifford? How many of us really despise Lester's life? Our experience today is that the instant wealth earned by talented athletes does not make them ethical role models for our youth. Throughout their lives, some of them seem above the law, and they appear happy to lead this type of life. Wealthy business executives like those in Enron and Worldcom seem to be the able to covertly exploit stockholders, citizens, and other businesses for their own greed, power, and prestige. Even when caught red-handed, the wealthy buy their way out of trouble and crime. "Murder will out," replied Judah's father to the great Aunt May, but we witness cases like the O.J. Simpson trial, and we question that apparent truth. Some wealthy citizens, it seems, with the help of our flawed judiciary system and with the assistance of high-priced, celebrity lawyers get away with murder.

Intelligence, talent or lack of it, is not our real danger in the world, as Plato tried to reveal in his dialogues, it's *ethos*—the Greek word for "character." Sometimes men are caught. But some forever escape justice. Whether these people are caught or not, though, Socrates would say that evil is a result of ignorance of how to develop and maintain the harmonious soul. True virtue is invisible to them, and their ignorance of it is what makes these unhappy men their own worst enemy and a danger to other citizens.

Interestingly, we know that *Crimes and Misdemeanors* is not a tragedy. Clifford tells us so. In Dostoevsky's *Crime and Punishment*, a real tragedy, the murderer ultimately confesses. There is suffering and agony for all, but in the end there is redemption for the individual. If Allen's *Crimes* were a tragedy, Judah would end up like Raskolnikov. However, the film neatly turns the tables. At the end of the story, at the wedding of Ben's daughter, Judah meets Clifford quietly sitting by himself, distressed after discovering that Halley is engaged to Lester. Judah, noting that Clifford is a writer, discusses with him a perfect murder scenario. Clifford politely replies that real tragedy requires that the murderer confess. But as Judah gets up to return to and embrace his loving wife, he responds to outcast Clifford that those kinds of endings happen "only in the movies." Drink in hand, Clifford is left with very little hope. Devoid of wife, job, friends, wealth, or status, Clifford is left to return to only his luckless widowed sister, her young innocent daughter, his "Singin' in the Rain" movie, and, what Socrates believes truly is important, his good nature. We realize that the successful, immoral Lester and the murderer-embezzler Judah will continue to prosper and gain honor. Is Clifford really the Socratic happy man?

Though in *Crimes and Misdemeanors* Woody Allen pokes fun at philosophical systems by having a "life-affirming" philosophy professor commit suicide, his film still remains philosophical. As we reflect on the film's pessimism, our thoughts and feelings are curiously provoked and heightened. They are a mixture of the wonders and paradoxes of our own human nature and existence. Plato's Gyges story in his *Republic* and Allen's *Crimes and Misdemeanors* encourage us in our lives to continue a search for justice and moral enlightenment. In this wonderful mysterious, examined life, then, maybe we could hesitatingly claim, "It's not *all* darkness."

14

Self-Knowledge in
Another Woman

JILL GORDON

Inscribed on the walls of Apollo's temple at Delphi some 2,500 years ago were the words "Know Thyself."[1] This cryptic imperative continues to stimulate philosophical thought. What does it mean, exactly, to have self-knowledge? How does one go about getting it? And why should one want to have it?

Woody Allen's film, *Another Woman*, treats the issue of self-knowledge through the transformation of its main character, Marion Post. Allen thus follows in a well-worn path, traceable as far back as the ancient Greeks. Plato (427–347 B.C.E.) addresses the importance of self-knowledge in several of his dialogues, perhaps most creatively and beautifully in a metaphor he creates in the dialogue called *Alcibiades I*, and his treatment illuminates what transpires in Allen's film. And it is with that beautiful metaphor I begin.

The Self-Seeing Eye

Although arrestingly handsome and ambitious, the youthful Alcibiades is not yet ready to assume the powerful position he aspires to occupy in Athens. What he lacks, as a backdrop to many other shortcomings, is self-knowledge. Socrates attempts

---

[1] [For further discussion of this expression and of the oracle at Delphi, see William Irwin's "Computers, Caves, and Oracles," in *The Matrix and Philosophy* (Chicago: Open Court, 2002) —THE EDITORS.]

to convince Alcibiades that only he, Socrates[2], can help him to satisfy his ambitions in life. Most important to Alcibiades's success, Socrates advises, is self-knowledge. But how can a self come to know itself?

> SOCRATES: If the [Delphic] inscription [to "know thyself"] took our eyes to be men and advised them, "See thyself," how would we understand such advice? Shouldn't the eye be looking at something in which it could see itself?
>
> ALCIBIADES: Obviously.
>
> SOCRATES: Then let's think of something that allows us to see both it and ourselves when we look at it.
>
> ALCIBIADES: Obviously, Socrates, you mean mirrors and that sort of thing.
>
> SOCRATES: Quite right. And isn't there something like that in the eye, which we see with? . . . I'm sure you've noticed that when a man looks into an eye his face appears in it, like in a mirror. We call this the "pupil," for it's a sort of miniature of the man who's looking.
>
> ALCIBIADES: You're right.
>
> SOCRATES: Then an eye will see itself if it observes an eye and looks at the best part of it, the part with which it can see. . . . But it won't see itself if it looks at anything else in a man, or anything else at all, unless it's similar to the eye.
>
> ALCIBIADES: You're right.
>
> SOCRATES: So, if an eye is to see itself, it must look at an eye, and at that region of it in which the good activity of an eye actually occurs, and this, I presume, is seeing.
>
> ALCIBIADES: That's right.
>
> SOCRATES: Then if the soul, Alcibiades, is to know itself, it must look at a soul, and especially at that region in which what makes a soul good, wisdom, occurs, and at anything else which is similar to it (132c–133b).[3]

---

[2] [For further discussion of Socrates as a character in Plato's dialogues, see William Irwin's "Jerry and Socrates," in *Seinfeld and Philosophy* (Chicago: Open Court, 1999) —THE EDITORS.]

[3] *Alcibiades I*, in John M. Cooper, ed., *Plato: Complete Works*, (Indianapolis: Hackett, 1997). Hutchinson notes that the word for "pupil" in Greek also means "doll," which enriches the image of a miniature of oneself which is being reflected back to oneself.

Socrates's image of the self-seeing eye suggests that one gains insight into oneself, at least in part, by entering into some reflective relationship with another who can mirror a true image back to oneself. Just as the self-seeing eye looks into another eye to see itself, so the self-knowing soul looks into another soul to know itself, and this aptly describes the phenomenon being depicted in Woody Allen's film. After a life of self-deception and delusion, Marion Post (Gena Rowlands) comes to see herself more clearly, more honestly, and in a new light. She does so through a mirroring relationship with "another woman" (Mia Farrow), and by the end of Allen's film, there is reason to hope that her newfound self-knowledge can and will be a vantage point from which she moves forward to make changes in her self and her life. It is Marion's relationship to this stranger, ironically, that provides her with a mirror in which she sees, perhaps for the first time in her adult life, an accurate reflection of herself, and is consequently motivated to change. But we meet Marion at a point far away from this insight when the film begins.

Marion

> If someone had asked me when I reached my fifties to assess my life, I would have said that I had achieved a decent measure of fulfillment, both personally and professionally. Beyond that, I would say I don't choose to delve. Not that I was afraid to reveal some dark side of my character, but I always feel if something seems to be working, leave it alone. My name is Marion Post, I am director of undergraduate studies in Philosophy at a very fine women's college, although right now I am on leave of absence to begin writing a book.[4]

Thus Marion's voice opens the film, narrating directly to the viewer her thoughts, perceptions, feelings, and eventually, her transformation. In addition to the facts that she divulges about herself, Marion's opening narrative indicates that she is not yet in a position to engage in any type of self-examination, espe-

---

[4] This and all other passages quoted from the film come from *Another Woman*, written and directed by Woody Allen, Orion Pictures Corporation, 1988. Videocassette (Orion Home Video, 1989).

cially one that might prove difficult and demanding. She prefers not to delve too deeply because her life seems to be "working."

The film soon reveals that Marion's perception in this regard is mistaken, however, and something in her life is deeply, sorrowfully wrong. Marion's narrative voice, especially in the film's opening scenes, is flat, detached, and it seems to lack much of an emotional range. Her delusion about the quality and functionality of her life will turn out to be rooted in a deep emotional repression—a kind of fear of her own passions—and her consequent need to keep an analytical distance from meaningful, close relationships. But as long as Marion is kept from delving further into the quality of her life, she will not discover the depths of her emotional deprivation nor see her life and its relationships for what they truly are. Marion's deepest problem, therefore, is her lack of self-knowledge.

We become acquainted with Marion's lack of self-knowledge through repeated instances in which her perception of herself, as well as her perception of how others perceive her, are presented as incongruous with reality. This incongruity is played out serially in the film in Marion's various personal relationships: with her husband, Ken (Ian Holm), her one-time lover, Larry (Gene Hackman), her step-daughter Laura (Martha Plimpton), her brother and sister-in-law, Paul and Lynn (Harris Yulin and Frances Conroy, respectively), and her childhood friend, Claire (Sandy Dennis). The abyss between Marion's perceptions and the reality of each of these relationships reveals the depth, breadth, and type of self-delusion from which she suffers.

Marion's married life is the first in the film to be exposed as rather bleak and empty. While at a party, Marion and Ken listen to their friends, Lydia (Blythe Danner) and Mark (Bruce Jay Friedman), relate a story of being caught having sex on their living room floor when the building superintendent let himself into their apartment unannounced. Later in the evening at the party, Marion opens a conversation with Ken about their own sex life and intimacy.

MARION: Would you ever think of making love to me on the
    living room floor?
KEN: Would you want me to?
MARION: I don't know, would you want to?

KEN: I don't know. Actually, I don't see you as the hardwood
     floor type.
MARION: Really?
KEN: Nuh-uh.

When Ken leaves Marion to return to the party, it appears that
these were not the answers she had hoped to elicit. It is not
clear, however, that Marion knows what she hoped would come
from the conversation, just as she doesn't know whether she
would, in fact, want Ken to make love to her on the living-room
floor. Perhaps she longs for more spontaneity and passion in
their relationship, and that is what motivated her to ask Ken in
the first place, but more than that, this scene forces Marion to
wonder whether she is "the hardwood floor type," or more generally, whether she wants and is she capable of having a freer,
less rigid relationship. Just what type is she? Thus, this early
scene sets the tone for one relationship that will later become
pivotal in the film's narrative, and which lies at the center of a
web of Marion's other troubled relationships.

Marion and Her Brother

One of Marion's most enduring relationships is with her brother,
Paul. In one scene, we see Marion on the street trying to hail a
cab, and her sister-in-law, Lynn, arriving out of breath. When
Lynn pleads with Marion for a few minutes of her time to talk,
Marion replies, "I've just got to be disciplined when I'm writing,
Lynn, otherwise I'm just not going to get it done." It turns out
that Lynn had requested this meeting with Marion in order to
ask her for financial assistance, especially now that she and Paul
are thinking of splitting up. Lynn is clearly in a difficult and dis-
advantaged position, having arrived late to a meeting which she
has asked for, with a woman who "has always disapproved" of
her, and then having to ask for money while Marion impatiently
hails a cab. After Lynn conveys to Marion the reason for asking
to meet with her, Marion asks why Paul has not come to her
himself to ask for the money.

LYNN: Don't you know how he feels about you?
MARION: Sure, we've always been very close.
LYNN: You're deluding yourself. Of course in a way he idol-
     izes you, but he—he also hates you.

MARION: I'm sorry, I don't accept that.

LYNN: You're such a perceptive woman. How can you not understand his feelings?

The utter incongruity between Marion's claim that she and Paul have always been "very close" and Lynn's description of Paul's hatred is striking, but Marion refuses to accept what Lynn tells her about her brother's feelings. Rather than being surprised, hurt, or even curious about Lynn's claim that Paul hates her, Marion meets Lynn's claim with obduracy. We might say that, beyond being deluded, Marion displays resilience to the truth.

Lynn thinks Marion's lack of insight about herself and her relationships belies her high intelligence and perceptiveness, and yet it is more likely that they are really two sides of the same coin: Marion's intellectual acuity is a mask for an emptiness underneath—for Marion's fears of her own emotions—and her intense intellectual life obscures from Marion her avoidance of deep thought or consideration about herself. The intellectual focus of Marion's life and her intense engagement in cerebral matters is exactly the locus of her emotional repression. We see here, also, Marion's dearth of compassion. Her treatment of Lynn is dismissive, condescending, even paternalistic, and she fails to register even the faintest measure of kindness or sympathy for someone going through a difficult separation and in financial need, someone willing to humble herself and ask for help. Marion leaves the scene with steely resolve to continue her philosophical writing. "The encounter with my sister-in-law had left me a little angry, but I refused to let it interfere with my work."

A Passionate Lover

Marion had a chance for a more emotionally open, even passionate, relationship with Larry, a friend of her husband, Ken, whom she met shortly after her engagement to Ken. Larry is immediately drawn to her, and he eventually confesses his love for her. In one scene, we witness what begins as a passionate kiss between Larry and Marion in Ken's kitchen at the engagement party one week before Marion's wedding to Ken. At first Marion and Larry are equally passionate, but then she tries to pull away from Larry's embrace. After she insists that "this is just

crazy, I'm marrying Ken and that's all there is to it," Larry tells
her that he loves her and that he knows assuredly that she loves
him, too.

> MARION: Well, I, I, it's, I'm, well, you're wrong, and I'm sorry
>   if I misled you.
> LARRY: It's you you're misleading.
> MARION: I'm surprised at you. I mean, Ken is your close
>   friend.
> LARRY: I love everything about you. I want you to come live
>   with me. Please.
> MARION: Stop it. That's disgusting. Just go away.

Then, there is a reprise later at the party:

> LARRY: What can I say to change your heart?
> MARION: I'm really amazed at you. He's your friend.
> LARRY: Yes he is my friend. But he's a prig and he's cold and
>   he's stuffy. Can't you see that? . . . and he's a snob.
> MARION: He's a wonderful man. He's a terrific doctor. He's
>   cultured and he's honorable. I love to be with him and I,
>   I, I love reading books with him.
> LARRY: It's all up here [pointing to his head].

It's clear to us, and possibly to Marion, that her reasons for marrying Ken ring hollow. Nowhere does she say how she *feels*
about Ken, unless one includes loving "to be with him" and to
read books with him.

> MARION: And he's sexy! . . . He would never try to undermine
>   you!
> Larry: Even if he loved a woman passionately?

Marion's claim about Ken's sex appeal sounds silly here,
expressed as a defensive, desperate afterthought, hardly convincing as it appears last in a litany of more clinical descriptions
of Ken's qualities. Even at this early moment, Marion is aware of
the lack of passion in her relationship with Ken and the alternative that Larry could offer, but she persists nonetheless.
Flustered and defensive, Marion tries to shame Larry by accusing him of undermining his friendship with Ken by pursuing

her. Larry conjectures, "Maybe I was wrong about you. Maybe you're two of a kind." She sharply retorts, so as to avoid taking what he says seriously, "Maybe you've had too much champagne." Larry responds knowingly, "Maybe this conversation is scaring you."

Of all the characters in the film, really, Larry seems to know Marion best, to understand things about her that she herself can't (yet) see. In a flashback that occurs later in the film, we witness the first intimate contact between Marion and Larry. They meet by chance, buying tickets for a concert, and then have lunch together and walk through Central Park. They escape a downpour by seeking shelter in a tunnel, and Larry kisses Marion for the first time.

> Her kiss was filled with desire and I knew I couldn't share that feeling with anyone else. And then a wall went up, and just as quickly, I was screened out, but it was too late because I now knew that she was capable of great passion, if she would just one day allow herself to feel.

Ken's Daughter

Perhaps the healthiest relationship Marion has, if only by comparison with the others depicted in the film, is with her stepdaughter, Laura, Ken's daughter from his first marriage, who appears to be in her late teens. Although not without its own problems, this relationship seems to be built on mutual respect and affection of some sort. Laura will listen to Marion's advice even when Ken proves unable to persuade her; the two women are close enough that Laura goes with Marion one evening to visit Marion's father (John Houseman) at his house outside the city; the two seem to talk frankly about various topics; and Laura is eager for Marion to meet her boyfriend and join them for a drink one night. But despite this relative closeness, Laura discloses a fundamental distrust at the root of the relationship that is revealing of Marion's character.

In a scene in which Laura has presumably just had sex with her boyfriend in Ken and Marion's apartment, she expresses concern over their coming home to find them. Her boyfriend says that he thought Laura said that Marion was "sophisticated," and "hip." "Yeah she is, she's great . . . it's just that she's . . . um

... she's a little judgmental. She sort of stands above people and evaluates them. I've heard her make remarks about her brother, and I always think she's going to judge me that way." [5] We see this same type of reaction in Lynn, Marion's sister-in-law. Lynn knows that Marion has never really approved of her because Marion has apparently made that clear in some way, probably not subtly. Laura clearly experiences her relationship with Marion similarly; she fears Marion's judgment despite their relative closeness.

One irony in Laura's fear of being judged by Marion, however, is that Marion's own relationship with Ken, Laura's father, began as an illicit affair while he was still married. The young woman's actions should, for this reason alone, not be subject to Marion's judgment. Clearly this type of judgment, inferiorization, and distancing mediates many of Marion's relationships, although she remains oblivious to the manner in which her judgment truncates those relationships. If Marion were to react judgmentally to Laura's actions it would be by turning a blind eye to her own actions, motivations, and behaviors. Without an insight into her own choices and actions, or into her own flaws, weaknesses, and shortcomings, she inauthentically stands in judgment of others and therefore distances herself from them. Greater self-knowledge would be one key to gaining an honest vision of herself and thus to improving her relationships with others.

A Childhood Friend

In a chance meeting on the street, Marion runs into her childhood friend, Claire, whom she has not seen in many years. Claire is now an actress, currently performing in a production in town, and she is with her husband, Jack (Jacques Levy). At Marion's behest, but clearly against Claire's desires, the three

---

[5] The filming of this scene is interestingly ambiguous. It could be a flashback of Marion's in which it is implied that Marion and Ken did indeed come home when Laura and her boyfriend were still there, and Marion overheard this conversation between them, in which case the flashback might depict a newfound impact that the recalled memory now has on Marion. It is also possible to read the scene between Laura and her boyfriend as having happened, though without Marion's overhearing it, in which case it is part of a layering of scenes through which Marion's persona and its effects on others is revealed.

head to a local bar for a drink. While Jack is charmed by Marion as they discuss philosophy, theater, and the arts, Claire grows increasingly agitated and intoxicated. "My husband is very impressed by certain things which I cannot give him. . . . We've been in this situation before where you [Marion] so innocently wound up causing me to doubt my whole life."

Claire recalls an adolescent relationship with a young man whom she loved, but who was attracted to Marion. Marion insists that she never encouraged him nor accepted his overtures. Claire, who sees more clearly than Marion, says that even if she did refuse these overtures, Marion already had what she wanted, which was to have gotten the attention and admiration of the young man. Claire encourages Marion to "think about it some time," to consider whether on a subconscious level she really did want this attention. "Maybe you didn't even know you were doing it." When Marion claims emphatically, "That's so untrue!" Claire retorts, "*You* should be the actress."

Despite Claire's bitterness and intoxication, her description of Marion's behavior with the young man has a good measure of credibility insofar as it resembles to some degree Marion's behavior with Larry. As in that situation, Marion charmed a man and wholly won him over, only to reject his overt advances. Moreover, Marion's own motivations remain opaque to her, and any attempt to make them more transparent meets again with resilient refusal to believe. In keeping with her obliviousness, Marion perceives that she and Claire had simply "drifted apart" over the years; Claire counters with the truth of the matter: "We didn't just drift apart, Marion. I withdrew." This possibility never occurred to Marion, but the viewer knows that Claire was not the only person in Marion's life to withdraw from her.

"Be Honest with Me, Paul"

Paul, Marion's brother, also withdraws from her. After a troubling afternoon in which Marion is haunted by emerging doubts about her life and relationships, she finds herself taking a walk and unconsciously, aimlessly ending up at her brother's office. Seeking her brother out on this occasion signals the beginning of the transition in Marion's life, which I shall discuss in detail below, but Paul's reaction is revealing. Probably because she had never before come by to see him for any reason, his first words to her when she enters his office are, "What's happened?!"

MARION: I don't know.

PAUL: Well, what are you doing here? (*Marion shakes her head while tears well up in her eyes.*) Something must be wrong.

MARION: Oh, don't say that.

PAUL: Marion, you don't seek out my company very often. You must need something.

MARION: Yes, I do need something, only I don't know what it is, exactly.

PAUL: What do I have that I can offer?

MARION: Be honest with me, Paul. You and I were so close when we were young.

PAUL: How honest do you want me to be?

Marion realizes that they haven't spoken in quite some time, and Paul tells her that he gave up pursuing her because he realized how uncomfortable he made her feel. Like Claire, Paul withdrew. But more in keeping with Laura's insight about Marion, Paul pulled away because of Marion's condemning judgment of him, although in his case the judgment is not just anticipated, but actual. When Paul claims to realize that he disappoints and embarrasses Marion with how he lives, whom he marries, and who he is, Marion repeats her now familiar refrain when confronted with someone else's unpleasant yet accurate insight about her: "That's not true!"

Paul recalls the time when he showed her something he had written. Before he can remind Marion of the details of the event, which she does not remember, she conjectures that whatever she said, she was "just trying to be truthful." Paul replies dryly, and with an irony that Marion seems not to detect, "Yes, I'm sure." Paul then recounts for Marion that she described his writing as overblown, too emotional, maudlin, and that while his dreams might be meaningful to him, to the objective observer they were "so *embarrassing.*" Marion incredulously demands, "I said that?!" Paul replies, "Exactly your words."

Marion's reaction is that of a woman who is disconnected from herself, who does not know herself. An event that painfully remains with Paul for many years and was a pivotal event in his relationship with his sister is not even a dim memory for Marion. Moreover, she questions, at least in surprised disbelief, that she actually behaved as she did. She made her crushing comments to Paul thoughtlessly, unaware of the damage she left in her wake. She lacked emotional sensitivity about how her words affected others who themselves are not as emotionally walled off as she and who are therefore vulnerable to her judgment.

Marion's Influence on Others

Others are vulnerable to Marion's judgment because, despite her emotional insensitivity, her ability to alienate and hurt those closest to her, and her refusal to examine her life, Marion is nonetheless deeply respected and admired. Twice in the film others are described as "idolizing" her.[6] In one powerful scene, Marion is approached by a former student from twenty years earlier while she is at dinner with friends. The woman enthuses about the meaningful influence Marion had on her, claiming at one point, "You changed my life." She turns to the rest of Marion's dinner table and says, "She was the inspiration to all the women in the philosophy department." Marion appears uneasy with the praise, as though her student's emotional reaction is embarrassing to her, perhaps like Paul's emotional writing is an embarrassment. Also like Paul, this student recalls a particular occasion that was meaningful to her—a powerful lecture on ethics and moral responsibility— but is perhaps not even a dim recollection for Marion. When others at Marion's dinner table ask her if she remembers the lecture, she uncomfortably gives a non-response and returns to her meal. It is also possible that Marion, feeling unsettled by her earlier interactions with Paul and perhaps in the earlier stages of her transformation, might feel unworthy of the accolades, sensing the incongruity between her positive influence on other people and her ability to hurt and dismiss them, as well.

Even Claire's description of Marion, albeit somewhat venomous, makes it clear that Marion possesses many talents and gifts. Despite her core of repressed emotion, coldness toward

---

[6] Ken says that his daughter, Laura, idolizes her, and Lynn says it about Paul— although in his case, "in a sense he also hates her."

others, and the opacity of her own inner life, Marion is engaging, intelligent, accomplished, seductive, alluring, and charming. Marion equally leaves in her wake those devastated by her insensitivity and judgment, as well as those inspired by her brilliance, her wit, and her charisma. The unifying point here is that Marion remains impervious to both her bad and her good influence on all of these relationships, both the intimate and the more distant. Her impenetrable core, impenetrable even by herself, alienates her from all these people. The eventual breakthrough and reconciliation in Marion's life is, quite unexpectedly, aided by a stranger, an other.

Another Woman

> I felt very tired, and I lay my head down and closed my eyes, and I guess I dozed off. I don't know exactly how long I was asleep, but . . . . I gradually became aware again of a voice. It was a woman's voice. And it was such an anguished, heart wrenching sound that I was totally arrested by its sadness.

And thus begins Marion's obsession with another woman.

The flat that she has rented during her leave of absence is located next door to a psychiatrist's office. Marion is able to hear the voices from the office through her vent, and this one voice in particular proves distracting to an otherwise singularly focused Marion. As she tells us early in the film, "A new book is always a very demanding project, and it requires that I really shut myself off from everything *but* the work." Marion fails to do that, however, so compelling is the other woman and what she says.

The several days during which Marion listens to the other woman become a painful distraction, as they force her to reflect on her own life. The anguished, heart wrenching sound that arrests Marion's work—and life—is the slightly muffled voice of the other woman:

> I began having troubling thoughts about my life—like there was something about it not real, full of deceptions, that these deceptions have become so many, and so much a part of me now, that I couldn't even tell who I really was....And only after a long time did I get my bearings, but for one moment earlier, it was like a cur-

tain had parted, and I could see myself clearly. But I was afraid of what I saw.

Marion's reaction to what she hears behind the wall appears on her face as a combination of deep fear and yet compelling curiosity. She parts the door separating her flat from the psychiatrist's office to look at the patient, a thirty-something, vulnerable looking pregnant woman. The opening of the door signals an opening up of Marion to herself. The episodes that the other woman narrates from within the therapist's office mirror Marion's life and force her to confront herself in ways that she has not before. Just like Socrates' description of the self-seeing eye, the other woman becomes a mirror in which Marion sees herself, and she will see herself most clearly when looking at another. The other woman will mirror Marion's own anguish and sadness back to her, providing her an opportunity for self-knowledge, and while the process is difficult and disturbing for Marion, it ultimately proves to be valuably transformative.[7]

"Lately, I've had odd feelings about my marriage. It's as if it's been coming apart, and in so many ways I've just been denying it. I must admit I have moments when I question whether I've made the right choice. I told you there was someone else once." This is not Marion speaking, but the other woman, though, Marion, too, has had odd feelings about her marriage. We saw her try to repress her doubts and feelings in the scene she plays out with Larry, Marion's own "someone else." Now, provoked by the other woman's words, and in an agitated state, Marion is set to remembering her brief time with Larry.

> I often wonder about real love. I should say, I keep myself from thinking about it. I don't mean the kind I've experienced. It's something much deeper and much more intense. And then I become frightened because I feel too much.

---

[7] Arostegui notes that the opening scene of the film depicts Marion gazing into a mirror as she readies herself to leave home. Asensio Arostegui, "Hlenka Regained: Irony and Ambiguity in the Narrator of Woody Allen's 'Another Woman'," *Miscelánea: A Journal of English and American Studies*, Volume 15 (1994), pp. 1–14.

Again, this is the voice of the other woman, but in Marion's recollection, Larry tells her essentially the same thing about herself,
that although he knows she is capable of great passion, he suspects she is also fearful of it. Marion gives up the chance for
passionate love because of that fear.

As the therapy narratives resonate more and more with her
own life, and as they get more deeply troubling to Marion, she
becomes haunted by the other woman. At one point Marion
sees the other woman walking down the street, and she obses-
sively tries to follow her, eventually losing track of her. Marion
is no longer the intensely and impatiently focused scholar we
meet in the early scenes of the film. One day, Marion actually
sits by the vent attentively waiting for the other woman to speak
during her session. But she is silent that day and has "nothing
to say." The other woman's silence signals, perhaps, a period of
reflection when words can't adequately serve as therapy, but a
turn inward is called for at a point of disturbing insight.[8]

The Dream

Marion, too, turns inward on this day and is cast into a deep,
waking reverie. There are several deep memory and dream
sequences in the film which depict Marion's beginning to wres-
tle with the issues she is presented with through listening to the
other woman. Marion's dreams are filled with images that sym-
bolize her alienation from herself (and others) and the poor
state of her life as a result: acting, masks, cages. Marion is not
sleeping very well, if at all, during these troubling days spent
reflecting on her life and choices.

After several sleepless days, Marion succumbs to sleep during the middle of the day and has a vivid dream. This particular dream, like her visit to her brother, Paul, is a turning point.
In it, she articulates several insights about herself and her life,
and in the film's narrative, it is after this dream that Marion's
transformation manifests itself in action. I shall, consequently,
discuss this dream in some detail and assess its various parts
insofar as they reveal aspects of Marion's move toward self-
knowledge.

---

[8] The silence could also signal deep anger, as we shall see later in the film.

In her dream, Marion enters the psychiatrist's office at the end of the other woman's session. As she was in Marion's waking perception, the other woman is silent that day in Marion's dream; the other woman is "too choked with rage to speak," as the psychiatrist says, and he asks her what "enrages" her. Marion hears only a litany of things—life, the universe, the cruelty, the suffering of humanity, illness, aging, death. The psychiatrist tells the other woman to stop worrying about humanity and get her own life in order. The other woman then leaves the session, walking right past Marion as though she weren't there, and the psychiatrist turns to Marion and speaks directly to her:

PSYCHIATRIST: What would you say she was suffering from?
MARION: Self deception.
PSYCHIATRIST: Good, but that's a little general.
MARION: But I don't think she can part with the lies.
PSYCHIATRIST: No? Too bad.
MARION: Not that she doesn't want to . . .
PSYCHIATRIST: It's precisely that she doesn't want to. When she wants to she will.
MARION: It's all happening so fast.
PSYCHIATRIST: I have to hurry. I'm trying to prevent her from killing herself.
MARION: You don't think she would?
PSYCHIATRIST: She's already begun.
MARION: She has?
PSYCHIATRIST: Oh, not dramatically; that's not her style. She's been doing it slowly and methodically—and has been since she's very young.

Marion's responses to the psychiatrist (almost like classroom responses), as well as his descriptions of the "patient," seem really to be about Marion as much as they might be about the other woman. At least in her dream consciousness, Marion shows some insight, some self-knowledge. The psychiatrist's words are really Marion's words insofar as they appear in *her* dream, so she is beginning to articulate to herself some of the problems that she has kept deeply submerged until now. She is beginning the process of self-knowledge from reflection occasioned by the other woman.

Next in this same dream sequence, Marion's father enters the psychiatrist's office and confesses his regret over various aspects of his life, now that he is nearing its end. He regrets that he has been too demanding with his daughter and did not give her enough feeling; he regrets that there is no love between him and his son, Paul; and he regrets that the woman he shared his life with was not the woman he loved the most deeply. Although he had "achieved some eminence in [his] field" as an historian—words that mimic Marion's opening narrative about her own academic life—he ultimately sizes up his life as having been "unhappy." This part of Marion's dream is another reflection of herself, perhaps cast toward the future, a mirroring that forces her to turn inward and to see these same patterns in her own life.[9] She, too, has many regrets, some of which parallel those expressed by her father, but she can't dwell on these regrets yet, for the dream moves rapidly to another scene.

From the psychiatrist's office, Marion's dream now takes her to the neighborhood where she ran into Claire near the theater where Claire was performing. Marion enters the theater and she observes a "rehearsal" in which various scenes from her own life are acted out on a stage. In the first scene Claire plays Marion in a re-enactment of her conversation with Ken about having sex on the hardwood floor, only this time, Claire-as-Marion speaks more truthfully than Marion did. She speaks as though she actually knows her own mind.

> No! that's a pretty insulting thing to say. I think it's you that's not the type to make love anywhere but in the bedroom with all the

---

[9] There is a portion of this film to which I have given insufficient attention in order to focus more narrowly on the mirroring function of the other woman for Marion. Marion's father is at the center of a family dynamic that is largely responsible for many of the problems that exist between Marion and her brother, Paul, and many of the problems that Marion has in her own right. Her father is himself remote, dispassionate, and wholly absorbed in his work. He is an academic historian of some note who clearly favored his intellectually promising daughter over his son and used the example of Marion to shame and belittle Paul. We might infer, also, that he was a mismatch for Marion's mother for whom nature and poetry were her "whole existence." I shall discuss Marion's mother briefly at the conclusion of the paper, but the family dynamic portrayed in *Another Woman* is certainly worthy of another, separate writing project.

lights out . . . Look let's just try being honest with one another. There's not much passion left in this marriage anymore. Don't be so aloof. I'm trying to tell you something: It's not erotic anymore.

Claire-as-Marion says things that Marion did not or could not say, things that perhaps she felt but repressed. Claire-as-Marion is much more forthcoming, more emotionally expressive. This part of the dream does seem to help Marion to confront the reality of her marriage and to express her emotions more authentically since that night she does exactly that, demanding of Ken why they're not sleeping together nor having any kind of intimate emotional lives. "I hadn't realized how much of that had slipped away until today," she says. Presumably, her dream helped her to make that realization and to act on it in her waking life. Marion is provided another opportunity to say and feel what she so far can't in her waking life in the next segment of this dream.

The dream then moves to depict a reunion with Larry who is now married. Claire plays Larry's wife, and after introductions she graciously leaves Marion and Larry together since they "have a lot to talk about."

MARION: I see your by-line now and then in magazines.
LARRY: Did you read my novel? . . . You inspired one of the characters.
MARION: Oh? I hope you weren't too rough on me.
LARRY: Aah, I wrote of you with great love.
MARION: Your wife is lovely.
LARRY: Yes, I met her right after you said goodbye to me. Her name is Jennifer. She's also quite a good writer.
MARION: Do you have any children?
LARRY: Yes. We have a daughter. It's been the greatest, most beautiful experience of my life.
MARION: Do you ever think of me?
LARRY: Do you ever think of *me*?
MARION: Once in a while.
LARRY: I hope you're happy with Ken. I ran into him on the street not too long ago. He must have told you.
MARION (*with tears welling up in her eyes*): I think of you *more* than once in a while.
LARRY: But without regret, please! Don't tell me you have any regret.

Just as in the part of the dream in which Marion speaks directly to the psychiatrist, her conversation with Larry is coming from her own mind. Larry's words are her words to herself in her own dream. Like her father, Marion has passed up the opportunity to be with a man she truly loved and perhaps "loved the most." Like her father, she has reason to regret this, but unlike her father, Marion still has the opportunity to make a change in her life, to gain self-knowledge about her own shortcomings and to begin living in a different way that, among other things, might make her more open to passionate love some time in her life.

In the "second act finale," the director of the vignettes in Marion's dream, (Claire's husband, Jack) introduces the scene depicting the suicide of Marion's first husband, Sam (Philip Bosco), fifteen years after their divorce. Sam had been one of Marion's professors, and he is clearly much older than she. The director says that it's unclear whether Sam's death was really a suicide, but the evidence—he was alone in a hotel room with alcohol and pills—would seem to point in that direction. Marion emphatically denies that his death was suicide and says he was a wonderful man—they "had such lovely times together." The viewer is left to wonder whether this description of Sam and their relationship is yet another of Marion's misperceptions. The director asks Marion to stick around, "there's another important scene between you and Sam," but Marion responds, "No, No more . . ." And thus her long dream ends.

The scene Marion perhaps wants to avoid seeing in this dream is depicted in a flashback presented later in the film. In this flashback, Marion has apparently just had an abortion, and she and Sam are arguing fiercely about it. Sam is obviously deeply hurt, but Marion responds that it was *her* decision and that it would be *her* career, not his, that would be negatively affected by having the baby. In the face of all Marion's reasons for not wanting the child, Sam exclaims, "To be capable of such a lack of feeling!" naming the affliction that she now wrestles with.

The significance of Marion's dream, with or without this scene included, lies in the various ways in which Marion appears to be gaining insight. All of the dialogue by all of the characters who populate her dream comes from Marion's own psyche. All the pointed remarks about regret, passion, self-deception, and repression, are Marion talking to herself, and are thus the beginning of her transformation to better self-knowledge. The transition from imagining possibilities in her dreams to carrying out such actions in Marion's waking life, putting her newfound self-knowledge into action, is further advanced and fully precipitated by a face-to-face meeting between the two women.

Two Women Meet

While shopping for a gift for Ken on their anniversary, Marion runs into the other woman in an antique store, and they meet and speak for the first time. The other woman is crying while looking at a print of an August Klimt painting. The painting depicts a pregnant woman who looks remarkably like the other woman did when Marion first laid eyes on her, parting the door between her flat and the psychiatrist's office. When Marion sees the other woman crying in front of the painting, Marion tells her that it is actually an optimistic work, that it is called, "Hope," and that she herself loves Klimt. "Of all the paintings Klimt did during this period, this is the most positive." As they talk, we learn that the other woman was a painter, just as Marion used to be, and that neither of them has painted for a very long time. We might imagine that a very long time ago signifies a time in both their lives when they were not afraid to feel emotion and express themselves freely, a time before the repression and self-alienation began.

The two women leave the antique store, go to an art gallery, and have lunch together. Marion ends up dominating their conversation, focusing on the trauma she experienced at turning fifty. "You suddenly look up and see where you are," Marion says. The other woman thinks Marion is in "a pretty good spot." Marion responds, "I thought I was, and then there's chances gone by that you can't have back again. . . . Maybe it would be nice to have a child. . . . I've never said it before . . ." Although after this confession Marion specifically recalls the abortion she had, her lament about chances gone by could also describe the missed opportunity for a passionate love with Larry, her lost friendship with Claire, a better relationship with Paul, and possibly even more time absorbed in painting and poetry as she did when she was much younger. The meeting was deeply meaningful for both women, and it becomes the

subject of conversation in the other woman's next session with
her therapist that very afternoon. This will be the last session
that Marion listens to, and the final reflection of herself that
Marion sees is horrifying:

> I feel . . . I feel a little depressed. I met a really sad woman today,
> a woman you'd think would have everything, and she doesn't. She,
> she has nothing. And it made me feel frightened because I feel—I
> feel if I don't stop myself, as the years go by I'm going to wind up
> that way. She can't allow herself to feel, so the result is she's led
> this cold cerebral life and has alienated everyone around her. Well,
> you know, we've talked about this before, how I only hear and see
> what I want to. That's exactly what she does. She's pretended for
> so long that everything's fine, but you can see clearly how lost she
> is. She had an abortion years ago which she regrets; she rational-
> izes it in many ways. But I think the truth is she was afraid of the
> feelings she would have for a baby. She's a very bright woman,
> very accomplished. But like me, you know, emotions have always
> embarrassed me. I've run away from men who I felt threatened me
> because the intensity of their passions frighten me. I guess you
> can't keep deep feelings closed out forever, you know, so . . . I just
> don't want to look up when I'm her age and find that my life is
> empty.

Marion's face is deeply pained and almost horror struck when
she hears these words about herself through the vent. The mirror held up to her life is now one into which it is painful to look.
The life that seemed to Marion "to be working" only days ago
appears now to be alienating, emotionally empty, and filled with
regret. The woman who "chose not to delve" any further behind
the false exterior of her life has now been plunged headlong
into deep self-examination.

The other woman's voice-over continues, and she relates that
while the two women were at lunch, Marion discovered that
Ken was there having lunch, and apparently also having an
affair, with their friend, Lydia. The next scene in the film is
Marion deeply weeping, which is the most emotion that we
have so far seen her display. Seeing Ken with Lydia and hear-
ing the other woman describe Marion's life so intimately proved
to be the breaking point, the point at which she could no longer
look away from herself. Self-knowledge comes at a painful cost
for Marion, but it will move her toward some kind of healthier

and happier transformation. Marion's tears reveal her pain. But they also signal hope.

The viewer is reminded of the tears Marion discovers staining the pages of her mother's volume of Rilke's poetry. In reminiscing about her youth and Rilke's poetry, to which her mother had introduced her, Marion speaks of two poems in the course of the film. The first is "The Panther," which Marion remembers having written about for a school project when she was sixteen. This poem describes a powerful animal who is caged behind bars beyond which there is no world for it. The panther's energetic circles inside the cage prove exhausting, but are the sign of a great will which has become numbed. Occasionally, the panther's eyes slide open and images enter from the world outside, only to vanish forever in its heart. Several of Marion's reveries in the film contain the image of the caged panther. As though drawn to the haunting words that secretly describe herself, Marion might have written her paper on "The Panther" just at the point in her young life when the bars of her own cage were being put up around her.

It is possible that Marion's mother, too, was caged up and never allowed to live freely enough to exert her innate power. The tears that stain the pages of Marion's mother's collection of Rilke's poetry fell on "Archaic Torso of Apollo," which was her mother's favorite poem. This poem describes the headless, truncated stone statue of Apollo and conjectures that the truncated body nonetheless reveals what we can't see in a head or face, so strong and powerful is its posture, and so much can we infer and imagine there. The stony, fragmented statue actually imbues Apollo with life and light and fecundity in a manner that a fuller representation would not, and hence presence is revealed in absence.[10] Similarly, the last two lines of the poem describe the power of sight in a seemingly sightless stone. Marion notices her mother's tears have fallen across these very lines, and they prove sorrowful and arresting for Marion, too: "for here there is no place that does not see you. You must change your life."

----

[10] Marion's mother has a kind of presence through absence as well in this film. Marion's father looms large in the film, and yet Marion's mother is not depicted at all. Her strong presence is ultimately felt, nevertheless, through the gifts of poetry and painting she gave Marion—things to which she might presumably return. In this way, Marion's mother could also be considered "another woman" who gives Marion an opportunity to look more honestly at herself.

Hope

There is no place that does not see Marion; she must change her life. The place from which she had been most invisible—from her own eyes—is now flooded with light and she lays open and exposed to herself. She sees herself now through another woman, and given what she sees, she must change her life. "Hope" is the name of the August Klimt painting that is admired by Marion and the other woman when they meet in the antique store. Allen names the character of the other woman, "Hope," only in his credits. The other woman represents Marion's hope for self-knowledge and a better, fuller, and more authentic life that might come from such insight.

We see Marion fulfill that hope the evening she returns from this last, frightening glimpse of herself on the night of her anniversary with Ken. Marion finds the strength to confront him about his affair with Lydia and about their failing marriage. Her claim that "if [she'd] had any perception" she would have known or suspected the affair with Lydia implies that she has now gained some perception. Marion now stands distinct from Ken, different from his cold, unemotional, judgmental superiority. They are no longer "two of a kind," as Larry had described them, but rather Marion's newfound self-knowledge separates and distinguishes them.

> MARION: I feel sorry for you Ken because in your way you've
>   been as lonely as I have.
> KEN: Have we been lonely?
> MARION: At least I've come to recognize it.

This is the beginning of Marion reassembling her life.

For the next few days Marion does not get any work done, nor does she seem concerned about that. She just walks and thinks, and tries to get her life back in order. She visits Paul again, and commits to starting over and spending more time with him, Lynn, and their children. Marion also speaks with Laura, and it seems that this relationship will carry on, bringing Marion a kind of surrogate maternal fulfillment, even though she has passed over, and can't regain, the chance to have children of her own.

Those missed chances are not sentimentalized, however, by the film's hopeful final note. Though she gains self-knowledge, Marion still accepts the price of those missed opportunities. Although she ultimately moves on to have better relationships with Paul and Laura, the relationship with Larry is one that can't be regained. The child that she chose to abort can't be a part of her life. This irreparable loss is a price that Marion pays. But there is still hope that she might have future relationships that involve passionate love. At least now, she might be less fearful of them.

In a final mirroring, Marion seems to complete her "therapy" at the same time the other woman disappears.[11] Marion knocks on the door of the psychiatrist's office to tell him that she can hear his sessions, and to inquire about the other woman; she would like to get in touch with her. The psychiatrist responds, "Oh yes, she's terminated her treatment. She's gone away. I don't have any way to reach her." In a parallel manner, the old Marion has also gone away, no longer hermetically sealed against her own entry into her internal life, nor blind to her own emotions and identity. Marion has become "another woman" by the end of the film.[12]

---

[11] The film is actually ambiguous about the reality of the other woman. Since she is first introduced as Marion is slowly emerging from sleep, it is possible that Allen is signaling to us that the other woman *is* Marion, another self confronted in her dream world or her subconscious. Seen this way, the film can be the story of Marion's own "therapy," and the exposure and revelation of her psyche through that process. Several other aspects of the film evoke a dream-like quality, for example, the "chance" meetings between Marion and Claire outside the theater, between Marion and the other woman at the antiques store, and Marion's discovery of Ken's affair with Lydia at the very restaurant where she goes with the other woman. Nonetheless, the story is still one of self knowledge gained through the process of mirroring or reflection, whether it takes place in Marion's waking or dreaming consciousness, and whether the other woman is truly other or merely an element of Marion's own consciousness.

[12] Asensio Arostegui, "Hlenka Regained: Irony and Ambiguity in the Narrator of Woody Allen's 'Another Woman'," *Miscelánea: A Journal of English and American Studies*, Vol. 15 (1994), pp. 1–14. Perhaps Marion also served as a mirror to the other woman, if she really existed, and her therapy has been terminated because she, too, has been sufficiently moved by the projected image

While Allen's presentation of Marion's struggle is steeped in
a twentieth-century existential and psychoanalytic idiom (of
authenticity, identity, consciousness, dreams, and therapy), it
nonetheless resonates beautifully with Plato's ancient, Greek
sense of the importance of self-knowledge. Self-knowledge is
among the most fundamental virtues; it must be prior to the
development of any others,[13] and it can be cultivated through
self-reflection occasioned by seeing oneself clearly through mirroring by another.[14] From the ancient temple of Apollo, where
the Greeks might have read the divine command inscribed on
the walls, to Rilke's haunting poem, "Archaic Torso of Apollo,"
the command to know and see thyself resonates throughout this
film. Marion gains insight into her bereft emotional life, and is
transformed from an otherwise unfeeling woman with "a decent
measure of fulfillment" to another woman with authentic and
more transparent feeling. Marion narrates the closing of the film
as she did its opening, but now with a more genuine description of her inner life, her feelings. We now hear from a more
ambivalent but psychically healthier Marion who recognizes and
mourns the irrecoverable loss in her life, but who also casts her
gaze forward as she becomes another women, a woman of
renewed health gained by self-knowledge. "I was filled with a
strange mixture of wistfulness and hope. And I wondered if a
memory is something you have or something you've lost. For
the first time in a long time I felt at peace."

---

of herself to change her life. That is, the other woman is motivated to change
by her fear of waking up one day and finding that she has become like
Marion, just as she expressed that fear to the psychiatrist

[13] Plato, *Phaedrus*, 230a.

[14] Plato, *Alcibiades I, passim*.

15

Woody Allen's *Film Noir* Light: Crime, Love, and Self-Knowledge in *The Curse of the Jade Scorpion*

MARY P. NICHOLS

The Curse of the Jade Scorpion (2001) occurs in the shadow of Bogart. Set in 1940, Allen's film about private investigator C.W. Briggs (Woody Allen) replays the classic Bogart detective film, *The Maltese Falcon* (1941). Like C.W. Briggs, Sam Spade (Humphrey Bogart), is a private detective. Both are accused by the police of a crime they are investigating. Both suspect the woman they love of the crime. Both relentlessly track down the guilty and bring them to justice. Moreover, each film involves the issue of the moral status of the private detective who pursues criminals. Finally, each involves the issue of trust.

The Curse of the Jade Scorpion responds to *The Maltese Falcon*, and presents a more positive understanding of how moral character, supported by love and the self-knowledge love fosters, offers an alternative to the corrupt *film noir* world Bogart inhabits. Like Allen's earlier protagonist Allan Felix (Woody Allen) in *Play It Again, Sam* (1972), who finds a way to imitate yet transcend his hero Bogart,[1] Allen finds a way to imitate yet transcend the *film noir* of an earlier epoch in American cinema.

---

[1] See my analysis of this film in *Reconstructing Woody: Art, Love, and Life in the Films of Woody Allen* (Lanham: Rowman and Littlefield, 1998), Chapter 2, especially pp. 26–28, and also that of Sam B. Girgus, *The Films of Woody Allen* (Cambridge: Cambridge University Press, 1983), esp. pp.18–19 and 22.

The Criminal World of *The Maltese Falcon*

The Maltese Falcon's hero is a loner, and a somewhat shady character. When his partner Miles Archer (Jerome Cowan) is murdered, Spade is the prime suspect, for the police have heard of an affair between him and Archer's wife. As Spade tells the ruthless "Fat Man" Kaspar Gutman (Sydney Greenstreet), he does not simply represent his clients, he also represents himself. When the jewel-studded falcon for which the Fat Man and Joel Cairo (Peter Lorre) are looking—and killing—is discovered to be a fake, Spade has impressed the villains as sufficiently one of them that they invite him to join them in continuing the search for the bird. And although Spade knows enough not to trust Brigid O'Shaughnessy (Mary Astor), who turns out to be Archer's murderer, he is not above falling in love with her. It is therefore not surprising that she supposes that he will not turn her in.

And we ourselves can't be sure what Spade is going to do. When he does turn Brigid over to the police, he tells her "don't be sure that I'm as crooked as I'm supposed to be," for "that sort of reputation might be good business, bringing me higher paid jobs and making it easier to deal with the enemy."[2] Unlike the police detective, who is a public servant and thus owes his allegiance to the community, the private eye serves the interests of his clients as well as his own. His job is, as Spade says, a "business" in which he looks for high paying jobs. It may be for this reason that it is a police detective (Barton McLane) who is most suspicious of Spade, although it is also the case that the police detective is the least intelligent character in the film, at least when it comes to solving crime.

What, then, distinguishes Spade from the enemy with whom he deals so well that he seems to belong among them? Gutman does not hesitate very long to accept Spade's proposal that he offer Wilmer (Elisha Cook, Jr.) to the police as the fall guy, although he "feels towards Wilmer," he says, "just exactly as if he were my own son." There is no loyalty among thieves, whereas Spade tells Brigid that "If a man's partner is killed, he's supposed to do something about it." He nevertheless adds that in his line of work "it's bad business to let the killer get

---

[2] *The Maltese Falcon* (1941).

away with it." He certainly does not act out of any regard for Archer: in pursuing the one who killed his partner, he explains, "it doesn't make any difference what you thought of him." Most importantly, Spade rejects the pleas of the woman he loves, for he knows she would always hold over him his withholding evidence against her. He will not listen to her pleas, he tells her in a fit of passion, "because all of me wants to, regardless of consequences."[3] He must preserve his freedom and independence.[4]

One of the most telling moments of the film occurs when Spade's secretary replaces the names "Archer and Spade" on the door of their office with "Samuel Spade, Confidential Investigator" in larger letters. The irony of his title is clear from the many echoes of "trust" in the film, or rather its lack: Spade, for example, will not trust Brigid, although she constantly asks for his trust as she repeatedly deceives him. Gutman claims to trust only "a man who tells you right out he's looking out for himself." Spade does not join the villains because he does not trust them. He also knows the futility of their search for happiness: the falcon, he says is "stuff dreams are made of." He is more of a cynic, less an idealist than the crooks, and if he questions the value of the falcon, perhaps it is because he questions all values. He turns them all in at the end, but we are not sure why. An example of the *film noir*, *The Maltese Falcon* leaves unanswered the question of the moral character of those like Sam Spade who are tough and competent enough to afford society the protection it needs from crime. In the end, Spade remains a lone hero, who has

---

[3] It was this scene from *The Maltese Falcon* that absorbed Allan Felix at the beginning of Allen's play, *Play It Again, Sam*. When he wrote the screenplay for the film, Allen substituted the final scene from *Casablanca* for this scene from *The Maltese Falcon*. The beginning of the film then foreshadowed its end, when Allan Felix chooses to imitate the patriot Bogart rather than the hard-nosed cynic. The beginning of the play, in contrast, highlighted the fact that there were different Bogart characters who might be chosen as models by Allan Felix. Allen's shift from the play to the film thus parallels his protagonist's shift from the cynical to the patriotic Bogart, a move that Rick himself makes in *Casablanca*.

[4] Sam Girgus observes that Bogart tells Astor that she has "to take the fall for her crimes in spite of—or perhaps because of—his love for her," *The Films of Woody Allen*, p. 17.

his integrity but little else. And society remains without any firm reason to trust its heroes.

The Criminal World of the Jade Scorpion

The problem of the "private" detective is not one that escapes Allen in his response to the *film noir*. Nor does the issue of trust. Just as we see the name of Spade's business of "Confidential Investigator" on the door of his office, so we see that of C.W. Brigg's "North Coast Casualty and Fidelity Insurance Company." Near the beginning of the film, two of its employees, C.W. Briggs and Betty Ann Fitzgerald (Helen Hunt), each reveal to their friends that there is something about the other that they do not trust.

In the first scene of *The Curse of the Jade Scorpion*, two employees of the investigative division of North Coast discuss a recent theft. Although "the cops want to nail the guy who stole it too," one observes, "the difference is we have to make good the 30,000 bucks, they don't. To them, it's just another heist."[5] The contrast to which Allen draws our attention by means of this opening remark, however, is ambiguous. The insurance investigators suppose that the police are less eager than they themselves are to catch the thief because they lack any personal interest. By this same reasoning, however, nothing prevents the police from doing their duty to solve the crime and apprehend the criminal. The "personal" interest of the insurance company, on the other hand, guarantees the vigilance of its agents against the thieves, only if they identify their interest with the insurance company's. Of course, their company pays them to do so, but why should they be loyal to their employer when a better opportunity arises, if their only bond is a paycheck? As owner of the company Chris Magruder (Dan Aykroyd) observes of his employees, "These guys earn their living exposing all kinds of exotic schemes to defraud and rob people. Sometimes they start thinking, 'Hey, I'm on the inside, I know why these schemes fail. I won't make the same mistakes."

Allen also highlights the problem of the similarity between the private detective and his criminal nemesis. Several times in

---

[5] *The Curse of the Jade Scorpion* (2001).

the course of the film, he alludes to the old adage, "It takes a thief to catch a thief." North Coast's ace investigator, C.W. Briggs, attributes his success to his ability to "put myself in the criminal's position" and "think like him." As C.W. observes, "I'd hate to have me after me." But if C.W. can think like a thief, why does he not become one? He does not hesitate to rifle through the desk of his fellow employee when he suspects her of the crime, and even to break into her apartment, even after his friend and co-worker Al (Brian Markissan) warns him that "it's unethical."

In these instances, however, C.W. is not much of a threat to the law because he bungles: Betty Ann catches him looking through her desk, and the only "crime" he discovers by breaking into her apartment is her sordid affair with their sleazy boss. Evidence for the jewel theft eventually points to C.W.—his footprint matches that of the jewel thief at the Kensington estate, a hair found at the crime scene matches his, and his fingerprint is found on a matchbook dropped by the thief. But could a "stupid little twerp" like C.W. pull off a jewel theft? If society is safe from Sam Spade because his cynicism shields him from the dreams that move thieves, perhaps society is safe from C.W. Briggs because like other Woody Allen characters over the years he is "a loser." C.W. finds out at the beginning of the film that the horse he bet to win came in seventh. He also has trouble with women. Although the beautiful and "fast-living" heiress Laura Kensington (Charlize Theron) does show up on his doorstep, she still refers to him "as a myopic insurance clerk," and Allen renders C.W.'s "seduction" ridiculous.[6] That losers are not threats, however, does not address the problem posed to

---

[6] Critics have pointed out how Theron is "essentially playing Martha Vicker's role of Carmen Sternwood from *The Big Sleep*. One of the highlights of *Scorpion* is the *Big Sleep*-inspired pitter-pat dialogue exchange between Theron and Allen when their characters try to seduce each other," in George Wu, CULTUREVULTURE.NET. Allen's film thus also incorporates allusions to Bogart's role in the 1946 detective film *The Big Sleep*. When Marlowe (Humphrey Bogart) meets Vivian Sternwood (Ingrid Bergman), Vivian supposes that private detectives exist only in books, or else they are "grimy little men snooping around hotel corridors." "I'm not tall either," Marlowe replies. When Laura Kensington refers to C.W. as "one of those grubby little private detectives," C.W. does not exactly speak up for himself either: "I'm a grubby little insurance investigator. Private eyes are romantics. I'm just grubby."

society by those who are not losers. Besides, in the end, C.W. is not a loser, even though Allen uses his "loser" status to evoke our sympathies.

The Stuff Dreams are Made Of

While in *The Maltese Falcon* the audience sees only through the eyes of Sam Spade, as we follow C.W. Briggs in *Scorpion* we see more than he does. We know from the outset, for example, the guilty party and his criminal methods that C.W. discovers only near the end. The effect, curiously enough, is to soften our view of C.W. as compared to Spade. We see his vulnerabilities, the extent to which he does not understand the web in which he is caught, and the ways in which he is not in control. As we saw, Spade is too hard-nosed to fall under the curse of the Maltese Falcon, for he knows it is the "stuff dreams are made of." C.W. Briggs, in contrast, is vulnerable to dreams. He comes under the spell of the jade scorpion, used by the sinister magician Voltan Polgar (David Ogden Stiers) to hypnotize subjects as part of a magic show.[7] By casting its spell through hypnosis, the scorpion does literally what the falcon, with its riches, does more metaphorically.

Again reminding us of *The Maltese Falcon*, Allen has Polgar awaken C.W. with the claim that "every dream must return to reality." Polgar nevertheless retains the power to recall C.W. into a hypnotic state, again and again, by pronouncing the word "Constantinople." The hypnotized C.W. will then do his bidding—which is to burglarize the wealthy estates insured by North Coast and to turn over the jewels to him. Polgar of course commands that C.W. have no memory of anything that occurs while in the trance. Unbeknownst to himself, C.W. is indeed the thief whose crimes he is attempting to uncover.

We glimpse the power of the jade scorpion when C.W.—and also Betty Ann Fitzgerald—are first hypnotized in the magic show. Although both claim they "can't be hypnotized," they immediately succumb to the charm. Both speak their inner feel-

---

[7]The jade scorpion, Polgar explains, was a gift presented many years ago to the emperor of China. Allen's device thus parallels the Maltese falcon, a gift to the king of Spain from the Knights Templar of Malta.

ings: "I can't stand her," C.W. says of Ms. Fitzgerald, who describes him as "a sleazy little megalomaniac who's frightened of women." To the audience's delight, Polgar pronounces the couple man and wife, "deeply, deeply in love," in "a tropical paradise," and C.W. and Betty Ann declare their passionate love for each other. For Polgar, this "illusion" of love is only part of his ruse to get the couple under his power for the jewel robberies, for which he employs Betty Ann as well. Their love, which he himself suggests to them, is a "dream" from which he commands them to awaken "to reality."

For the couple, however, Polgar's deception is the beginning of their coming to understand their love, and the image Polgar created for his own purposes happens to reveal the truth of which the couple are unaware. We should not suppose that their love is only an illusion stemming from Polgar's suggestive power, an illusion to which the couple eventually succumbs even in their non-hypnotic state. Al later observes the chemistry between C.W. and Betty Ann: "you can't hate someone that much without there being at least a little bit of attraction underneath it all." He claims to have "always known" that C.W. had a crush on her, just as he had told C.W. earlier that Betty Ann "has some real feelings for you." Allen's film demonstrates the power of magic or art, not the power to create reality, but to bring what is not yet realized to fruition. What Polgar does inadvertently, presumably, someone like Allen might do more deliberately.

The Power of the Jade Scorpion

Whenever Polgar recalls C.W. or Betty Ann back into their hypnotic states to command their jewel thefts, they also remember their love, which Polgar first induced them to admit under hypnosis. But their declarations go beyond what Polgar originally commanded. They become aware of and acknowledge why they have such trouble expressing their love. "I resisted because down deep I thought you might hurt me," C.W. admits to Betty Ann as he meets her in his trance-like state on his way to carry out Polgar's instructions. "A terrible marital experience," we learn from his boss Magruder, "turned [C.W.] off from women except little no-threat secretaries and barflies." Betty Ann's situation is similar: her husband left her, and she still dreams of his affair with her best friend. When she returns in a hypnotic state with the jewels from the Adrian Greenwood Mansion, she proclaims to C.W. that "my passion for you is so intense it scares me." "Can't you see I've submerged it under a mask of hostile acts and cruel words? Couldn't you see I was just protecting myself?"

Their revelation of their fears is nothing that Polgar commands, or even knows anything about. What Polgar thinks is true, and what they reveal when first hypnotized-their hostility toward each other-is in fact an illusion they create for themselves. And what Polgar thinks is an illusion that he creates for them, their love, is a truth they come to discover and acknowledge. They attain the truth about themselves not primarily by admitting it to themselves while hypnotized but by seeing in their wakeful states their reflections in the other. In C.W.'s case, even he acknowledges this openly to Betty Ann. When the hypnotized Betty Ann, for example, tells C.W. that she loves him but that she hides it out of fear, C.W. admits that "all these things you said rang a very deep bell with me." C.W. sees himself in the self-revelations Betty Ann makes while hypnotized.

Moreover, the news they reveal to each other when hypnotized is not all bad. They see not only their own fears in the other, but also how much the other loves them. C.W. is loved not by "a no-threat secretary" or "barfly," but by "a brilliant woman," who thinks that he is "what [she's] been searching for all [her] life." Betty Ann is loved by a man who finds her "the most beautiful woman [he has] ever met." More important, even when not hypnotized, C.W. tells Betty Ann that her choices of men are unworthy of her. He has a higher opinion of her than she has of herself. The lovers receive from each not only images of their own fears but images of themselves they might live up to.

The jade scorpion thus unleashes forces of which its dishonest possessor is unaware, forces that uncover as well as cover, and that will eventually prove benign rather than harmful. The power of the jade scorpion therefore connects the film's detective story with its love story, the discovery of the crime's solution with the discovery of the protagonists' love, and their recovery of the jewels with their recovery of themselves.

Opposites Attract?

C.W. and Betty Ann at first seem most unlike. Their different views of criminal investigation, for example, put them at odds early in the movie. Placing himself in the criminal's position, C.W. adopts an "intuitive" approach, whereas Betty Ann is an efficiency expert hired to streamline the office. She maintains that "we're moving into a decade of scientific investigation" that has little place for C.W.'s "street ways" and "hunt and peck methods." To Betty Ann, C.W. is "disorganized," and the pair almost come to blows when she attempts to get rid of his "antiquated file system." C.W. proceeds on the level of the personal, whether he pays a not so blind beggar for information, or, like another ace insurance investigator, Barton Keyes (Edgar G. Robinson) in *Double Indemnity* (1944), follows the hunch of "the little man who lives inside me."

C.W.'s intuition tells him that the crime committed at the Kensington Estate is an inside job. And when the identical crime is repeated at the Dilworth Mansion, he infers that the inside job must come from "inside our company." His suspicions naturally turn to Betty Ann, whom he doesn't trust, and who is the only new employee with North Coast. After all, she is "a smart woman," and "is always saying that she can do anything a man can do." He would of course never suspect himself. He may be "a scummy vermin," as Betty Ann accuses him, but he knows that he is "an honest scummy vermin" and that he served as "a Boy Scout for three years."

C.W.'s intuition is therefore successful only up to a point. When Betty Ann recommends "fresh techniques" and expanding the investigation by bringing in an "outside" detective agency to help C.W., C.W. objects that Betty Ann's Coopersmith Detectives (Michael Mulhoren and Peter Linari) are "submental." But C.W. would have ignored all the evidence the Coopersmiths find that leads to himself. Without the "outside" investigation of the Coopersmiths, the evidence against him would have never been discovered. He would have "[forgotten] about logic and [given himself] the benefit of the doubt," as he asks Betty Ann to do. And without understanding his own part in the crime, he would have never been led to Polgar and the crimes' solution. C.W. comes to realize the value of logic as well as intuition when he rehearses with his friends in the office all the strange events in the hope that by thinking them through something will make sense.

Betty Ann also has something to learn. Her scientific efficiency and logic have not shown her Magruder for what he is.

When C.W. breaks into her apartment to look for evidence, he finds Betty Ann and Magruder together, and overhears Magruder announce that he is not keeping his promise to leave his wife. When, after Magruder leaves, Betty Ann is about to jump out of the window, C.W. comes out of hiding to save her life. He tells her that she "makes all the wrong decisions," because she relies on her head rather than on her heart, on "gray cells, [which] just lay there and think," rather than on blood, which "gets around and knows what the score is." Betty Ann does learn to be guided by her intuitions, for even when all the evidence points to C.W., "it doesn't feel right" to her that he is the thief. After all, she "was a bit touched that [he] stayed up all night watching [her]" after she attempted suicide, and began thinking that he might not be the scummy little vermin he seems to be. Her "instincts," even when it comes to men, are better than she supposes they are.

Betty Ann, however, is not ready to admit her affection for C.W. He could not be the jewel thief, she insists, because he is not "romantic enough" and lacks "the flair and imagination" for it. Nor is he "man enough to be a cat burglar." But Betty Ann's distinction between "wormy little ferrets" and daring "cat burglars" is not an exhaustive presentation of human types. The criminal is not the only romantic. And Betty Ann knows this on some level. When she is hypnotized, for example, she calls C.W. "a very romantic man." Even their never hypnotized fellow worker Jill (Elizabeth Berkley) feels the same. After listening to C.W. declare his love for Betty Ann, Jill "hope[s] somebody talks to [her] like that some day."

The Limits of Hypnosis

One who falls between the romantic jewel thief Betty Ann imagines and the "twerp" who never dares anything, in fact, is the man who can catch a thief, who must possess some of the thief's acumen and daring. And catching thieves is C.W. Briggs's strength. When the evidence points to him, he knows he didn't commit the crimes, that there must be a bigger picture, which he doesn't yet see. He gets a clue from one of his street contacts, the name of Eddie Polgar, although he does not connect it with the magician who hypnotized him. He gets another clue from the "blind" beggar in an earring dropped at the crime scene in the latest theft, whose match he saw in Betty Ann's apartment. He goes to the office to read the Coopersmith report. As he goes over the events with Al and George (Wallace Shawn), the latter observes that C.W.'s description of Betty Ann's declaration of love to him sounds like what they heard her saying during the magic show, and mentions that the magician's name is Polgar. These crucial clues lead C.W. to "theoriz[e] on an incredible sequences of events." Indeed, as Al observes, he "look[s] like [his] Uncle Jerry after a United Parcel Service truck hit him." Describing to C.W. what happened when he was hypnotized on stage, Al happens to say the word with which Polgar revives CW's trance. C.W. goes into his hypnotic state before their eyes.

Fortunately George is an amateur magician, and can command C.W. "to recall everything" when he wakes up. George reverses Polgar's command, "your memory will be clear, crystal clear" and "all the events of the past week will come to you vividly." With George's help he sees at a glance what he had been piecing together. As the film moves to a close, we see the extent to which its resolution is a group effort. C.W. is no lone hero, like Sam Spade; nor does he remain alone in the end. And magic is now in the service of memory rather than forgetting, of truth rather than illusion. C.W. goes to find Betty Ann, who in her hypnotic state leads him to Polgar. And C.W. lets Al know the address, so that he can ensure police support.

When C.W. confronts Polgar, even Polgar must admit that he "underestimated" C.W. But it is Betty Ann who is ecstatic. "You are the bravest, most brilliant, most courageous man I ever met," Betty Ann tells C.W., and "I'd go to the end of the earth with you." C.W. kisses her, and Betty Ann "feels those fireworks they tell about." Since she is still in her hypnotic state, about which she has been told by Polgar to forget everything when it is over, C.W. supposes that when she "wake[s] up from this fabulous illusion," "the ugly curtain of reality [will drop] on both of [them]." And yet it is not simply a "fabulous illusion," for the events that have occurred are real. C.W. has solved the mystery, pursued Polgar, and risked his life. When Betty Ann wakes up, she will be under the illusion that none of this happened. But she did kiss C.W. and experience fireworks. Amateur magician George, who knows enough about hypnosis to "deprogram" C.W., claims that "a person will not do anything under hypnosis they will not do in real life." We glimpse a better end for this couple. But if George is right about the limits of hypnosis, are C.W. and Betty Ann thieves as well as lovers? Not surprisingly, as we shall see, the film's theme of love sheds light on this issue of crime, as becomes clear, if not crystal clear, as the film approaches its end.

More Than Hope

Once she comes out of the hypnotic state, Betty Ann plans to marry Magruder, who has finally stirred himself to leave his wife. Lest we have any sympathy for Magruder, however, Allen has him confide to C.W. "between us boys" that once he and Betty Ann are married she "will have to retire whether she wants to or not," for he'll have no wife of his working in the office. Al, who recognizes how C.W. feels, urges him "to take the bull by the horns," for she is about to leave with Magruder. His friend thus bolsters his resolve, just as Al and George helped him solve the crime. When proclaiming his love and proposing marriage doesn't work, C.W. invokes the charm of the jade scorpion by uttering Betty Ann's trance word, "Madagascar," which Polgar had given her. Betty Ann goes into a trance, and tells Magruder that she is staying with C.W.

Al hands C.W. the jade scorpion as "a going away present." But does this mean Betty Ann will love him only when in a hypnotic state, which C.W. must constantly evoke by saying "Madagascar" every morning when they wake up? "You're the most wonderful man in the world," she declares to him, as the happy office workers look on. "You're the handsomest, the most brilliant, the sexiest," she continues. Although C.W. is delighted, it is not enough, and he holds out the hope for something beyond the illusion: "some day I'll make you feel those things, just really feel them." Earlier Allen films may have ended with hope,[8] but *The Curse of the Jade Scorpion* offers more than hope. "I made you feel that way and I didn't even have to say 'Constantinople,'" she tells him. But if she were in her hypnotic state, she would have no awareness of trance words or of their power.

---

[8] See my analysis of *Another Woman*, for example, in *Reconstructing Woody: Art, Love, and Life in the Films of Woody Allen*, Chapter 9, especially pp. 146–47.

We see C.W.'s "detective" mind trying to piece together the implications of her statement, as he looks back and forth between Betty Ann and his office mates. The crucial supportive role of the office workers in the lives of C.W. and Betty Ann, which we have seen from the beginning, now becomes clear. C.W. does not merely look to himself, in seeking to understand, but to his friends and co-workers. They have from the outset served as a kind of chorus and audience for the action, commenting on new developments, providing information-to both C.W. and to us-and for the most part cheering C.W. on. Moreover, it is from his friends and co-workers in the office that C.W. receives recognition and congratulations at the beginning of the film on his solving the case of the stolen Picasso. It is from them that he learns his horse came in seventh. It is with them he celebrates George's birthday-and meets Polgar the magician. It is George and Al who help him figure out the crime. It is George who rescues him from the magician's power by means of magic of his own. And it is Al who understands his and Betty Ann's affection, and who urges him to act. The "North Coast Casualty and Fidelity Company" that Allen portrays in this film is not a mere financial organization, whose employees are united only by self-interest. It is a "company," that suffers its share of casualties but also deals in trust. C.W. is the company's hero at the beginning (Magruder says he is his "best man" in solving crime) and is acknowledged as such at end. "You are our hero," Al says to C.W. in the name of all of them. Nothing more clearly illustrates Allen's use of the Casualty and Trust Company as a model for an association that transcends self-interest, as the proclamation of C.W.'s fellow workers that if he quits they will go with him.

When George reveals to those in the office that he has "deprogramed" Betty Ann the previous night, we understand why Betty Ann's memory is also crystal clear. She may have "a crazy look in her eye," as Magruder notices, but she "never felt more normal in [her] life." She too has found the courage to act without illusion, although she at first pretends she is hypnotized. C.W. demonstrates that he has figured out this puzzle as well, when he too walks away with her as if he were in a hypnotic state. After all, the last word he has heard is "Constantinople," although his hypnotic state is delayed until he figures out the meaning of her words. As they walk away together, they are in a way back in the tropical paradise in which Polgar first asked them to imagine themselves.

Criminals, Lovers, and Friends

When the couple walk away together down the hall from their office, the employees of North Coast watch them through their office's glass door, which serves as a frame for their exit. Given the frame and the glass, which recalls the lens of a movie camera, Betty Ann and C.W. are "on the screen," just as they were "on stage," during the magic show, then too watched by an audience that included their friends from work. When Allen's camera follows C.W. and Betty Ann as they walk off, our vision at the end of the film is identical to that of the employees who are also watching the couple through the door. C.W.'s and Betty Ann's audience within the film merges with the audience of Allen's film. By this device, the film expresses the hope that the community represented by the North Coast Casualty and Fidelity Company might expand to include its audience as well. The name of the company is on the glass door through which we view C.W. and Betty Ann. It is a community, we remember, that takes C.W. as its hero, a hero more vulnerable than Sam Spade, one more like us, and therefore more within our reach. While the advocate of modern efficiency Betty Ann comes to appreciate C.W.'s "old-fashioned" ways, Allen's viewer must come to appreciate his "modern" hero more than that of the old-fashioned *film noir*.

Critics have compared C.W. and Betty Ann's sparring antagonism to that of Cary Grant and Rosalind Russell in an earlier epoch of film, and also to that of Tracy and Hepburn. In Allen's movie, *film noir* meets romantic comedy. While the result is something lighter than the former,[9] it is something more serious than the latter, for without the jade scorpion, and

---

[9] The most obvious difference between a *film noir* and *Scorpion* is that Allen's film is in color rather than in black and white. According to Dennis Schwartz, "instead of being in B&W [*Scorpion*] is a lazy color version of it. It's the kind of faded out coloring that would have been used to make a 1940 film noir, if they were made in color," *Ozus' World Movie Reviews*. But then, they were not made in color.

its "power to darken men's minds," they might never have had the courage to understand themselves and to declare their love. Unlike *The Maltese Falcon*, the *Scorpion* ends with its lovers going off together. Of course that is possible because neither of them intended any crime, whereas Brigid O'Shaughnessy murdered someone. But it is not simply that they can be lovers because they are not criminals. It is also that they are not criminals because they are lovers. By that I mean that they have experiences of friendship and love, and a community that supports those experiences, which help to form their characters by teaching them their connections with others. Thus it is true that, as Al says to his friend, C.W. "has a little bit of larceny in [him]." Presumably we all do. The remedy is not rejecting dreams, in the manner of Sam Spade, but dreaming in the context of a world where friends and associates offer experiences of concern, affection, and courageous risk that support moral deeds and decent behavior. It is such a world that can risk letting those with more than "a little bit of larceny in them" catch thieves.

C.W. does not hesitate to save Betty Ann's life, nor does Betty Ann hesitate to come to his apartment to warn him about the case the Coopersmiths are building against him. Their experiences teach them what they owe to others, even if Allen mocks Betty Ann's pronouncements of life's lessons at the beginning of the film when she demands that C.W. enter her office "like a human being," or at least "an orangutan," which "would be a step up." Their experience of others gives them in turn the courage to risk the trust that Spade and O'Shaughnessy never have.

When C.W. proposes marriage to Betty Ann, even though she is about to go off with Magruder, "I'm putting my heart in your hands." This is something that the self-sufficient Sam Spade would never do, and when Brigid seems to do so ("I'm so alone and afraid. I've got nobody to help me if you won't help me."), Spade merely observes that "You won't need much of anybody's help. You're good." Just as Allan Felix in *Play It Again, Sam* rejects the *film noir* Bogart in favor of the patriot of *Casablanca*, C.W. and Betty Ann emerge untainted from the involvement in the criminal underworld that rubs off in different ways on Spade and O'Shaughnessy.

Love and Self-Discovery

Allen's film addresses not only film history, however, but even earlier antecedents. Like Sophocles's *Oedipus*, C.W. is responsible for investigating a crime and protecting his company from disaster, and in spite of his astuteness fails initially to recognize his own involvement. And as in the case of Shakespeare's Benedick and Beatrice in *Much Ado about Nothing*, a deception brings a sparring couple to the truth about their love.[10] Self-discovery through romantic love produces a happier outcome than in classic tragedy.

Comedy is not "tragedy plus time," so that we can laugh at the pain, as the pretentious Lester (Alan Alda) pontificates in Allen's *Crimes and Misdemeanors* (1989). If Lester were right, comedy would involve forgetting rather than remembering. But the jade scorpion, finally, commands those under its spell to "recall everything." That at least is what George does for C.W. and Betty Ann, when he "set[s] them free from the trance for good." By their "crystal clear" memory they escape the curse. Their self-knowledge gives them the courage to acknowledge their love to themselves and to each other. Nor are they ashamed to do so in public, so to speak, as their fellow workers congratulate them on their announcement that they will be married. "So much passion in a lousy insurance office," Jill happily observes.

The jade scorpion provides the opportunity for self-knowledge, but C.W. and Betty Ann must do the work themselves. The charm begins its life in the hands of Polgar as a device to involve others in a crime, it then sets the lovers on a path to self-discovery whereby they recognize and affirm their love, and it ends as a harmless token, apparently deprived of its power over them. Yet it remains as a reminder of all that has transpired. It is in this way that *Scorpion* responds to *The Maltese Falcon*: the earlier film shows us only "the stuff that dreams are made of," as "the ugly curtain of reality drops" before its characters. Allen's film shows us how with courage and love and persistent sleuthing, even or especially when we ourselves are its objects, the dream can become the stuff of reality.

---

[10] I am grateful to Paul Kirkland for alerting me to the parallel with Beatrice and Benedick and to the Shakespearean themes in *Scorpion*.

Entertainment for Intellectuals: A Woody Allen Filmography

What's New, Pussycat? (As writer and costar; directed by Clive
   Donner) 1965
What's Up, Tiger Lily? (Original director: Senkichi Taniguchi; original
   screenplay: Hideo Ando) 1966
Casino Royale (As costar; directed by John Huston, Kenneth Hughes,
   Val Guest, Robert Parrish, Joseph McGrath; written by Wolf
   Mankowitz, John Law, Michael Bayers) 1967
Don't Drink the Water (As writer, with R.S. Allen and Harvey Bullock,
   based on the stage play by Woody Allen; directed by Howard
   Morris) 1969
Take the Money and Run (Co-written with Mickey Rose) 1969
Bananas (Co-written with Mickey Rose) 1971
Play it Again, Sam (Directed by Herbert Ross; based on the stage
   play by Woody Allen) 1972
*Everything You Always Wanted to Know about Sex (But Were Afraid
   to Ask)* 1972
Sleeper (Co-written with Marshall Brickman) 1973
Love and Death 1975
The Front (As Co-star; directed by Martin Ritt; written by Walter
   Bernstein) 1976
Annie Hall (Co-written with Marshall Brickman) 1977
Interiors 1978
Manhattan (Co-written with Marshall Brickman) 1979
Stardust Memories 1980
A Midsummer Night's Sex Comedy 1982
Zelig 1983
Broadway Danny Rose 1984

The Purple Rose of Cairo 1985
Hannah and Her Sisters 1986
Radio Days 1986
September 1987
Another Woman 1988
Crimes and Misdemeanors 1989
Oedipus Wrecks (from *New York Stories*) 1989
Alice 1991
Scenes from a Mall (Co-star; directed by Paul Mazursky; written by
    Roger L. Simon and Paul Mazursky)
Shadows and Fog (Based on the stage play, "Death," by Woody
    Allen) 1992
Husbands and Wives 1992
Manhattan Murder Mystery 1993
Bullets over Broadway 1994
Mighty Aphrodite 1995
Everyone Says I Love You 1996
Deconstructing Harry 1997
Celebrity 1998
Antz (Voice; directed by Eric Darnell and Lawrence Guterman; writ-
    ten by Todd Alcott and Chris Weitz) 1998
Sweet and Lowdown 1999
Small Time Crooks 2000
Picking Up the Pieces (Costar; directed by Alfonso Arau; written by
    Bill Wilson) 2000
The Curse of the Jade Scorpion 2001
Hollywood Ending 2002
Anything Else 2003
Melinda and Melinda 2004

All These Great Minds . . .

JEROLD J. ABRAMS is Assistant Professor of Philosophy at Creighton University, Omaha, Nebraska. He has previously published essays on aesthetics, film, and logic, including "Cinema and the Aesthetics of the Dynamical Sublime: Kant, Deleuze, and Heidegger on the Architecture of Film," *Film and Philosophy* (forthcoming); "Solution to the Problem of Induction: Peirce, Apel, and Goodman on the Grue Paradox," *Transactions of the Charles S. Peirce Society*, 2002; and "Aesthetics of Self-Fashioning and Cosmopolitanism: Rorty and Foucault on the Art of Living," *Philosophy Today*, 2002. In addition to writing on these topics, Jerold also buys art by the yard.

LOU ASCIONE received his Ph.D. in Philosophy from Temple University and is currently a professor at DeVry University in Pomona, California where he teaches both philosophy and humanities. He is the author of a critical thinking text entitled *Rational Problem Solving: Integrating Procedure and Logic* (Houghton Mifflin, 2002), but more importantly his pet raccoon has hepatitis.

PER F. BROMAN is Assistant Professor of Music Theory at Butler University in Indianapolis. He is the author of *Back to the Future: Towards an Aesthetic Theory of Bengt Hambræus* (Gothenburg University, 1999) and the chapter "Sweden" in *New Music in the Nordic Countries*, ed. by John White (Pendragon, 2002). He writes about twentieth-century music and aesthetics. His goal is to be nominated to the Academy of the Overrated.

MARK T. CONARD is Assistant Professor of Philosophy at Marymount Manhattan College. He was a contributor to *Seinfeld and Philosophy* (Open Court, 2000), and a contributor to and co-editor of *The Simpsons and Philosophy* (Open Court, 2001). In addition, he has published a number of essays on Kant and Nietzsche. He is also the author of the novels, *Dark as Night*, and the forthcoming *Williams Bucket*, both published by Uglytown Press. Mark is dating a girl wherein he can beat up her father.

DAVID DETMER is Professor of Philosophy at Purdue University Calumet. He is the author of *Challenging Postmodernism: Philosophy and the Politics of Truth* (Humanity Books, 2003) and *Freedom as a Value: A Critique of the Ethical Theory of Jean-Paul Sartre* (Open Court, 1988), as well as essays on a variety of philosophical topics. He wants to be paid in small, unmarked bills—or large, marked ones, if you want to go that route.

JILL GORDON is Professor of Philosophy at Colby College. She is author of *Turning Toward Philosophy: Literary Device and Dramatic Structure in Plato's Dialogues* (Penn State Press, 1999), plus several articles in ancient Greek philosophy and several articles in social and political philosophy. She is currently working on the role of eros in Plato's metaphysics. For the first time in a long time she feels at peace.

JASON HOLT is Assistant Professor of Philosophy at Concordia University. He is author of a number of philosophical articles, the book *Blindsight and the Nature of Consciousness* (Broadview Press, 2003), the novel *Fragment of a Blues* (Famous Thursday Press, 2001), and three books of poetry, including *A Hair's Breadth of Abandon* (AB Collector Publishing, 2002), and *Memos to No One* (AB Collector Publishing, 1999). While he admits that his whole fallacy is wrong, he has no plans to visit Königsberg.

IAN JARVIE is Distinguished Research Professor of Philosophy at York University, Toronto, where he has taught philosophy of science for many years. His film publications include *Movies and Society* (Basic Books, 1970); *Window on Hong Kong* (University of Hong Kong Press, 1977); *Movies as Social Criticism* (Scarecrow Press, 1978); *Hollywood's Overseas Campaign* (Cambridge University Press, 1992); and (with Garth S. Jowett and Kathryn H. Fuller) *Children and the Movies* (Cambridge University Press, 1996). Close to retirement, he asks, "Is it over? Can I go now?"

JIM LAWLER teaches philosophy at SUNY/Buffalo. He is the author of *The Existentialist Marxism of Jean-Paul Sartre* (Grèuner, 1976) and *IQ, Heritability, and Racism* (International Publishers, 1978), editor of *The Dialectic of the U.S. Constitution: Selected Writings of Mitchell Franklin* (MEP Publications, 2000), and a contributor to *Market Socialism: The Debate Among Socialists* (Routledge, 1998). He is currently working on the philosophy of Immanuel Kant. While more recent sales in a fickle North American market have been "disappointing," Jim's books are eagerly devoured by the French, who continue as always to recognize his genius.

SANDER H. LEE is a professor of Philosophy at Keene State College in Keene, New Hampshire. He is the author of *Eighteen Woody Allen Films Analyzed: Anguish, God and Existentialism* (McFarland, 2002) and *Woody Allen's Angst: Philosophical Commentaries on His Serious Films* (McFarland, 1997). He edited *Inquiries into Values* (Mellen, 1988). He has also written numerous essays on issues in aesthetics, ethics, social philosophy, and metaphysics. If necessary, he will always choose God over the truth.

TOM MORRIS is Chairman of the Morris Institute for Human Values, an organization that brings philosophy to the broader culture. He is the author of such books as *If Aristotle Ran General Motors*, *Philosophy for Dummies*, and *The Stoic Art of Living*. Unlike Ike Davis, he's never had a Manhattan friend named "Yale," but he did get a Ph.D. in philosophy and religious studies from the homonymous university (and yet he asks that we not think of him as a graduate of Homonymous U). During fifteen years of teaching at Notre Dame, he always wanted his classes to evoke various Woody Allen movies, with the one notable exception of *Sleeper*.

MARY P. NICHOLS is Professor of Political Science at Baylor University. She has published widely in ancient and modern political theory, and politics and literature. Her books include *Socrates and the Political Community* (SUNY Press, 1987), and *Citizens and Statesmen: A Study of Aristotle's Politics* (Rowman and Littlefield, 1992). Most recently, she discusses the films of Woody Allen in *Reconstructing Woody: Love, Life, and Art in the Films of Woody Allen* (Rowman and Littlefield, 1998). She is astounded by people who want to know the universe when she finds it hard enough to find her way around Chinatown.

JOHN G. PAPPAS teaches philosophy at DeSales University and St. Joseph's University, both in Pennsylvania. His primary areas of research are ancient Greek metaphysics, Aristotle's conception of mind, and the history of science. He's trying to get his heart and head to be friends again.

AEON J. SKOBLE is Assistant Professor of Philosophy at Bridgewater State College, in Massachusetts. He is co-editor of *Political Philosophy: Essential Selections* (Prentice-Hall, 1999) and *The Simpsons and Philosophy* (Open Court, 2001), and author of *Freedom, Authority, and Social Order* (Open Court, 2005). He writes on moral and political philosophy for both scholarly and popular journals. He wants to be sure that when he thins out, he'll be well thought of.

JAMES B. SOUTH is Associate Professor of Philosophy at Marquette University in Milwaukee, Wisconsin. He is the editor of *Buffy the Vampire Slayer and Philosophy* (Open Court, 2003), and has published a number of essays on Late Medieval and Renaissance Philosophy. James does not respond well to mellow.

JAMES M. WALLACE is Professor and Chair of English at King's College, Pennsylvania. He has published on American literature, is the author of *Parallel Lives: A Novel Way to Learn Thinking and Writing* (McGraw-Hill, 1997), and is the co-author of *Critical Thinking: A Student's Introduction* (McGraw-Hill, 2002). His "A (Karl, Not Groucho) Marxist in Springfield" appeared in *The Simpsons and Philosophy* (Open Court, 2001). He is currently swelling to maculate giraffe, as usual.

Index

Index